The Vygotsky Anthology

A Selection from His Key Writings

Edited by Myra Barrs and John Richmond

LONDON AND NEW YORK

Designed cover image: © Marxists Internet Archive

First published 2024
by Routledge
4 Park Square, Milton Park, Abingdon, Oxon OX14 4RN

and by Routledge
605 Third Avenue, New York, NY 10158

Routledge is an imprint of the Taylor & Francis Group, an informa business

© 2024 selection and editorial matter, Myra Barrs and John Richmond; individual chapters, the contributors

The right of Myra Barrs and John Richmond to be identified as the authors of the editorial material, and of the authors for their individual chapters, has been asserted in accordance with sections 77 and 78 of the Copyright, Designs and Patents Act 1988.

All rights reserved. No part of this book may be reprinted or reproduced or utilised in any form or by any electronic, mechanical, or other means, now known or hereafter invented, including photocopying and recording, or in any information storage or retrieval system, without permission in writing from the publishers.

Trademark notice: Product or corporate names may be trademarks or registered trademarks, and are used only for identification and explanation without intent to infringe.

British Library Cataloguing-in-Publication Data
A catalogue record for this book is available from the British Library

Library of Congress Cataloging-in-Publication Data
Names: Vygotskiĭ, L. S. (Lev Semenovich), 1896–1934, author. | Barrs, Myra, editor.
Title: The Vygotsky anthology : a selection from his key writings / edited by Myra Barrs and John Richmond.
Description: First edition. | New York : Routledge, 2024. | Includes bibliographical references and index.
Identifiers: LCCN 2023051499 (print) | LCCN 2023051500 (ebook) | ISBN 9781032581859 (hbk) | ISBN 9781032581842 (pbk) | ISBN 9781003448938 (ebk)
Subjects: LCSH: Philosophical anthropology—Russia (Federation) | Psychology. | Educational psychology. | Arts—Psychological aspects. | Child development.
Classification: LCC BD450 .V96 2024 (print) | LCC BD450 (ebook) | DDC 370.15—dc23/eng/20231226
LC record available at https://lccn.loc.gov/2023051499
LC ebook record available at https://lccn.loc.gov/2023051500

ISBN: 9781032581859 (hbk)
ISBN: 9781032581842 (pbk)
ISBN: 9781003448938 (ebk)

DOI: 10.4324/9781003448938

Typeset in Bembo
by Apex Covantage, LLC

The Vygotsky Anthology

The Vygotsky Anthology brings together, for the first time, a selection of extracts from the best translations available of Vygotsky's writings, spanning the entire arc of his career.

Vygotsky was arguably one of the greatest educational psychologists of the 20th century. Grounded in his experience as a teacher, an expert in special education, a research psychologist and an outstanding theorist, the editors of this unique anthology chart his enormous influence on professionals working in education and child development around the world. The extracts are introduced by the editors' commentaries, helpfully setting them in the context of Vygotsky's life and work, providing a collection of work that adequately represents his writing, and conveying some of the great pleasures of reading him. In the passages selected here, his voice is clearly heard, the intellectual brilliance of his insights is reflected, his line of argument is clear, and his humour and humanity are evident.

With its inclusion of recent translations of essential texts, this anthology will help students to understand the full diversity of Vygotsky's influence on today's classrooms. Seen as a companion volume to Myra Barrs' previous work *Vygotsky the Teacher* (Routledge, 2022), the value of this text to teachers, educational psychologists, and other practitioners working in the field of education and child development will be significant and lasting. It is a key reference book for new generations of Vygotsky students.

Myra Barrs was the author of many books and other publications on language and learning in education. She was Honorary Senior Research Associate at the UCL Institute of Education, UK, and former director of the Centre for Literacy in Primary Education, UK. Her book *Vygotsky the Teacher: A Companion to his Psychology for Teachers and Other Practitioners* was published by Routledge in 2022. She died in 2023.

John Richmond has been an English teacher, an adviser of teachers and an educational broadcaster. He has published books and articles on English teaching and language and learning.

To all students of Vygotsky

Contents

Figure	viii
Acknowledgements	ix
Introduction	xi

1	Vygotsky's roots in psychology: extracts from *Educational psychology*	1
2	Vygotsky's passion for literature and drama: extracts from *The psychology of art*	10
3	Vygotsky the defectologist	22
4	On the crisis in psychology	38
5	Discovering the power of the sign: extracts from *Tool and symbol in child development*	56
6	In pursuit of a unified psychological structure: extracts from *The history of the development of higher mental functions*	72
7	Vygotsky the pedologist	89
8	Play, imagination and creativity	108
9	The zone of proximal/proximate development	124
10	Word meaning develops: extracts from *Thinking and speech*, Chapters 1, 2, 4 and 6	135
11	The final 'why': extracts from *Thinking and speech*, Chapter 7, 'Thought and word'	153

Index	167

Figure

6.1   The relationship between tool and sign   74

Acknowledgements

Acknowledgements are due to the following owners of copyright material:

The MIT Press, for extracts from *The psychology of art*, by L.S. Vygotsky, introduction by A.N. Leontiev, pp. 22–24, 132–135, 152–155, 189–195, 213–215, 249. © 1971 Massuchusetts Institute of Technology.
Springer Nature Group, for extracts from the following volumes of *The collected works of L.S. Vygotsky*: Volume 1, *Problems of general psychology*, 1987; Volume 2, *The fundamentals of defectology*, 1993; Volume 3, *Problems of the theory and history of psychology*, 1997; Volume 4, *The history of the development of higher mental functions*, 1997; Volume 5, *Child psychology*, 1998; and for extracts from 'The problem of the environment in pedology' in Volume 1 of *L.S. Vygotsky's pedological works*, 2019, 'The problem of age periodisation in child development' and 'The crisis at three years of age' in Volume 2 of *L.S. Vygotsky's pedological works*, 2021, both volumes translated and with notes by D. Kellogg and N. Veresov.
The editors of *International Research in Early Childhood Education*, for extracts from Vygotsky's 'Play and its role in the mental development of the child', translated by N. Veresov and M. Barrs, which originally appeared in edition 7(2).
Taylor and Francis, for extracts from *Imagination and creativity in childhood* in *Journal of Russian and East European Psychology*, 42(1); and (with C. Mitchell) for extracts from 'The problem of teaching and mental development at school age' in *Changing English*, 24(4), translated by S. Mitchell.
The Marxists Internet Archive, for the cover photograph.
The editors would be glad to hear from the copyright holder(s) of the English translation of *Tool and symbol in child development*, by L.S Vygotsky and A.R. Luria, as it appears in *The Vygotsky reader*, edited by R. Van der Veer and J. Valsiner, and published by Blackwell in 1994, whom they have been unable to trace.
The editors would be glad to hear from the copyright owner of the English translation by R. Silverman of Vygotsky's *Educational psychology*, © 1997 by CRC Press LLC, whom they have been unable to trace.

The editors thank Luciano Mecacci for permission to reprint sentences from his Italian translations of two of Vygotsky's works: '*Il problema dell'insegnamento/ apprendimento e dello sviluppo mentale nell'età scolare*' ('The problem of teaching and mental development at school age'), and *Pensiero e linguaggio* (*Thinking and speech*).

Introduction

Myra Barrs

Part 1

Vygotsky's name is one of the most frequently cited in the field of developmental and educational psychology, yet paradoxically his work is not easy to access. Many of his works are as yet unavailable in English translation, while many others are currently out of print.

There is a terrible irony in Vygotsky's publishing history. In his own lifetime much of his work was unpublished, either because he did not put it forward for publication, perhaps sometimes to avoid political censure (as might have been the case with *The historical meaning of the crisis in psychology* [Vygotsky, 1997d]), or because, by the early 1930s under Stalin, it would definitely have met with official disapproval. This particularly applies to Vygotsky's pedological writings, some of which are only just now appearing in English, in new translations by Kellogg and Veresov (Vygotsky, 2019, 2021 and 2022). Pedology was an interdisciplinary approach to the study and care of children, which united paediatricians, school doctors, child psychologists, researchers in child development, teachers (including special-needs teachers) and parents. This movement was coming under increasing political scrutiny and suspicion in the late 1920s and early 1930s as a Western bourgeois science. Two years after Vygotsky's death in 1934, a Decree by the Central Committee of the Communist Party denounced it as an 'anti-Soviet pseudo-science' (Byford, 2021). Thereafter, its publications were banned and its institutions dismantled.

After his death, and more particularly after the death of Stalin in 1953, two ex-colleagues of Vygotsky, Alexei Leontiev and Alexander Luria, published new editions of some of his works, notably *Thought and language* (or *Thinking and speech*). These editions contained quite extensive editorial cuts and changes, including the omission of any reference to pedology. Vygotsky's *Collected works* did not appear in Russian until 1982–84, and contained the same kinds of omissions and changes as had appeared in the editions of the 1950s and 1960s. The Russian *Collected works* are now out of print, but a new and much more comprehensive version is planned in Russia. The work on this is proceeding slowly, however; Elena Kravisova, Vygotsky's granddaughter, who was leading this project, died in 2022.

In the UK and USA, some books were published separately. An incomplete translation of *Thought and language*, with an introduction by Jerome Bruner, appeared in 1962 (Vygotsky, 1962). Luria had made the Russian original available to the translators, who decided that Vygotsky's substantial critique of Piaget in the book was excessive and cut most of it. In later years, more works (e.g. *The psychology of art* [Vygotsky, 1971]) appeared in English translation, before the *Collected works* in English were published between 1987 and 1999. But there were changes and distortions in these volumes, too, reflecting those present in the Russian originals. These ranged from deletions and suppressions of names or passages to actual insertions (Van der Veer and Yasnitsky [2011] term them 'outrageous insertions') of editorial views into Vygotsky's own text, in ways that were not uncommon in the Stalinist era. The *Collected works* in English are now out of print, as are several of Vygotsky's works which were not included in the *Collected works* but were published separately, such as *Educational psychology* (Vygotsky, 1997c) and *Imagination and creativity in childhood* (Vygotsky, 2004).

Rationale for this book

For interested readers of Vygotsky, there is therefore a real difficulty in getting hold of primary texts. Of course, Vygotsky's works are available for readers who have access to academic or specialist libraries, but without academic affiliations it is difficult, or expensive, for readers to access even online texts. (The honourable exception here is the excellent Marxists Internet Archive [www.marxists.org].) That is why it seemed important to us as editors to make available a book which would provide a selection of substantial extracts from Vygotsky's main publications, chiefly those discussed in Myra Barrs' book *Vygotsky the teacher* (Barrs, 2022). While working on that book we became acutely aware of the lack of any such 'reader' (apart from the unsatisfactory *Mind in society* [Vygotsky, 1978] and the excellent, but partial, *The Vygotsky reader* [Van der Veer and Valsiner (eds) {1994}]). So we formulated the idea of an anthology of extracts which would serve as an introduction to a wide range of Vygotsky's works, from his earliest books, such as *Educational psychology*, to his last book, *Thought and language/Thinking and speech* (Vygotsky, 1962 and 1987b).

We were aware of the difficulties inherent in this project. A book of extracts cannot do more than select a group of passages from each work which, taken together, give an impression of the main line of Vygotsky's arguments in that work, while only hinting at the complexity of those arguments. The work of selecting the extracts is itself very demanding, as Vygotsky is an expansive writer, often given to digression or pausing his argument so as to compare his thinking with that of other psychologists.

Another likely problem of such an undertaking is the cost of seeking permissions for the extracts selected. Though some publishers set reasonable permission fees, a good many others have made a business out of charging excessively high prices for extracts even from a book whose author died ninety years ago, and which has been out of print for years. We knew we had no hope of recouping these high fees, but we chose to proceed with the project in the hope that it would prove possible.

Principles

Our working principles in putting this reader together have been as follows:

- We have drawn on the best texts available in English, in the most up-to-date versions. So, for instance, we have been able to select pedological texts from Kellogg and Veresov's translations of Vygotsky's *Pedological works,* Volumes 1 and 2 (Vygotsky, 2019, 2021).
- We have, where possible, referred to excellent translations in other languages in order to provide a wider perspective on the English translation we are using. In the case of *Thinking and speech,* which we have based on the translation in Volume 1 of the English *Collected works,* we have frequently referred to the Italian translation of this book by Luciano Mecacci (Vygotsky, 1992) – the only translation in any language to be based on the original 1934 publication. We have also been able to refer to the translation of certain pedological works into French by Leopoldoff Martin and Schneuwly (Vygotsky, 2018).
- We have done as little cutting as possible within the passages selected; we did not want to present the reader with a patchwork text. So our concern was to identify longer extracts which provided a coherent statement of each part of the overall argument of the book, and to group the extracts in such a way that, together, they gave as full as possible an idea of the thesis of the book as a whole.
- In making our selection following these principles, we have hoped to provide the reader with a collection of extracts which give an adequate representation of Vygotsky's texts, and also convey some of the great pleasures of reading him. We have favoured passages where his voice is clearly heard, where the sheer intellectual brilliance of some of his insights is reflected, where the line of his argument is clear and where his humour and humanity are present in the writing.

Part 2

As became apparent in *Vygotsky the teacher,* the value of a chronological approach which takes Vygotsky's major texts in order, from his earliest work to the last texts, is that the full range and scope of his work becomes apparent. We can follow the recurrence of key themes and observe their development and their interactions. It becomes irrelevant to talk about phases or 'periods' in Vygotsky's work, especially given that most of it was produced within the space of about fourteen years. Throughout these years, though his interests developed, certain themes were constant or formed part of the developing pattern of his thinking.

In this part of the Introduction, we attempt to identify and relate the elements in this pattern.

Consciousness

One fundamental theme is that of consciousness, sometimes thought of as belonging to the later work. But Vygotsky's preoccupation with consciousness is there from the start; it appears in *Educational psychology* (Vygotsky, 1997c), perhaps his earliest book, based on the lectures in the psychology course that he gave at Gomel Teachers' College. Extracts from the book form our Chapter 1. Given the state of psychology at this time, with reflexology as the dominant discipline, this reaching beyond what reflexologists deemed to be capable of study, towards one of 'the most difficult questions in all of psychology' (ibid., p. 33) is extraordinarily bold. The nature of consciousness continues to be known as the 'hard problem' for psychology today, though materialist neuroscientists are satisfied to see consciousness principally as a function of brain activity.

Art and emotion

A second major theme appears in another early book, *The psychology of art* (Vygotsky, 1971), which reputedly had its origins in his doctoral thesis. Extracts from the book form our Chapter 2. Literature, and the way it works on us, is the main topic of this book and Vygotsky's lifelong love of literature, particularly drama and poetry, permeates the text. He thought that literature, with its power to explore and express inner states, should be a legitimate source of evidence in psychology. These themes do not return in force until his later writing on imagination, creativity and the inner planes of thought. In the first and last chapters of *Thinking and speech*, he underlines the inextricable relationship between emotion, or affect, and cognition. He also emphasises the way 'the affective-volitional tendency stands behind thought', becoming 'the final "why" in the analysis of thinking' (Vygotsky, 1987b, p. 282). But in *The psychology of art* he was above all preoccupied with the social role of art in enabling us to live through and contemplate emotions: 'Art is the social technique of emotion, a tool of society which brings the most intimate and personal aspects of our being into the circle of social life' (Vygotsky, 1971, p. 249).

'Defects' and 'detours'

Vygotsky's lifelong experience as a practising defectologist (a psychologist of children with special needs) is not usually given enough credit in accounts of his psychology. But his experience of working as a teacher and clinician with special-needs children and their teachers made him unique in the world of experimental psychology, and greatly influenced both the formation of his theory and the development of his methodology. His practice in defectology developed rapidly; he soon realised that the social integration of children with 'defects', though important, was only a start. He saw that 'defects' could become challenges that would stimulate development. Finding 'detours', or ways round the 'defect', usually through language and other sign systems, would give them access both to higher mental functions and to full cultural development, which were not dependent on the 'organic deficit'. Vygotsky went on using the insights gained in his defectological experience in his other work in psychology, especially in experimental design, methodology and assessment. He developed detailed observation-based frameworks for the descriptive assessment of children with special needs – a field which was generally dominated by purely quantitative assessment. Extracts from some of his numerous writings on defectology form our Chapter 3.

Psychology reimagined

In order to start on the next part of his work, Vygotsky had to reimagine psychology. The texts in our Chapter 4 show him doing this. In 'Consciousness as a problem in the psychology of behaviour' (Vygotsky, 1997b), he demolished the argument that subjective experience and consciousness had no place in scientific psychology by showing that, in the impeccably objective science of neurology, subjective experience was accepted as evidence where it was the only source of information. The science of psychology must not ignore the facts of consciousness but 'materialise them, translate them into the objective language of the objectively existing' (ibid., p. 67) and incorporate them in its body of knowledge.

In *The historical meaning of the crisis in psychology* (1997d), Vygotsky began by deploring the lack of consensus in the discipline and arguing the need for a general science, operating at a high level of generality and abstraction and capable of providing a common framework for disparate sub-disciplines, several of which aspired to become a general science despite being unable to offer such an overview. One characteristic of a general psychology would be a focus on the development of appropriate methodologies; Vygotsky felt psychology needed to 'emancipate itself from narrow empirical naturalism' and he advocated more analytic approaches, such as the identification of 'units of analysis' and the use of 'interpretive methods that allow for the investigation of the invisible' (Hyman, 2009). The decisive moment in the book is Vygotsky's rejection of the idealistic psychology of William James, whom he admired, and his determination to work for the development of a scientific psychology of which the test would be 'praxis' – its relevance to applied psychologies (such as educational psychology).

The instrumental method

Tool and symbol in child development (Vygotsky and Luria, 1994), extracts from which form our Chapter 5, is a short but significant work which gives insight into Vygotsky and Luria's theory of child development. The authors analysed studies of the comparative development of young apes and children, and showed that children began to overtake apes decisively in practical tasks as soon as their language developed. The 'instrumental method' the researchers used involved children in tasks which were initially too hard for them, but which they could learn to solve with the use of 'signs' – e.g. coloured or picture cards. The researchers measured the increase in the children's egocentric speech as they engaged with these tasks. Vygotsky applied to the design of the game-like experiments, which were intended to be challenging, all he had learned from his study of 'detours' in defectology.

It was noticeable that children viewed these play experiments as *social* situations and regarded the experimenters observing them as participants in the play, with whom they often shared their feelings or to whom they turned for help. Vygotsky and Luria stressed the interactive nature of development, which was achieved through social relationships; hence, also, their emphasis on the role of language in mental development. So many ideas are launched in this short text, from the instrumental method as a shortcut to the development of higher mental functions, to the internalisation of those functions, and the role of language and of will, or self-control, in these developments. It is an invaluable summary of what was achieved by the team assembled by Vygotsky and Luria, which Vygotsky, reaching ever into the future, was about to go beyond.

Higher mental functions

The history of the development of higher mental functions (Vygotsky, 1997e), extracts from which form our Chapter 6, is a huge compendium of ideas and research to date, probably intended for a readership of psychologists. It complicates the picture presented in *Tool and symbol* (Vygotsky and Luria, 1994) in several ways. For one thing, it sets mental developments in the context of three lines of development – biological (evolutionary), historical and ontological – each of which is described in detail and contributes to individual inheritance.

A section on research in the first part of the book discusses in detail the role of signs and of language in higher mental functions, and clearly differentiates between tools and signs in human activity. Both are means of mediation. Tools mediate work, enabling human beings to change nature and build their environment; they are outwardly directed. Signs mediate psychological activity, enabling us to direct and develop our thinking; they are inwardly directed.

Vygotsky also redefines higher mental functions in this book, suddenly including in the familiar list of *voluntary* attention, *logical* memory and so on, a group of 'cultural languages', such as spoken and written language, and the language of mathematics, the use of which supports the development of these higher functions. In the second half of the book, chapters are devoted to all these functions, with priority given to the cultural languages. As children develop higher mental functions, they also develop the capacity to control them, and the book has chapters on self-control and on child-rearing which deal with these broader aspects of development. This summing up of Vygotsky's work in psychology to date is preparation for the new leap that follows.

Pedology

While working as a clinician at the Moscow Experimental-Defectological Institute, from about 1927 onwards, Vygotsky was also drawing on the insights of pedology, the wider study of the child, in which attention was given not only to mental development but also to physical and emotional growth. Extracts from five of Vygotsky's pedological works form our Chapter 7.

The first text, 'On psychological systems' (Vygotsky, 1997f), was a lecture given by Vygotsky to his colleagues in experimental psychology, proposing a new agenda. He himself had been broadening his experience through his pedological work with adolescents, and his increasing interest in the breakdown of mind in illnesses such as aphasia and Parkinson's disease. He now saw that higher mental functions were not discrete but continually developing and interacting, and he proposed to his colleagues that they should turn to the investigation of these 'psychological systems'.

Vygotsky's important review (2021a) of different age periods in childhood, in which stable periods are shown alternating with 'crises', was rooted in pedological practice and illustrated by examples from case studies. A pedological text based on an illuminating family case history is the lecture 'The problem of the environment in pedology' (Vygotsky, 2019a), which focuses on the very different emotional experiences that three children of different ages take from their upbringing by an abusive, mentally ill mother. Emotional experience, or '*perezhivanie*', and how it can vary greatly from one individual to another, is a key aspect of the study of the wider personality. Vygotsky also published a major textbook on the psychology of adolescence, *Pedology of the adolescent* (Vygotsky, 1998a), in which he emphasised emotional development, and particularly identified concept development as opening up the deep structures of knowledge. Concept development (linked to language development) was fundamental to all intellectual development.

Pedology, with its wider perspective, gradually became Vygotsky's main specialism, though simultaneously he worked as a teacher and researcher in psychology. But, as we have seen, the discipline itself was regarded with increasing political suspicion as a 'bourgeois' science, and soon after Vygotsky's death it was banned, with many of its publications being destroyed.

Play and the imagination

The three texts from the early 1930s, extracts from which form our Chapter 8, provide an account of the development of the imagination from early-childhood play, through school age and into adolescence. The third text broadens this picture to explore the role of art, creativity and invention in social life. These themes are central to Vygotsky's psychology and point back to his early interest in drama as well as forward to his final statements about literature, affect and the internalisation of language.

'Play and its role in the mental development of the child' (Vygotsky, 2016)

Vygotsky sees play as an acting-out of children's unrealisable desires and a way of being 'a head taller' (in a way that links it to the zone of proximal/proximate development; see below). Through play, children become able to detach objects from their names and give them other names, thus learning to play with meanings and create imagined worlds. This makes play 'the highest level of preschool development' (ibid., p. 18).

'Imagination and its development in childhood' (Vygotsky, 1987a)

In this lecture, the imagination is viewed developmentally, and the development of speech is what enables the child to imagine more freely, to articulate and develop imaginative ideas, and to plan imaginary worlds and then create them (as in 'utopian constructions'). Although feelings are obviously part of the imaginary scenarios that children think into being, Vygotsky argues vigorously that imaginary thinking also informs realistic thinking. In fact, when the imagination joins with thinking in this way, the results can be seen as a 'psychological system' which brings together several mental functions, including emotional aspects, in a new unity. He sees imaginative thinking as enriching realistic thinking and enabling it to become more speculative and original.

Imagination and creativity in childhood (Vygotsky, 2004)

This longer text, part of a correspondence course for teachers, goes further in describing how imagination can become part of reality by being realised in technical inventions and works of art. Vygotsky sees all these artefacts as representing the 'crystallised imagination', in which the productions of inventors and artists form part of the social environment, available to be used and studied. Once 'crystallised', in this way they become part of a cycle by which children (and adults) absorb their influence and learn from the ingenuity and beauty they represent, perhaps themselves being inspired towards creative or inventive activity.

Education (and the zone of proximal/proximate development)

Our Chapter 9 consists of extracts from three texts providing accounts of Vygotsky's theory of the zone of proximal/proximate development (ZPD), culminating in the most recent translation (Vygotsky, 2017) of the 1935 article 'The problem of teaching and mental development at school age', which, in its *Mind in society* translation (Vygotsky, 1978), has become the most commonly known. It was necessary to devote a separate chapter to this topic, because it has been given such disproportionate prominence in Vygotsky's work and is undoubtedly the concept most frequently associated with his name. Perhaps this is mainly because it has been closely associated with assessment.

But, if we pull back from the detail of the ZPD and look at the broader questions raised in the article, what do they show about Vygotsky's educational focus? It is clear that *all* of Vygotsky's work, in one way or another – from his first book to his last, whether classed as defectology, psychology or pedology – was related to human development and to education. His views about education are always supported by examples of how development can be furthered and how learners can be encouraged to overcome challenges and learn to access the higher mental functions and cultural languages. 'Pedagogy' is a frequent word in the article (although it is entirely absent from the commonly known version).

Some of the key features of 'The problem of teaching and mental development at school age' (Vygotsky, 2017) are the following:

- Its consistent use of the word '*obuchenie*' to describe the process of teaching, or learning with a teacher. The *Mind in society* (Vygotsky, 1978) version uses 'learning' to translate this word, but it is apparent that the word actually conflates teaching and learning in a complex process.
- The central place given to imitation puts this important strategy for learning in its original, prominent place in the argument, and thus links the article to Vygotsky's writings about play and drama.
- The article was a pedological work in which Vygotsky, in the closing paragraphs, argued that the ZPD provided a means of observing development in the context of the classroom, thus enabling pedology to research and develop a 'science of teaching'. In the commonly known version, pedology is not mentioned.
- The relationship between teacher and learner is at the centre of this article, and the challenges posed to learners are viewed as fundamental to the 'self-propulsion' that has to happen if challenges are to be overcome. The references back to the 'defects' and 'detours' of Vygotsky's work in defectology are inescapable.

The kind of 'future-directed' pedagogy featured here is fundamental to Vygotsky's vision of what is possible when teaching 'engages the child with life, awakens and puts in motion a whole range of inner developmental processes' (Vygotsky, 2017,

p. 368) in the course of interaction with children who 'do what they do not (yet) know how to do' (Schneuwly, 1994, p. 287). Both teacher and child need to believe that this is possible. Vygotsky has no doubt of it.

Thinking and speech *(Vygotsky, 1987b)*

Vygotsky's final book, extracts from which form our Chapters 10 and 11, is a long, complex exploration of the relationship between language and thought. His chosen 'unit of analysis', the element which retains the property of the whole, is *word meaning*, and his thesis throughout explores the relationship between word and meaning – not a fixed relationship, because *word meaning develops*. The development discussed is a long-term process, because Vygotsky wants to look at what happens, not only in childhood and at school age, but into adolescence and adulthood.

After an initial chapter on the development of word meaning, Vygotsky essentially divides the book into two parts. The first, which takes up chapters 2 to 6, follows the route that 'external' speech takes as children's understanding of the cognitive and denotative meanings of words grows through experience and teaching. This enables children to map their knowledge of the world and clarify their ideas, which in time form personal 'spontaneous' concepts in many areas. Vygotsky draws on the several studies of concept development that he has worked on or directed, from Sakharov's cross-age studies of children, to later studies of how children encounter and master 'scientific' concepts in school settings. Throughout, he sees the development of scientific concepts, which are more abstract in nature and which restructure students' existing knowledge, as the key to intellectual growth.

Scientific concepts can only be understood, Vygotsky says, through 'conscious awareness' and 'voluntary control'. These concepts are not acquired easily but are formed with the help of instruction and 'through an extraordinary effort of [the student's] own thought'. The development of scientific concepts therefore opens the gate both to conscious awareness and to more developed forms of thinking.

'External speech' leads outwards; the aspect of language that Vygotsky explores in the second part of the book (chapter 7) is its 'semantic' aspect, where meanings are initially apprehended (by young children) as whole connotative meanings, surrounded by associations. The route followed by this personal and affective aspect of language leads away from external speech and inwards. Vygotsky's theory of the internalisation of language is counterpoised to Piaget's view of the process, with which he profoundly disagrees. Whereas Piaget sees very young children's language and their egocentric speech as 'autistic' (private and personal, essentially uncommunicable), gradually falling away and 'dying off' when replaced by 'social' speech based on that of adults, Vygotsky argues urgently that the beginnings of speech are always social, and that this speech is then taken over into pretend play as egocentric speech.

Vygotsky's explanation of the progress of this form of speech, which gradually becomes more fragmented and harder to interpret, is that it becomes 'inner speech'. From here he hypothesises a progression by which inner speech becomes 'verbal thought', and then 'non-verbal thought'. We become aware that his model of these progressions can be visualised as a succession of inner planes where thought becomes less verbal and more formless, with the inmost plane being made up of emotions and feelings, images and sensations. These are the expressions of affect, which is seen as a key element in this inner core of thought.

Vygotsky uses examples from literature and drama to illustrate these hypotheses, for instance drawing on Stanislavsky's method for producing a scene from a play by asking the actors to infer the unspoken motives behind the words of the script. The multiple examples taken from literature, and particularly from poetry, in his chapter 7, remind us of his determination in *The psychology of art* (Vygotsky, 1971) to use literature as authentic evidence of the workings of mind in his psychology.

In addition, in describing how thought can be externalised as external speech and writing, Vygotsky draws on his substantial studies of writing to trace the experience of bringing a remote or half-formed idea, first into verbal thought or inner speech, and then into external speech or writing. This enables him to trace the progress of thought as it travels both outwards and also, by analogy, inwards.

Consciousness, affect and emotion, art and literature, methodology, the higher mental functions and the cultural languages, will and self-control, the ZPD and pedagogy, imagination and creativity, language development and concept development, and of course language and thought – all Vygotsky's main themes explored through his life's work are present in *Thinking and speech*. The book is both a retrospective, reviewing his great body of work, and is also forward-looking, setting an agenda for future investigations and for education.

References

Barrs, M. (2022). *Vygotsky the teacher*. Abingdon, Oxon and New York, NY: Routledge.

Byford, A. (2021). 'Pedology as occupation in the early Soviet Union', in *A history of Marxist psychology: the golden age of Soviet science*. Yasnitsky, A. (ed.). London: Routledge, pp. 109–127.

Hyman, L. (2009). 'Vygotsky on scientific observation'. Berlin: Max-Planck-Institut für Wissenschaftsgeschichte. Available online: www.mpiwg-berlin.mpg.de/sites/default/files/Preprints/P375.pdf

Schneuwly, B. (1994). 'Contradiction and development: Vygotsky and paedology'. *European Journal of Psychology of Education*, 9(4), pp. 281–291.

Van der Veer, R. and Valsiner, J. (eds) (1994). *The Vygotsky reader*. Oxford, UK and Cambridge, MA: Blackwell.

Van der Veer, R. and Yasnitsky, A. (2011). 'Vygotsky in English: what still needs to be done'. *Integrative psychological and behavioral science, 45*, pp. 475–493.

Vygotsky, L.S. (1962). *Thought and language* [1934]. Trans. E. Hanfmann and G. Vakar; intro. J. Bruner. Cambridge, MA: MIT Press.

Vygotsky, L.S. (1971). *The psychology of art* [1925]. Intro. A.N. Leontiev; commentary V.V. Ivanov. Cambridge, MA: MIT Press.
Vygotsky, L.S. (1978). *Mind in society*. Cole, M., John-Steiner, V., Scribner, S. and Souberman, E. (eds). Cambridge, MA: Harvard University Press.
Vygotsky, L.S. (1987). *The collected works of L.S. Vygotsky. Volume 1, Problems of general psychology*. Trans. and intro. N. Minick; Rieber, R.W. and Carton, A.S. (eds). New York, NY: Plenum Press.
Vygotsky, L.S. (1987a). 'Lecture 5: Imagination and its development in childhood' [1932], in Vygotsky, L.S. (1987), *The collected works of L.S. Vygotsky. Volume 1, Problems of general psychology*, pp. 339–349.
Vygotsky, L.S. (1987b). *Thinking and speech* [1934], in Vygotsky, L.S. (1987), *The collected works of L.S. Vygotsky. Volume 1, Problems of general psychology*, pp. 37–285.
Vygotsky, L.S. (1992). *Pensiero e linguaggio* [1934]. Trans. L. Mecacci. Bari-Roma: Gius. Laterza e Figli Spa.
Vygotsky, L.S. (1997). *The collected works of L.S. Vygotsky. Volume 3, Problems of the theory and history of psychology*. Trans. and intro. R. Van der Veer; Rieber, R.W. and Wollock, J. (eds). New York, NY: Plenum Press.
Vygotsky, L.S. (1997a). *The collected works of L.S. Vygotsky. Volume 4, The history of the development of higher mental functions*. Rieber, R.W. (ed.). New York, NY: Plenum Press.
Vygotsky, L.S. (1997b). 'Consciousness as a problem in the psychology of behaviour' [1925], in Vygotsky, L.S. (1997), *The collected works of L.S. Vygotsky. Volume 3, Problems of the theory and history of psychology*, pp. 63–79.
Vygotsky, L.S. (1997c). *Educational psychology* [1926]. Trans. R. Silverman. Davydov, V.V. (ed. and intro.). Boca Raton, FL: CRC Press.
Vygotsky, L.S. (1997d). *The historical meaning of the crisis in psychology: a methodological investigation* [1926–7], in Vygotsky, L.S. (1997), *The collected works of L.S. Vygotsky. Volume 3, Problems of the theory and history of psychology*, pp. 233–343.
Vygotsky, L.S. (1997e). *The history of the development of higher mental functions* [1931], in Vygotsky, L.S. (1997a), *The collected works of L.S. Vygotsky. Volume 4, The history of the development of higher mental functions*, pp. 1–251.
Vygotsky, L.S. (1997f). 'On psychological systems' [1930], in Vygotsky, L.S. (1997), *The collected works of L.S. Vygotsky. Volume 3, Problems of the theory and history of psychology*, pp. 91–107. Also available online in the Marxist Archive: www.marxists.org/archive/vygotsky/works/1930/psychological-systems.htm
Vygotsky, L.S. (1998). *The collected works of L.S. Vygotsky. Volume 5, Child psychology*. Rieber, R.W. (ed.). New York, NY: Plenum Press.
Vygotsky, L.S. (1998a). *Pedology of the adolescent* [1930–31], in Vygotsky, L.S. (1998), *The collected works of L.S. Vygotsky. Volume 5, Child psychology*, pp. 3–184.
Vygotsky, L.S. (2004). *Imagination and creativity in childhood* [1930]. *Journal of Russian and East European Psychology*, 42(1), pp. 7–97. Also available online in the Marxist Archive: www.marxists.org/archive/vygotsky/works/1927/imagination.pdf
Vygotsky, L.S. (2016). 'Play and its role in the mental development of the child' [1933]. Trans. N. Veresov and M. Barrs. *International Research in Early Childhood Education*, 7(2), pp. 3–25. Also available online at https://files.eric.ed.gov/fulltext/EJ1138861.pdf
Vygotsky, L.S. (2017). 'The problem of teaching and mental development at school age [1935] (*'Problema obucheniya i umstvennogo razvitiya v shkol'nom vozraste'*). Trans. S. Mitchell. *Changing English*, 24(4), pp. 359–371. Also available online in the Marxist Archive: https://www.marxists.org/archive/vygotsky/works/1931/school-age.htm
Vygotsky, L.S. (2018). *La science du développement de l'enfant: Textes pédologiques (1931–1934)*. Leopoldoff Martin, I. and Schneuwly, B. (eds and trans.) Berne: Peter Lang.

Vygotsky, L.S. (2019). *L.S. Vygotsky's pedological works. Volume 1, Foundations of pedology*. Trans. and notes D. Kellogg and N. Veresov. Singapore: Springer.

Vygotsky, L.S. (2019a). 'The problem of the environment in pedology' [1935], in Vygotsky, L.S. (2019), *L.S. Vygotsky's pedological works. Volume 1, Foundations of pedology*, pp. 23–42.

Vygotsky, L.S. (2021). *L.S. Vygotsky's pedological works. Volume 2, The problem of age*. Trans. and notes D. Kellogg and N. Veresov. Singapore: Springer.

Vygotsky, L.S. (2021a). 'The problem of age periodisation in child development' [1932–4], in Vygotsky, L.S. (2021), *L.S. Vygotsky's pedological works. Volume 2, The problem of age*, pp. 15–38.

Vygotsky, L.S. (2022). *L.S. Vygotsky's pedological works. Volume 3, Pedology of the adolescent I: pedology in the transitional age*. Trans. and notes D. Kellogg and N. Veresov. Singapore: Springer.

Vygotsky, L.S. and Luria, A.R. (1994). *Tool and symbol in child development* [1930], in *The Vygotsky reader* (1994). Van der Veer, R. and Valsiner, J. (eds), pp. 99–174.

Chapter 1

Vygotsky's roots in psychology
Extracts from *Educational psychology*

Educational psychology (Vygotsky, 1997) was one of the few of Vygotsky's books published in his lifetime. It was probably written between 1921 and 1923 and may have its origins in Vygotsky's notes for the psychology course he taught at Gomel Teachers' College. It begins with a fairly conventional account of reflexology: the theory which states that all behaviours are learned through interaction with the environment in a system of learned responses – 'conditional reflexes' – to stimuli. 'Reflexology' was the scientific approach to psychology pioneered by Pavlov, which dominated experimental psychology at the time the book was written. Part of the fascination of Vygotsky's argument lies in the fact that, although it opens with relatively orthodox reflexological statements, it soon begins to push against the boundaries of reflexology. For example, Vygotsky points out that the term 'reflex' should really only be used for animals that possess a nervous system. Human behaviour, which is infinitely more complex, is best described in terms of 'reactions'. Throughout the book's pages, there are hints of the arguments that Vygotsky will use in future writing and in later developments of his theory. Notable among these is Vygotsky's early conviction of the centrality of consciousness and social experience in distinguishing the behaviour of humans from that of non-human animals. These ideas are developed further in Chapter 4.

From *Educational psychology*, Chapter 3, 'The most important laws of higher nervous activity in man'

Animal behaviour and human behaviour

For modern natural science the common origin and common nature of man and animal is no longer open to question. For science, man is only a higher and far from the ultimate species of animal. Similarly, there is much in common in the behaviour of man and animals. One might say that man's behaviour grows out of the roots of animal behaviour and, quite often, is only the 'behaviour of an animal that has assumed an upright position'.

DOI: 10.4324/9781003448938-1

In particular, the instincts and the emotions, i.e. the inherited forms of behaviour, are so similar in man and the animals that they doubtless share a common origin. Certain naturalists are not inclined to make any essential distinction between human and animal behaviour, and tend to reduce all the differences between the two to different degrees of complexity and subtlety of the nervous system. The proponents of this viewpoint believe it is possible to explain human behaviour exclusively from the standpoint of biology.

However, it is not hard to see that this is not so. There is a fundamental distinction between human and animal behaviour, as is apparent from the following argument. From the standpoint of the study of conditional reflexes, all of an animal's experience, his entire store of behaviour, may be reduced to inherited reactions and conditional reflexes. All of an animal's behaviour may be expressed by means of the following formula: (1) inherited reactions + (2) inherited reactions x by individual experience (conditional reflexes). That is, the behaviour of an animal is composed of these inherited reactions plus the inherited reactions multiplied by the quantity of new relations that are present in the individual animal's experience. It is obvious that this formula does not cover human behaviour even in the slightest degree, however.

By comparison with animal behaviour, human behaviour displays, above all, an expanded use of the experience gained by prior generations. Man makes use of the experience of prior generations not only to the extent it is reinforced and transmitted by physical inheritance. Everything we use in science, in culture, and in everyday life is enriched by the vast quantity of experience accumulated by prior generations but not transmitted by means of physical inheritance. In other words, unlike the animals, man possesses a history, and this historical experience, i.e. not physical inheritance, but social inheritance, distinguishes him from the animals.

The second new term in our formula is that of collective social experience, which is also a new phenomenon in man. Each person makes use not only of those conditional reactions that have formed in his or her individual experience, as happens also with animals, but also by means of conditional relations that have formed in the social experience of other people. In order to establish a conditional reflex to light in a dog, it is necessary that the two effects, of light and of a piece of meat, 'intersect', i.e. occur simultaneously, in the individual dog's personal experience. Man, in contrast, uses in his everyday experience reactions which evolved in, and became part of, someone else's experience. I may know about the Sahara without ever having left my native city, or I may know quite a bit about Mars without ever having looked through a telescope. Those conditional reactions of thought or of speech in which these pieces of knowledge are expressed are part not of my own experience, but of the experience of people who have lived in Africa or have, in fact, looked through a telescope. Those new forms of adaptation, which we encounter for the first time in man, are the most essential feature which distinguishes human behaviour from the behaviour of animals.

The animal adapts passively, responding to changes in the environment by varying his own organs and the structure of his body. He changes himself in order to adapt to the conditions of existence. Man, on the other hand, adapts nature to himself deliberately. Instead of his own organs undergoing changes, bodies in nature are altered by man, becoming tools for him. He responds to cold not by growing a protective coat of wool, but by making deliberate adaptations to the environment, through the production of dwellings or of clothing, i.e. by adapting nature to himself.

According to one researcher, the whole difference between man and the animals may be summed up by saying that man is an animal that makes tools. From the moment labour, in the human sense of the term, i.e. the deliberate and intentional intervention in the workings of nature on the part of man, for the purpose of regulating and controlling vital processes between nature and himself, became possible – from this very moment mankind ascended a novel biological stage, and something novel that was foreign to his animal ancestors and to his fellow creatures became part of his experience.

It is true that we encounter in animals purposive adaption in rudimentary form, for example nest building in birds, the construction of dwellings in beavers, and so on. These examples all recall labour activity in man, but nevertheless occupy such a small place in the experience of the animal that, on the whole, it alters the basic character of passive adaption only slightly. The main point is that, despite all apparent similarity, the labour of an animal differs from human labour in the most decisive and categorical respects. This difference was expressed by Marx [1867] with consummate force, in *Das Kapital*.

> A spider conducts operations that resemble those of a weaver, and a bee puts to shame many an architect in the construction of her cells. But what distinguishes the worst architect from the best of bees is this, that the architect raises his structure in imagination before he erects it in reality. At the end of every labour-process, we get a result that already existed in the imagination of the labourer at its commencement.

The fact is that the spider's weaving of a web or the bee's construction of the cells in its hive constitutes the same passive, instinctive, inherited forms of behaviour as do all its other passive reactions. The labour of the least experienced human weaver or architect constitutes deliberate forms of adaptation simply because the weaver or architect is conscious.

What constitutes the conscious aspect of human behaviour and what is the psychological nature of consciousness – these questions are very nearly the most difficult questions in all of psychology, about which we will speak later. But even now it is clear that consciousness must be considered as consisting in the most complex forms of organisation of our behaviour, in particular, as Marx has shown, as a kind of doubling of experience, that makes it possible to predict in advance the results of labour and to direct one's own reactions to this end. This doubled experience also constitutes the third and final distinctive feature of human behaviour.

Thus, the entire formula of human behaviour, which is based on the formula of animal behaviour, complemented with new terms, assumes the following form: (1) inherited reactions + (2) inherited reactions x by individual experience (conditional reactions) + (3) historical experience + (4) social experience + (5) doubled experience (consciousness).

Thus, the decisive factor of human behaviour is not only the biological factor, but also the social factor, which brings with it entirely novel elements of behaviour. Man's experience is not just that of an animal that has assumed an upright position, but is rather a complex function of the entire social experience of mankind and of his individual groups.

The next two extracts from *Educational psychology* firmly justify the appearance of the first word in the book's title. Here Vygotsky plunges straight into the world of teaching and learning, drawing on his own experience as a teacher, and later a teacher of teachers, in Gomel, his home town. Engage the child's interest, he says (though he makes it clear that to engage a child's interest is not the same thing as merely seeking to entertain the child). And, crucially, let teaching be 'a labour of feeling'; 'an emotional component' is all too rarely regarded 'as an essential element of the educational process in the classroom'.

From *Educational psychology*, Chapter 5, 'The instincts as the subject, mechanism, and means of education', the section entitled 'The child's interest'

In childhood the basic mode of appearance of the instincts is in the form of interest, i.e. a special inclination of the child's psychic apparatus aimed at a particular object. Interests possess an all-encompassing importance in the child's life. Everything we do, even the most uninteresting, we nevertheless do out of interest, according to Thorndike,[1] though from negative interest, out of a fear of trouble. Thus, interest would appear to be the natural motive force of the child's behaviour; it is the true expression of instinctive striving, an indication that the child's activity coincides with his organic needs. That is why the fundamental rule demands that the entire educational system, the entire structure of teaching, be constructed on the foundation of children's interests, taken into account in exact fashion.

The psychological law simply says that before trying to get a child involved in some activity, get him interested in it, take care to discover whether he is ready for it, so that all the forces necessary for the activity are tensed, and the child is ready to act on his own, with the teacher left to simply guide and direct his activity. Even superficial imitation of interest clearly shows that interest is nothing other than the disposition and preparation of the organism for a particular activity, accompanied by an increase in overall vitality and a general sense of well-being. He who heeds his own interests, thus, holds his breath in, turns his ears in the direction of a speaker, does not lift his eyes from him, leaves aside all other cares, and avoids all movement, and, as the saying goes, 'is all ears'. This is also the clearest expression of an organism's focusing all its energies at a single point, as if transformed into a single kind of activity.

We should keep in mind an extremely critical danger the teacher encounters here. In striving to gain someone's interest in one thing or another, that person's interests may switch. There may be interest, but not the sort of interest which is needed, or this interest may not be pointed in the right direction. There is an eloquent story told in one of the American textbooks on psychology. A teacher in a public school who wished to teach geography had decided to begin by acquainting the children with regions that were nearby and accessible to them, and, moreover, were natural features, for example fields, hills, rivers and valleys in their environs. This the children found boring, however, and lacking all interest. It turned out that their previous teacher, out of a wish to arouse their interest, had brought in a rubber ball with a hole in it and filled it with water as a way explaining the nature of geysers. This she did by cleverly concealing the ball in a sand pile and then pressing down upon it with her foot at the proper spot. As a result she succeeded in causing a stream of water to shoot through the sand to the universal delight of the children. In her explanation of volcanoes, the same teacher employed a small piece of cotton dipped in sulphur and placed it in a pile of sand where she set it on fire, making it look just like the burning crater of a volcano. This aroused the liveliest interest in the children and to the new teacher they said, 'All of us know this, show us better fireworks than Miss N,' or 'how a syringe works,' said one of them to another.

This example easily shows how one interest may be falsely substituted for another. The first teacher had, undoubtedly, succeeded in arousing lively interest in the children, but it was an interest in a particular artifice, in fireworks and syringes, not in volcanoes and geysers. Such interest is not only not useful pedagogically, but is even profoundly harmful. This is because it not only does not contribute to the development of the various forms of activity we require from children, but instead creates a powerful rival to these activities in the form of strong interests and, consequently, causes the child's sense of readiness, which the teacher anticipates awakening, to slacken off. It is rather easy to arouse interest in history lessons by relating anecdotes, but it is difficult to tell whether the resulting interest has to do with history, and not the particular anecdote. The interest thus aroused by such supplementary techniques not only does not promote, but may even hold back, the development of the form of activity we require.

★ ★ ★

There are three important pedagogical conclusions that may be drawn from our study of children's interests. First, all the topics in a course must be interconnected, which is also the best way of ensuring that a common interest will be aroused and that this interest will collect around a single axis. Only then may we speak of a more or less prolonged, lasting, and deep interest, an interest that will not shatter into dozens of unrelated parts, making it impossible to grasp in a unified and general thought all the different subjects of study. The next conclusion has to do with that rule which said that everything has to involve recourse to repetition, to memorisation and assimilation of knowledge. But we all have come to realise how uninteresting is such repetition for children, how they dislike these lessons, even if they do not find them difficult. The reason for this is that here the fundamental rule of interest is violated and, consequently, repetition turns into mere dawdling, constituting the most irrational and un-psychological of all techniques.

The rule is to avoid repetition absolutely and to make instruction focused, i.e. to arrange the material in such a way that it may be gone over fully and all at once in the briefest and most simplified way possible; then the teacher may return to a topic, but not to just repeat what has been already gone over, but to review the same topic one more time in a more thorough and more all-inclusive form, complemented with a wealth of new facts, generalisations and conclusions, so that topics students have already studied are repeated anew, though unfolded from a new perspective, and this new aspect is so connected with what they are already acquainted with that interest is readily aroused all by itself. In this sense, in science just as in real life, it is only a new view about what is old that may arouse our interest.

... the third and final rule governing the employment of the child's interest mandates the construction of the entire educational system in the school in direct proximity to everyday life, to teach children in such a way as to interest them, to begin with what is familiar to the child and what arouses his interest in a natural way. Froebel points out that the child obtains his first bits of knowledge on the basis of his own natural interest in life and from the lessons he receives from adults. From earliest childhood, the son of a peasant, of a merchant or of a craftsman acquires a host of the most diverse bits of information in a natural way, in the course of observing his father's behaviour. At a later stage, therefore, it is essential to always take as a starting point for the development of a new interest one that already exists, and to proceed on the basis of what is known and familiar. This is the reason why classical education, which began all at once with mythology and the ancient languages and with subjects that had nothing in common with everyday life as it affected the child, was tedious. Thus, the basic rule is that before imparting new knowledge to the child and before fostering a new reaction in him, we must be sure to prepare the ground for it, i.e. arouse the appropriate interest. For an analogy, just think of how we loosen the soil before planting seeds.

From *Educational psychology*, Chapter 6, 'Education of emotional behaviour', the section entitled 'Education of the feelings'

Education in pre-revolutionary times rationalised and intellectualised our behaviour in infinite ways, resulting in that frightful hardheartedness, in that utter absence of all feeling, which became an inevitable trait of every person who passed through the educational system. In modern man, everything is mechanical to such an extent, his individual impressions are so associated with concepts, that life passes in tranquillity, neither engaging nor affecting his psyche, nor tingeing his relations with the emotional, and this joyless and untroubled life, without serious catastrophes, but also without great joys, creates a foundation for that fastidious gradation of feelings which, in literary language, has long been known as narrow-mindedness or philistinism.

Everything that we lost as a consequence of this education, the spontaneous sensation of life and, incidentally, the lifeless, uninspired method of teaching all the different subjects, played no small role in this disengagement from the world and in this destruction of feelings. Who among us has not thought of what an inexhaustible source of emotional stimulation is concealed in an ordinary course of geography, astronomy, or history? All we have to do is think of ways of teaching these subjects that go beyond all dry logical schemata and make of teaching not only an object and labour of thought, but also a labour of feeling.

Emotion is no less important a tool than is thinking. The teacher must be concerned not only that students think about and learn geography, but also feel deeply about it. Such a thought usually does not come to mind for one reason or another, and teaching that is emotionally felt is a rare visitor to our schools, and is associated, for the most part, with an impotent love for one's own subject on the part of a teacher who doesn't know of any way of imparting this love to his students and, therefore, usually has the reputation of being eccentric.

Meanwhile, it is precisely the emotional reactions that have to serve as the foundation of the educational process. Before communicating a particular piece of knowledge, the teacher should induce the appropriate emotion in the student, and take care to associate this emotion with the new knowledge. Only new knowledge that has passed through the student's senses may be inculcated. Everything else is lifeless knowledge that diminishes every vital relationship to the world. Of all the subjects taught in school, only in the teaching of literature, and there only to an insignificant degree, was the presence of an emotional component recognised as an essential element of the educational process in the classroom.

The ancient Greeks said that philosophy begins with wonder. Psychologically, this is true with regard to all knowledge, in the sense that every bit of new knowledge must be preceded by a certain sense of craving. A certain degree of emotional sensitivity, a degree of involvement must, of necessity, serve as the starting point of all educational efforts.

Vygotsky's abiding concern with the relationship between the individual and the social context, and with the origins of language and thought in this relationship, is already evident in this early work.

From *Educational psychology*, Chapter 9, 'Thinking as an especially complex form of behaviour', the section entitled 'Psychology of language'

… the most remarkable fact for the psychology of language is that language would seem to implement two entirely distinct functions. On the one hand, it serves as a means for the social coordination of the experience of individual people, and on the other, it is the most important tool of our thought.

We always think in some language, that is, we speak to ourselves and organise our behaviour within ourselves just as we organise our behaviour as a function of the behaviour of other people. In other words, thinking readily discloses its social character and demonstrates that our personality is organised according to the same model as is social intercourse, and that the primitive representation of the psyche as a double living inside man is the notion that is closest to our concepts.

Traditional psychological science has looked upon the understanding of the mind of another person as an insoluble conjecture, since none of my mental experiences is accessible to the perception of another person, and each of my mental experiences is disclosed to me only in introspection. I can only get to know my own joy through my own experiences, so how could I ever get to know another person's joy? In all psychological theories, despite all the differences in their construction, the question is always resolved on the basis of the thesis that we can get to know other people insofar as we can get to know ourselves. Whether we interpret the movements of other people by analogy with our own movements, whether we create a sense of empathy, i.e. induce in ourselves emotions appropriate to someone else's facial expression, we are always, as the psychologists put it, translating someone else's mind into the language of our own mind and getting to know another person through ourselves.

In fact, from the genetic standpoint of the development of the child's consciousness and from the standpoint of psychological knowledge of volitional acts, it would be more correct to think of this thesis as a contradictory assertion altogether. We have seen that the very understanding or awareness of our deeds arises as a relation between inner sensations and, like every conditioned-type relation, it arises out of experience in the simultaneity of different stimuli. Thus, before learning to understand other people, and only then on the basis of this model, the child learns to understand himself. It would be more correct to say that we know ourselves insofar as we know other people, or, more precisely, that we are conscious of ourselves only to the extent we are other for ourselves, i.e. somehow alien to ourselves. This is why language, this tool of social intercourse, is, in addition, also a tool of inner communication between man and himself.

The very consciousness of our thoughts and deeds must be understood as the very same mechanism responsible for the transmission of our reflexes to other systems or, speaking in terms of traditional psychology, as a feedback reaction.

Note

1. Edward Lee Thorndike (1874–1949) was an American behaviourist psychologist and one of the founders of educational psychology.

References

Marx, K. (1867). *Das Kapital*, Volume 1, Part III, Chapter 7, Section 1. Available online in the Marxist Archive: www.marxists.org/archive/marx/works/1867-c1/ch07.htm

Vygotsky, L.S. (1997). *Educational psychology* [1926]. Trans. R. Silverman. V.V. Davydov (ed. and intro.). Boca Raton, FL: CRC Press.

Chapter 2

Vygotsky's passion for literature and drama

Extracts from *The psychology of art*

The psychology of art (Vygotsky, 1971) was Vygotsky's first major work in psychology. The book was not published in Russian until 1965 and in English until 1971. It was probably written when Vygotsky was teaching in Gomel. He presented it in 1925 as his doctoral thesis.

The psychology of art speaks to Vygotsky's lifelong interest in literature, and foreshadows some of his later ideas, most particularly his insistence on the centrality of emotion in human consciousness. It is a rigorous attempt to identify the psychological laws of works of art and the systems by which they work.

After a preface, the book is divided into four parts. In the first, 'On the methodology of the problem', Vygotsky argues that 'the work of art, rather than its creator or its audience, should be taken as the basis for analysis' (ibid., p. 23).

From *The psychology of art*, Part I, 'On the methodology of the problem', Chapter 1, 'The psychological problem of art'

The psychological study of art has hitherto followed one of two trends: either the psychology of the creator (artist) was studied as it revealed itself in the work of art, or the psychology of the receptor (viewer, reader, etc.) was investigated. The imperfection and futility of both methods are sufficiently obvious. If we consider the extraordinary complexity of creative processes and the total lack of knowledge about the laws governing the expression of the artist's psyche in his work, it becomes clear that we cannot work back from the work of art to the artist's psychology unless we resign ourselves to being lost forever in conjectures.

* * *

… the work of art, rather than its creator or its audience, should be taken as the basis for analysis. While it is true that a work of art as such is not an object of psychology (having no psyche of its own), we must remember that a historian, studying for instance the French Revolution from materials that do not contain any of the objects of his study, finds himself faced with the necessity of actually creating the object of his study by means of indirect, that is, analytic methods. Indeed, this happens in a number of other disciplines and sciences. They search for the truth in a way similar to that of a court investigating a crime from leads, circumstantial or other evidence. Only a bad judge would pass a sentence on the basis of statements from either the defendant or the plaintiff, both of whom are prejudiced and bound to distort the truth. The psychologist operates in a similar fashion when he studies the statements of a reader or a viewer of a work of art. This does not mean, however, that a judge should not hear the interested parties – provided he takes their statements with a grain of salt. And the psychologist never refuses to use any material, even though he knows from the outset that it may not be correct. The judge establishes the truth by comparing various false statements, checking them against objective evidence, and so forth. The historian uses notoriously false or biased material most of the time; and like the historian or the geologist who first creates the object of his studies and only then subjects it to scrutiny, the psychologist is forced to resort to material evidence – the works of art – and create a corresponding psychology in order to be able to study the laws governing it. For the psychologist any work of art is a system of stimuli, consciously and intentionally organised in such a way as to excite an aesthetic reaction. By analysing the structure of the stimuli we reconstruct the structure of the reaction. Here is a simple example: we study the rhythmic structure of a philological excerpt and deal with non-psychological facts; but if we analyse it as being variously directed to cause a corresponding functional reaction, we create, proceeding from objective data, certain characteristics of the aesthetic reaction. It is obvious that the aesthetic reaction thus created is completely impersonal, that is, it does not belong to any single individual, nor does it reflect any concrete individual psychic process – which is its virtue. Thus we are able to determine the nature of aesthetic reaction in its pure form without confounding it with all the random processes accumulated with it in an individual's psyche.

This method guarantees a sufficient objectivity of results and of investigation, since it proceeds every time from the study of solid, objectively existing, accountable facts. Here is the formula of this method: from the form of the work of art, via the functional analysis of its elements and structure, recreate the aesthetic reaction and establish its general laws.

The task and the plan of the present book can be termed an attempt at applying this new method consistently and thoroughly to actual problems.

In Part II of the book, Vygotsky critiques three psychological theories of art: the school of 'art as perception'; 'art as technique' or formalism; and 'art and psychoanalysis', the work of the Freudians. This critique clears the way for Part III, in which Vygotsky applies the method he has proposed in Part I to three literary forms of increasing complexity.

The first literary form Vygotsky considers is the fable, and in particular some of the well-known fables of Ivan Krylov. The 'subtle poison' in the title of the chapter from which the following extract is taken refers to Krylov's ability to introduce a double meaning, a second level, into his stories. Vygotsky suggests that, for Krylov, 'this double meaning overcame the narrow horizon of the prosaic fable which Krylov detested' (Vygotsky, 1971, p. 137). Vygotsky finds this second level in each of the ten fables he analyses.

In 'The wolf in the kennel', a wolf has got into the hunting dogs' kennel by mistake, causing huge panic and confusion.

From *The psychology of art*, Part III, 'Analysis of the aesthetic reaction', Chapter 6, 'The subtle poison, a synthesis' – Krylov's 'The wolf in the kennel'

This is the most noteworthy of Krylov's fables. There is nothing equal to it in terms of emotion, form or style. It has no moral and no conclusion. Its stern verses have hardly any space for jokes or jibes. A faint joke in the mouth of the huntsman acquires such a contradictory and sinister meaning that it no longer seems funny.

Here we have, strictly speaking, not a fable but a small drama. This is what Belinskii[1] frequently called Krylov's style. In terms of its psychological meaning in this fable, we are dealing with the true seed of tragedy.

★ ★ ★

We will try ... to distinguish the two levels on which the action of the fable evolves, probably in opposite directions. The first thing that strikes us is the extraordinary state of alarm, close to panic, that takes up the first part of the fable and is so masterfully described by the poet. The first impression of the wolf's mistake becomes apparent by the incredible confusion in the kennel itself:

> The kennel was in an uproar as everyone
> sensed the intruder. The dogs were howling
> and tearing at their leashes for a fight.
> 'Boys, there's the thief!' the huntsman yelled
> and slammed the kennel gate.
> And then all hell broke loose –
> some ran around with guns;
> some ran around with clubs.
> 'Light! Give us light!' they screamed.

Each word in this section shows that hell had indeed broken loose. Then this loud, yelling, bouncing, confusing noise, which comes down on the wolf like an avalanche, suddenly changes to another level: it becomes long, slow, and calm, as the wolf is described.

> There was the wolf, pressed in a corner,
> gnashing his teeth, his hair abristle,
> rolling his eyes as if he wanted
> to devour everyone in sight.
> He saw that this was different from
> the fields and woods. He saw
> the reckoning before him for all the sheep
> he'd killed, and he decided, cunningly,
> to start discussions ...

The wolf, cornered, sets a specific mood. We realise that a struggle is impossible; the wolf has been brought to bay, his end is imminent and is taking place before our eyes. But instead of losing his head and panicking, he begins to speak in majestic verses, like an emperor: 'And he began: "Friends, why all this noise?"' The wolf speaks as if it were a festive occasion. He addresses the mob that is running with sticks and guns as 'Friends', and adds a highly ironical note with 'why all this noise?' It takes unusual poetic daring to reduce to a mere 'noise' all the hellish turmoil unleashed against the wolf. It is hard to find another example of such bold artistic technique in Russian poetry. This statement completely upsets the atmosphere and mood created at the beginning; it changes the entire situation and abruptly introduces the other level, so necessary for the further development of the fable. The words uttered subsequently by the wolf develop this plane with unusual poetic courage.

> 'I came to you in peace, not for a fight.
> Let us forget the past and set up a joint order!
> Not only will I henceforth not attack your herds,
> but I shall fight for them against all common foes.
> I am prepared to swear the oath of wolves
> that I ...'

The exalted tone of the speech is in open contradiction to the actual situation. The wolf's eyes want to devour everyone, but his words promise protection. They say that he came to seek peace and graciously offer protection for the herds, but in fact he is pressed into a corner, trembling. The dogs are ready to tear him to pieces, yet his words offer them protection. We are really looking at a thief, but his words offer an oath in which he majestically expresses the word 'I'. The contrast and contradiction between the two levels, as expressed in the experiences and emotions of the wolf and the true and false images, continue. The huntsman interrupts the wolf and answers him in a completely different tone. The wolf uses a lofty, slightly exalted popular language (as correctly pointed out by one critic), quite unique in its way. The huntsman, in contrast, uses rather pedestrian, common language, applicable to everyday facts and events. His familiar interjections, like 'neighbour', 'buddy' and 'guts', are of course in violent contrast to the solemnity of the wolf's words. The huntsman, however, is ready to talk; he accepts the wolf's proposition and answers him in this sense. He is willing to reach an agreement and make peace. But at the same time his words may have a completely opposite meaning. In the clever contraposition, 'You're grizzly, buddy; I, instead, am grizzled,' the distinction between the sounded *r* and the dull *d* [in the Russian words for 'grizzly' and 'grizzled' respectively] is particularly significant.[2]

★ ★ ★

The catastrophe of this fable combines the two contradictory levels, while at the same time they are revealed by the words of the huntsman:

'... Therefore I hold the view
that peace with wolves is made in one way only –
after they have been stripped of hide and hair.'
This said, a pack of wolfhounds he unleashed.

The last line tells us that the discussions have ended in an 'agreement', and that the hunt has resulted in death.

This fable, like the others, develops its action on two contrasting, and frequently opposing, emotional levels. It is obvious from the very beginning that the swift attack on the wolf is equivalent to his destruction. The threat of death is present at all times throughout the entire fable. But alongside it another theme develops. It is one of discussions, where one party wants to make peace and the other is at least agreeable to talking about it. The roles of the characters are inverted. The wolf promises to give protection to the herds and is willing to take a wolf's oath. These two levels are described with the utmost poetic realism, so much so that the author gives a dual characterisation to the participants.

Next, Vygotsky analyses 'Gentle breath', a short story by Ivan Bunin. (The story is reprinted complete in Vygotsky [1971].) We know right at the beginning that the central character, Olia Meshcherskaia, is dead and buried. We learn that Olia, a shallow schoolgirl, obsessed by her own appearance and attractiveness to men, has been murdered out of jealousy by the man who had seduced her when she teasingly revealed that she had already been seduced by another man. The only mourner who comes to Olia's grave is her schoolteacher, herself a person touched by tragedy.

Whereas in the simple form of the fable, the contradiction or struggle takes place on the level of the action itself, Vygotsky shows how in Bunin's story the form and the content pull against one another. The account of 'the insignificant and rather senseless life of a schoolgirl in a provincial Russian town' is on one level irredeemably bleak. And yet the plot, by its complex form, moves the story to another level and 'produces in us an effect that is almost diametrically opposed to the impression caused by the events themselves'.

From *The psychology of art*, Part III, 'Analysis of the aesthetic reaction', Chapter 7 – 'Bunin's "Gentle breath"'

If we take a look at the content of the story, its material taken per se and the system of events in it, we find that it all comes under the category 'troubles of life'. There is not a single bright spot in the entire story. There is nothing but the insignificant and rather senseless life of a schoolgirl in a provincial Russian town. It is a life that springs from obviously diseased roots; its outcome is inevitably unhealthy and sterile. Could it be that this troubled life has been idealised, or somewhat adorned, in the story? Could it be that its darker aspects have been made somewhat lighter so that it may appear to be as a 'pearl of creation', or could it be that the author represents them in a rosy light? Could it be that the author himself grew up in similar circumstances, and finds a certain charm in these events? Could it be that our evaluation differs from the one given these events by the author?

As we analyse the story, we find that none of these conjectures is justified. Not only does the author not attempt to conceal the gloom of life; he exposes it whenever he can, describes it with graphic precision, lets our sensations and emotions almost touch these events, and, figuratively, allows us to put our hand right into life's festering sores. He underscores the senseless emptiness of this life. This is what he says of the girl: '… her fame at school spread almost imperceptibly, and rumours began to circulate that she was frivolous, that she could not live without admirers, that the schoolboy Shenshin had lost his head over her, that she was also in love with him but was so capricious in her behaviour toward him that he attempted suicide …' Bunin uses harsh and brutal terms when he speaks of her liaison with the officer and reveals a truth of life which otherwise might have been somewhat concealed. '… Olia had seduced him, had had an affair with him, had promised to become his wife. But on the day of her murder, at the railway station, as she was seeing him off to Novocherkassk, she suddenly announced that she had never loved him, that all the talk about marriage was but a joke …' Then there is the cruel revelation of the truth as it appears in Olia's diary. Here, she describes her encounter with Maliutin: 'He is fifty-six, but still quite handsome and always well dressed – only I didn't like the cape he arrived in – it smells of English cologne, and his eyes are quite young and black, and his beard is carefully divided into two flowing parts and is entirely silver.'

There is nothing in this scene, as recorded in Olia's diary, that makes us feel the existence of any feeling, or somehow brightens the dark and gloomy picture formed in the reader's mind. The word 'love' is neither mentioned nor hinted at; one may well think that there is no word more alien to these lines than 'love'. Thus, the entire material, all the circumstances of life, all the everyday events, concepts and emotions are described in a subdued tone, without a single bright spot. Thus, as we have stated, the author does not conceal the facts of life but exposes them with a brutality that makes us realise the full impact of the truth upon which his short story is based. We say once again: the essence of the story, viewed from this angle, can be defined as life's troubles, or its turbid waters. Surprisingly, however, the effect of the story, as a whole, is somewhat different.

The story is, after all, called 'Gentle Breath'. It produces in us an effect that is almost diametrically opposed to the impression caused by the events themselves. The true theme of this story is the gentle breath, not the muddled life of a provincial schoolgirl. Its fundamental trait is the feeling of liberation, lightness, the crystal transparency of life, none of which can be derived from the literal events. The duality of the story becomes particularly obvious in the part concerning Olia's schoolteacher, which serves as a frame for the entire narrative. This teacher, who goes into a stupor-like trance as she beholds Olia's tomb, this teacher who is ready to give half her life if only the funeral wreath would disappear, this teacher who is basically as happy as anyone in love or possessed by a dream – it is she who suddenly gives a completely different meaning to the story. For a long time she has been living under delusions which she believes to be life. The author is bold enough to name three of them. The first was her brother, a poor, insignificant non-commissioned officer (this is reality) whom she expected to change miraculously her life and fate (this is the delusion). Then, she deluded herself that she was performing some sort of great work, or sacrifice, for an ideal; this served her as a substitute for life for some time. 'Olia Meshcherskaia's death provided her with a new dream,' says the author, and ranges this third self-deception beside the other two. With this technique, Bunin splits our emotions. He holds up a mirror to the story as he describes the new protagonist and breaks it up into several beams, as with a spectrum. As we read along, we are not only aware but fully convinced that the story reflects both reality and dreams. From here our mind proceeds easily to the structural analysis mentioned earlier. The straight line is reality as it appears in the story, and the complex structural curve of reality, which we called the composition of the novella, is its light breath. We realise that the events are connected in such a way that they lose their turbidity. They are associated as in a melody, and in their crescendos, diminuendos and transitions they untie the threads connecting them. They free themselves of the conventional bonds in which they are presented to us in actuality. They divorce themselves from reality, and associate in the same way as words associate and combine into a verse.

Now we can formulate our idea and say that the author's reason for tracing such an extremely complex curve is his intent to undo life's turbidity and transform it into a crystal transparency. He did this to make life's events unreal, to transform water into wine, as always happens in any real work of art. The words of a story or verse carry its meaning (the water), whereas the composition creates another meaning for the words, transposes everything onto a completely different level, and transforms the whole into wine. Thus, the banal tale of a frivolous provincial schoolgirl is transformed into the gentle breath of Bunin's short story.

In contrast to Krylov's fable and Bunin's story, the events in Shakespeare's play *Hamlet* require no introduction for most readers. Here, Vygotsky builds on the contradictions he analysed in the first two works: emotional contradictions in 'The wolf in the kennel' and the conflict between form and content in 'Gentle breath'. In analysing *Hamlet*, he adds to these a third conflict or contradiction: that between the plot and the protagonist.

From *The psychology of art*, Part III, 'Analysis of the aesthetic reaction', Chapter 8, 'The tragedy of Hamlet, prince of Denmark'

The formula of the story is that Hamlet kills the king to avenge the death of his father; that of the plot is that he does not kill the king. If the material of the tragedy tells us how Hamlet kills the king to avenge the death of his father, then the plot of the tragedy shows us how he fails to kill him and, when he finally does, that it is for reasons other than vengeance. The duality of the story and the plot accounts for the action taking its course on two different planes. Constant awareness of the pre-set path, the deviations from it, and the internal contradictions, are an intrinsic part of this play. Shakespeare apparently chose the most suitable events to express what he wanted to say. He chose material that definitely rushed toward a climax, but at the same time forced him to deviate from it. Shakespeare used a psychological method quite appropriately called the 'method of teasing the emotions' by Petrazhitskii,[3] who wanted to introduce it as an experimental method. In fact, the tragedy does nothing but tease our feelings. It promises the fulfilment of the task set from the very beginning, but deviates again and again from this goal, thus straining our expectations to the utmost and making us quite painfully feel every step that leads away from the main path. When the target is reached at last, it turns out that we have been brought to it from a completely different direction; we also discover that the two paths which led away from each other in apparent conflict suddenly converge at one point during the final scene (when the king is killed twice). The same motives that prevent the killing of the king finally lead us to his death. The catastrophe reaches a point of extreme contradiction, a short-circuiting of two currents flowing in opposite directions.

* * *

In addition to this contradiction, there is another one in the tragedy which is of equal importance for the artistic effect of the play. The dramatis personae chosen by Shakespeare somehow do not quite fit the action; moreover, Shakespeare convincingly disproves the widespread belief that the individual characters of the dramatis personae must determine their own actions.

* * *

Psychoanalysts are right in asserting that the substance of the psychological effect of a tragedy consists in our identification with the hero. It is quite correct that the author forces us to view all the other characters, actions and events from the protagonist's viewpoint. The hero becomes the point upon which our attention is focused, and simultaneously serves as a support for our feelings, which would otherwise be lost in endless digressions as we evaluate, empathise and suffer with every character. Were we to evaluate the king's and Hamlet's emotions or Polonius's and Hamlet's hopes in the same way, our feelings would suffer constant changes and oscillations in which one and the same event would appear to us to have completely contradictory meanings. The tragedy, however, proceeds in a different way. It shapes our feelings into a unity and forces them to follow the protagonist alone and to perceive everything through his eyes. It suffices to examine any tragedy, *Hamlet* in particular, to realise that all its characters are portrayed as the protagonist sees them. All the events are refracted by the lens of his soul. The author actually builds his tragedy on two planes: on the one hand, he sees everything with Hamlet's eyes; but then he also views Hamlet with his own – Shakespeare's – eyes, so that the spectator becomes at the same time Hamlet and his contemplator. This insight explains the important roles played by the characters of the tragedy, in particular Hamlet. We are dealing here with a completely new psychological level. In the fable we discovered two meanings within one and the same action. In the short story we discovered one level for the story (subject) and one for the plot (material). In the tragedy we uncover yet another level, the psyche and the emotions of the hero.

* * *

The new contribution of the protagonist is that *at any moment, he unifies both contradictory planes and is the supreme and ever-present embodiment of the contradiction inherent in the tragedy*. We have said that the tragedy is constructed from the viewpoint of the protagonist, which means that the tragedy is the force uniting the two opposing currents and combining in the protagonist two opposing emotions. Thus the two opposite levels of the tragedy are perceived as a single unit, for they merge in the tragic hero with whom we identify. The simple duality which we discovered in the [short] story is replaced in the tragedy by a much deeper and more serious one, because of the fact that not only do we view the entire tragedy through the protagonist's eyes, but we in turn look at the protagonist himself through our own eyes.

In the final part of the book, Vygotsky has two main purposes. His first is to find a theory of artistic response which can explain how art works on us. This involves him in developing his discussion of catharsis.

From *The psychology of art*, Part IV, 'The psychology of art', Chapter 9, 'Art as a catharsis'

We have seen from the foregoing that a work of art (such as a fable, a short story, a tragedy) always includes an affective contradiction, causes conflicting feelings, and leads to the short-circuiting and destruction of these emotions. This is the true effect of a work of art. We come now to the concept of *catharsis* used by Aristotle as the basis for his explanation of tragedy, and repeatedly mentioned by him with regard to the other arts. In his *Poetica* he says that 'tragedy imitates an important and finished action of a certain magnitude, with a speech whose every part has a different ornament, or with action, not narration, that performs a purification of such affects by means of pity and fear.'

No matter what interpretation we assign the enigmatic term 'catharsis', we must be sure that it corresponds to Aristotle's. For our purposes, however, this is irrelevant. Whether we follow Lessing,[4] who understands catharsis to be the moral action of the tragedy (the transformation of passions into virtues) or Müller,[5] for whom it is the transition from displeasure to pleasure; whether we accept Bernays'[6] interpretation of the term as healing and purification in the medical sense, or Zeller's[7] opinion that catharsis appeases affect: we will imperfectly and incompletely express the meaning we assign to this term. Despite the indefiniteness of its content, despite our failure to explain the meaning of this term in the Aristotelian sense, there is no other term in psychology which so completely expresses the central fact of aesthetic reaction, according to which painful and unpleasant affects are discharged and transformed into their opposites. Aesthetic reaction as such is nothing but catharsis; that is, a complex transformation of feelings. Though little is known at present about the process of catharsis, we do know, however, that the discharge of nervous energy (which is the essence of any emotion) takes place in a direction which opposes the conventional one, and that art therefore becomes a most powerful means for important and appropriate discharges of nervous energy. The basis for this process reveals itself in the contradiction which inheres in the structure of any work of art.

* * *

But then, in any work of art there are emotions generated by the material as well as by the form; the question is: how do these two kinds of emotion interrelate to each other? We already know the answer, for it derives from our preceding arguments. This relation is one of antagonism; the two kinds of emotion move in opposite directions. The law of aesthetic response is the same for a fable as for a tragedy: *it comprises an affect that develops in two opposite directions but reaches annihilation at its point of termination.*

This is the process we should like to call catharsis.

* * *

The contrast discovered by us in the structure of artistic form and that of artistic content is the basis of cathartic action in the aesthetic response. Schiller [2004] puts it like this: 'The secret of a master is to destroy content by means of form; the more majestic and attractive the content, the more it moves to the fore, and the more the viewer falls under its spell, the greater the triumph of art which removes the content and dominates it.'

A work of art always contains an intimate conflict between its content and its form, and the artist achieves his effect by means of the form, which destroys the content.

Let us now make some final statements. We can say that the basic aesthetic response consists of affect caused by art, affect experienced by us as if it were real, but which finds its release in the activity of imagination provoked by a work of art. This central release delays and inhibits the external motor aspect of affect, and we think we are experiencing only illusory feelings. Art is based on the union of feeling and imagination. Another peculiarity of art is that, while it generates in us opposing affects, it delays (on account of the antithetic principle) the motor expression of emotions and, by making opposite impulses collide, it destroys the affect of content and form, and initiates an explosive discharge of nervous energy.

Catharsis of the aesthetic response is the transformation of affects, the explosive response which culminates in the discharge of emotions.

Vygotsky's second purpose in the final part of the book is to consider the emotional power of art in our lives. Here he touches on the role of art in the development of the new society.

From *The psychology of art*, Part IV, 'The psychology of art', Chapter 11, 'Art and life'

A more complex and deeper meaning of the principle of economising emotions will become clearer if we try to understand the social significance of art. Art is the social within us, and even if its action is performed by a single individual, it does not mean that its essence is individual. It is quite naive and inappropriate to take the social to be collective, as with a large crowd of persons. The social also exists where there is only one person with his individual experiences and tribulations. This is why the action of art, when it performs catharsis and pushes into this purifying flame the most intimate and important experiences, emotions and feelings of the soul, is a social action. But this experience does not happen as described in the theory of contamination (where a feeling born in one person infects and contaminates everybody and *becomes* social), but exactly the other way around. The melting of feelings outside us is performed by the strength of social feeling, which is objectivised, materialised, and projected outside of us, then fixed in external objects of art which have become the tools of society. A fundamental characteristic of man, one that distinguishes him from animals, is that he endures and separates from his body both the apparatus of technology and that of scientific knowledge, which then become the tools of society. Art is the social technique of emotion, a tool of society which brings the most intimate and personal aspects of our being into the circle of social life. It would be more correct to say that emotion becomes personal when every one of us experiences a work of art; it becomes personal without ceasing to be social.

Notes

1. Visarion Belinskii (1811–1848) was a Russian literary critic.
2. 'The Russian word for 'grey' is *seriĭ*, with the stem *ser*; and, for 'grey-haired', *sedoĭ*, with the stem *sed*. The sounded *r* in the former gives the word, in the context of the fable, a slightly sinister sound or meaning, which can be rendered with 'grizzly'. There is an obvious reference to a growl.' (translator's note)
3. Leon Petrazhitskii (1867–1931) was a Polish philosopher, sociologist and legal scholar.
4. Gotthold Lessing (1729–1781) was a German philosopher, art critic and dramatist.
5. Adam Müller (1779–1829) was a German-Austrian philosopher, political economist and literary critic.
6. Jacob Bernays (1824–1881) was a German philologist and philosopher.
7. Eduard Zeller (1814–1908) was a German theologian and philosopher.

References

Schiller, F. (2004) 'On the aesthetic education of man' [1795]. Mineola, NY: Dover Publications.

Vygotsky, L.S. (1971). *The psychology of art* [1925]. Intro. A.N. Leontiev, commentary V.V. Ivanov. Cambridge, MA: MIT Press.

Chapter 3

Vygotsky the defectologist

The term 'defectology' had been in general use for decades in Vygotsky's day to describe what we might call 'the study of children with special educational needs', whether physical or intellectual. From the beginning of his career to the end, Vygotsky worked, and held official posts, in the field of defectology, but he recognised the negativity in the term. He regularly criticised practice in 'old-style' defectology as being condescending, mechanical and negative. He was also clear that the merely quantitative methods of diagnosing handicaps used in defectology were inadequate.

In this chapter, we present extracts from some of Vygotsky's numerous texts on defectology.

In the following two texts, Vygotsky takes blindness as the handicap on the basis of which he advances his argument.

From 'Introduction: The fundamental problems of defectology' (Vygotsky, 1993g), sections 1 and 2

A purely arithmetical conception of a handicapped condition is characteristic of an obsolete, old-school defectology. Reaction against this quantitative approach to all theoretical and practical problems is the most important characteristic of modern defectology. The struggle between these two attitudes toward defectology – between two antithetical ideas, two principles – is the burning issue in that positive crisis which this area of scientific knowledge is presently undergoing.

Viewing a handicapped condition as a purely quantitative developmental limitation undoubtedly has the same conceptual basis as the peculiar theory of preformed childhood operations, according to which post-natal childhood development is reduced exclusively to quantitative growth and to the expansion of organic and psychological functions. Defectology is currently undertaking a theoretical task which is analogous to the one once performed by pedology[1] and child psychology, when both defended the position that a child is not simply a small adult. Defectology is now contending for a fundamental thesis, the defence of which is its sole justification for existence as a science. The thesis holds that a child whose development is impeded by a defect is not simply a child less developed than his peers but is a child who has developed differently.

★ ★ ★

The dual role of a physical disability, first in the developmental process and then in the formation of the child's personality, is a fundamental fact with which we must deal when development is complicated by a defect. On the one hand, the defect means a minus, a limitation, a weakness, a delay in development; on the other, it stimulates a heightened, intensified advancement, precisely because it creates difficulties. The position of modern defectology is the following: any defect creates stimuli for a compensatory process. Therefore, defectologists cannot limit their dynamic study of a handicapped child to determining the degree and severity of the deficiency. Without fail, they must take into account the compensatory processes in a child's development and behaviour, which substitute for, supersede, and overarch the defect. Just as the patient – and not the disease – is important for modern medicine, so the child burdened with the defect – not the defect in and of itself – becomes the focus of concern for defectology ... Thus, the child's physical and psychological reaction to the handicap is the central and basic problem – indeed, the sole reality – with which defectology deals.

A long time ago, W. Stern[2] pointed out the dual role played by a defect. Thus, the blind child compensates with an increased ability to distinguish through touch – not only by actually increasing the stimulability of his nerves, but by exercising his ability to observe, estimate, and ponder differences. So, too, in the area of psychological functions, the decreased value of one faculty may be fully or partially compensated for by the stronger development of another. For example, the cultivation of comprehension may replace keenness of observation and recollection, compensating for a poor memory. Impressionability, the tendency to imitate, and so forth, compensate for weakness of motivation and inadequate initiative. The functions of personality are not so exclusive that, given the abnormally weak development of one characteristic, the task performed by it necessarily and in all circumstances suffers. Thanks to the organic unity of personality, another faculty undertakes to accomplish the task (Stern, 1921).

★ ★ ★

A. Adler[3] and his school posit as the basis of their psychological system the study of abnormal organs and functions, the inadequacy of which constantly stimulates an intensified (higher) development. According to Adler, awareness of a physically handicapped condition is, for the individual, a constant stimulation of mental development. If any organ, because of a morphological or functional deficiency, does not fully cope with its task, then the central human nervous and mental apparatus compensates for the organ's deficient operation by creating a psychological superstructure which shores up the entire deficient organism at its weakened, threatened point. Conflict arises from contact with the exterior milieu; conflict is caused by the incompatibility of the deficient organ or function and the task before it. This conflict, in turn, leads to an increased possibility of illness and fatality. The same conflict may also create greater potentialities and stimuli for compensation and even for over-compensation. Thus, defect becomes the starting point and the principal motivating force in the psychological development of personality. It establishes the target point toward which the development of all psychological forces strives. It gives direction to the process of growth and to the formation of personality. A handicap creates a higher developmental tendency; it enhances such mental phenomena as foresight and presentiment, as well as their operational elements (memory, attention, intuition, sensibility, interest) – in a word, all supporting psychological features (Adler, 1928).

★ ★ ★

'He will want to see everything,' Adler says about a child, 'if he is near-sighted; to hear everything, if he is hearing-impaired; he will want to say everything, if he has an obvious speech defect or a stutter ... The desire to fly will be most apparent in those children who experience great difficulty even in jumping. The contrast between the physical disability and the desires, fantasies, dreams, i.e. psychological drives to compensate, are so universal that one may base upon this *a fundamental law: via subjective feelings of inadequacy, a physical handicap dialectically transforms itself into psychological drives toward compensation and over-compensation*' (Adler, 1927, p. 57). Formerly, it was believed that the entire life and development of a blind child would be framed by blindness. The new law states that development will go against this course. If blindness exists, then mental development will be directed away from blindness, against blindness.

★ ★ ★

It would be a mistake to assume that the process of compensation always, without fail, ends in success, that it always leads from the defect to the formation of a new capability. As with every process of overcoming and struggle, compensation may also have two extreme outcomes – victory and failure – and between these two are all possible transitional points. The outcome depends on many things, but basically it depends on the relationship between (1) the severity of the defect and (2) the wealth of compensatory reserves. But whatever the anticipated outcome, *always and in all circumstances*, development, complicated by a defect, represents a creative (physical and psychological) process. It represents the creation and re-creation of a child's personality based on the restructuring of all the adaptive functions and on the formation of new processes – overarching, substituting, equalising – generated by the handicap, and creating new, roundabout paths for development. Defectology is faced with a world of new, infinitely diverse forms and courses of development. The course created by a defect – that of compensation – is the major course of development for a child with a physical handicap or functional disability.

The positive uniqueness of the handicapped child is created not by the failure of one or another function observed in a normal child, but by the new formations caused by this lapse. This uniquely individual reaction to a defect represents a continually evolving adaptive process. If a blind or deaf child achieves the same level of development as a normal child, then the child with a defect achieves this *in another way, by another course, by other means*. And, for the pedagogue, it is particularly important to know the *uniqueness* of the course, along which he must lead the child. The key to originality transforms the minus of the handicap into the plus of compensation.

From 'Defect and compensation' (Vygotsky, 1993c), section 3

The education and rearing of handicapped children should be based on the fact that along with a defect come combative psychological tendencies and the potential for overcoming the defect. Education of these children should take into account that precisely these tendencies emerge in the foreground of a child's development and must be included in the educational process as his motivating strength. Constructing the entire educational process on the basis of natural compensatory drives does not mean alleviating all difficulties that arise as a result of the defect. It means instead concentrating all strengths on the compensation of the defect, selecting, in the appropriate sequential order, those tasks which will bring about the gradual formation of the entire personality from a new standpoint.

What a liberating truth for the pedagogue! A blind child develops a psychological superstructure circumventing his impaired vision with only one goal in mind: to replace sight. Using every possible means available to him, a deaf child works out ways to overcome the isolation and seclusion caused by his deafness. Up to now we have neglected these psychological powers. We have not taken into account the desire with which such a child struggles to be healthy and fully accepted socially. A defect has been statically viewed as merely a defect, a minus.

Education has neglected the positive forces created by a defect. Psychologists and pedagogues have not been acquainted with Adler's law of the opposition between a physical handicap and the psychological drives to compensate. They have taken into account only the former, the defect. They didn't understand that a handicap is not just an impoverished psychological state but also a source of wealth, not just a weakness but a strength. They thought that the development of a blind child centres on his blindness. As it turns out, his development strives to transcend blindness. The psychology of blindness is essentially the psychology of victory over blindness.

Vygotsky argued that it was possible for handicapped children to circumvent or 'overcome the deficit' by gaining access to language – including, of course, specialist languages like Braille and the language of the deaf (which Vygotsky initially calls 'mimicry'). These means of communication, like those used by sighted and hearing people, are examples of cultural development. Vygotsky points out that a defect can act as a stimulus, spurring children on to find ways round it. Language is the main 'detour' by which handicapped children can circumvent their handicaps and gain access to higher mental functions and to the world of knowledge and culture. Even multiply handicapped blind deaf-mute children can learn to hear, speak, read and write, as long as they are encouraged to do so and introduced to different, appropriate means of communicating.

In the next four passages Vygotsky further discusses the specific needs of blind children and extends his discussion to the needs of deaf-mute and blind deaf-mute children. In an aside, he compares the merits of special schools with the value of integrating blind children into mainstream schools.

From 'The psychology and pedagogy of children's handicaps' (Vygotsky, 1993h), section 3

In education for the blind, or in any branch of special education, the leap that heals (*salto vitale*) goes beyond the limits of individual pedagogy, beyond that 'duet' between the teacher and the pupil, which has been the basis of traditional education. As soon as a new element – in this case the use of another's eyes, that is, collaboration with a sighted person – is drawn into the process of educating the blind, then we immediately find ourselves, in principle, on new ground: the blind person acquires his microscope and telescope, which infinitely widens his experience and closely intertwines him in the general weave of the world.

Psychologically, the task of educating the blind child boils down to combining all the special symbol and signal systems linked with the other sensory analysers: skin nerves, auditory nerves, and so forth. Only in this way does the education of the blind differ from the education of everyone else. A portion of the conditional associations is redirected to the skin or to any other part of the nervous system. A blind person reads, feeling the perforated dots with his fingers. What is important is that he reads *in precisely the same way as we do*; that he does this using different means, his fingers, not his eyes, cannot have any major significance. Does it make any real difference if you read a German text in Latin or Gothic script? Meaning is what is important, not the signs in themselves. We may change the signs but the meaning will be preserved.

From this, of course, it follows that the special education of blind children must occur in a special school which builds up the skills in this particular symbol system. The basic principle of pedagogy for the blind child will mean, then, the use of *a different symbolic system which maintains the same content as any other instructional or educational process.*

However, the special school systematically breaks off contact with the normal world; it isolates the blind child and puts him in a narrow, closed off, small world, where everything is calculated for and adapted to the defect, where everything reminds him of it. This artificial milieu has nothing in common with that normal world where the blind adult will ultimately have to live. In the special school, a close, hospital-like atmosphere and regime are soon created. The blind child moves in the narrow circle of the blind. This environment nurtures the defect and fixes the child's attention on his blindness, 'traumatising' him. Blindness is not overcome in such a school but is intensified. In such a school, not only is there no development of those strengths which could help the blind child enter the normal world; instead these strengths become systematically atrophied. Mental health and the normal formation of the psyche become disorganised and disintegrate; blindness turns into psychic trauma.

The special school by its very nature is antisocial and encourages antisocialism. We have to think about not isolating the blind person from life as soon as possible, but about introducing him into life as early and as extensively as possible. A blind person will have to live a normal life in the seeing world; he must, therefore, learn in a general (mainstream) school. Therefore, certain elements of his special education and upbringing must be taken beyond the special school and introduced into the mainstream school. In principle, Shcherbina's[4] proposed system of combining special and mainstream education should be created. In order to overcome the antisocial nature of the special school, scientifically based experiments must be conducted to integrate the education of the blind with that of the sighted, an experiment which possesses an enormous future.

From 'Defectology and the study of the development and education of abnormal children' (Vygotsky, 1993d)

...in the case of the blind, tactile print replaces visible print. The raised dots of Braille permit the blind to compose an entire alphabet, to read by touching these dots on a page, and to write by perforating the paper and poking out raised dots. In a similar way, dactylology (or finger spelling) allows the deaf-mute to substitute visual signs and various hand positions for the various signs of our alphabet and to compose a special way of writing in the air which a deaf child reads with his eyes.

Education has proceeded even further and teaches the deaf-mute child oral speech, inasmuch as his verbal apparatus is not usually damaged. A child who is deaf from birth becomes mute as a result of the fact that he is deprived of auditory perceptions. Education teaches a deaf child to understand oral speech by reading the lips of a speaking person, that is, by replacing the sounds of speech with visual images, movements of the mouth and lips. A deaf-mute learns to speak by using touch, by using signs to imitate, and by using kinetic sensations.

These specially devised roundabout paths of cultural development for the blind or the deaf-mute, this written and oral speech created especially for them, are extremely important in the history of cultural development from two perspectives. The blind and the deaf are seemingly nature's true experiment for revealing to us that the cultural development of behaviour is not necessarily connected with this or that organic function. Speech is not necessarily tied to the sound apparatus; it may be embodied in another sign system, just as the written language may be transferred from the path of vision to the path of touch.

Cases of abnormal development allow us to observe with the greatest clarity the divergence between cultural and natural development. This divergence essentially occurs in a normal child as well, but in the case of the deaf or blind child it appears with far greater distinctness precisely because a striking disparity is noted between those cultural forms of behaviour intended for the normal human psycho-physiological make-up, and those behavioural forms available to the handicapped child. Most important, however, the cultural forms of behaviour serve as the only path of education for an abnormal child. This path means the creation of roundabout ways of development at that point where it proves to be impossible to proceed by direct paths. Braille for the blind and writing in the air for the deaf-mute are just such roundabout psychological means of cultural development.

We have grown accustomed to the thought that a human being reads with his eyes and speaks with his mouth, and only a great cultural experiment demonstrating that it is possible to read with the fingers and speak with the hand can bring to light the entire complexity and dynamics of behaviour. Psychologically, these forms of behaviour succeed in overcoming that which is most important: they succeed in cultivating speech and writing in a blind or deaf child in the proper sense of these words.

It is important that a blind child be able to read just as we read, but this cultural function is performed by an absolutely different apparatus than is normally the case. Similarly, from the point of view of cultural development, what is most important for a deaf child is that universal human speech is made available to him by a completely different psychological apparatus.

And thus, these examples first teach us that cultural forms of behaviour do not depend upon a specific psycho-physiological apparatus. Second, it is clearly apparent from the example of deaf-mute children that the development of cultural forms of behaviour occurs spontaneously. Deaf-mute children, when left to themselves, develop a complex language of mimicry, a unique means of speech. This particular form of speech is not created for the deaf-mute but composed by the deaf-mute themselves. A unique language is created and it differs from all modern human languages more than these languages differ from each other, because this unique means of speech dates back to the most ancient proto-language of mankind, the language of gesture or even only of the hand.

Left to himself, deprived of any education, a child sets off on the path of cultural development; in other words, in a child's natural psychological development and in his surrounding milieu, in his need to communicate with this environment, we find all the ingredients necessary for cultural development, which occurs, as it were, like combustion. A spontaneous transition occurs in the child from natural to cultural development.

Both above-mentioned points, taken together, bring us to a radical re-evaluation of the present-day view of the education of an abnormal child. The traditional view proceeds from the position that a defect means a minus, a flaw, a deficit, which limits and constricts the development of the child who is characterised first and foremost from the standpoint of the failure of one or another function. The entire psychology of the abnormal child was founded upon methods intended for the functions which lapsed from the psychology of normal children.

In place of this conception, we find another, more dynamic examination of a handicapped child's development; it takes as its point of departure the basic premise that a defect has a twofold influence on a child's development. On the one hand, it is a deficit and operates directly as such, creating a flaw, an impediment, and difficulties in the child's adaptation. On the other hand, precisely because the defect creates obstacles and impasses to development, disrupting the normal equilibrium, it serves as a stimulus for the development of roundabout paths of adjustment, of substitute functions which build a superstructure and which strive to compensate for the deficit and bring the entire system of the disturbed equilibrium into a new order.

Thus, the new point of view prescribes taking into account not only the child's negative characteristics, not only his minuses, but also a positive contour of his personality. This view presents a picture of complex developmental paths. The development of higher psychological functions is possible only along paths of cultural development, whether or not this development proceeds along lines which master cultural means (speech, writing, arithmetic), or along the line of an internal perfection of psychological functions (the development of voluntary attention, logical memory, abstract thought, concept formations, volition, and so forth). Investigations have shown that an abnormal child is usually delayed precisely in this respect. Cultural development, then, does not depend on the organic deficit.

Thus, the history of child cultural development permits us to advance the following thesis: cultural development is the main area for compensation of deficiency when further organic development is impossible; in this respect, the path of cultural development is unlimited.

From 'The collective as a factor in the development of the abnormal child' (Vygotsky, 1993b), section 4

Psychological research, both experimental and clinical, agree in their demonstrations that polyglossia (that is, the mastery of several forms of speech) is an unavoidable and fruitful method of speech development and education for the deaf-mute child, given the current state of pedagogy for the deaf. In connection with this, radical changes should be made in the traditional view about the competition among a variety of forms of speech and about their mutually restrictive nature on the development of the deaf-mute child. We must also pose the theoretical and practical question concerning their coordination and structural composition at various stages of learning.

This latter question, in turn, demands a complex, differentiated approach to speech development and to the education of a deaf-mute child. The experience of the most advanced European and American pedagogues, especially the Scandinavians and Americans, testifies to the presence of a complex structure for combining different forms of speech, as well as a differentiated approach to speech education for the deaf-mute child. Rather than being simply acceptable, all this suggests in turn a whole series of problems and questions for the theoretical and practical pedagogy of the deaf. These might jointly be resolved, not at the level of methods, but at the level of the methodology of speech education. Their resolution absolutely demands an elaboration of the psychology of the deaf-mute child.

Only a serious investigation of the laws of speech development and a radical reform in the method of speech education can bring our schools to a real, rather than a minimal, victory over muteness in deaf children. This means that, in practice, we must make use of all possibilities for speech activity for a deaf-mute child. We must not approach mimicry with condescension and scorn, treating it as an enemy. Rather we must understand that different forms of speech do not only compete with one another or disrupt one another's development, but that they can also serve as steps on which the deaf-mute child climbs to the mastery of speech.

From 'Bases for working with mentally retarded and physically handicapped children' (Vygotsky, 1993a), section 7

Educating a blind deaf-mute child raises more difficulties and presents more obstacles than educating either a blind or a deaf child. Still, such a child has limitless possibilities for development and education, as long as the central circuitry of the nervous system and the mental apparatus are undamaged in a blind deaf-mute. The names of Helen Keller and Laura Bridgeman are universally recognised as two blind deaf-mutes who attained very high levels of mental development thanks to their education and teaching. Helen Keller succeeded in becoming a famous writer and proponent of optimism. The data about Laura Bridgeman are more modest, but also more trustworthy and scientifically accurate: she had a command of language, reading, writing, elementary arithmetic, geography and natural history.

The basis for training a blind deaf-mute child lies in teaching him speech. Only with the ability to speak can he become a social entity, that is, a human in the real sense of the word. Such a child establishes contact with his surroundings through touch. Through his sense of touch, he receives the signs of the deaf-mute 'finger alphabet' (dactylology) as well as the raised points of the Braille alphabet for the blind. In this way the child learns to understand speech and to read. Such a child can learn to speak with the aid of the 'hand alphabet' or using natural speech, learned through imitation. True, such learning is very complicated by comparison with the teaching of a deaf child, since a blind deaf-mute cannot see the articulating lip movements of the person with whom he is speaking and his imitation can be guided only by his sense of touch.

Not only was Vygotsky concerned to promote the most enlightened ways of helping children with a physical handicap to overcome, or circumvent, the handicap; he was also profoundly aware of the social implications of handicap. He and his colleagues had studied the ways in which handicapped children (in the specific example following, a hearing-impaired child) may respond to the social situation in which they find themselves.

From 'The difficult child' (Vygotsky, 1993f), section 1

I permit myself to begin with a concrete example which will clarify how modern psychologists are inclined to picture the formation of certain character traits, or a certain behavioural tendency. Let us say that we have before us a child who is afflicted with a hearing loss as a result of one or another cause. It is easy to imagine that this child will experience a series of difficulties in adapting to his surroundings. During play, other children will leave him in the background; he will lag behind on walks; he will be eliminated from active participation in children's festivities and conversations. In a word, a child with a hearing impairment will be placed, because of his simple organic deficiency, in a lower social position than other children. We want to say that in the process of adapting to the social milieu, this child will run up against more obstacles than will a normal child. How will this circumstance affect the formation of the child's character?

I think that the development of a child's character will proceed along the following fundamental lines: as a result of poor hearing, he will confront difficulties; therefore, a heightened sensitivity, attentiveness, curiosity, distrustfulness with respect to his environment will develop. Perhaps he will cultivate still another series of particular psychological traits, the appearance of which is understandable if we take into account that these character traits are the child's response to the difficulties encountered on his path. The child who, as a result of his deficiency, becomes the object of derision among his comrades will develop increased suspicion, curiosity, and caution, and an entire complex psychological superstructure. We understand this complex system of attitudes and behavioural modes to be a reaction, or response to the difficulties the child encounters in the process of adapting to his social environment.

We are able to note three basic types of such forms of reaction in the child. One of these is well known in psychiatry; in medicine, it is called the delirium of the hard of hearing. This group is so different from others that psychiatrists long ago singled it out. Those forms of response mentioned above begin to occur in the hard of hearing. Suspicion, distrust, over-anxiety and caution develop in the person who is beginning to lose his hearing. Each word from those surrounding him gives him cause for strong anxiety; it seems to him that people are thinking something bad about him. He loses sleep and begins to feel that he will be killed. He is ready to accuse others of conspiring against him. Each new face arouses suspicions in him. In the final analysis, he develops a persecution mania.

Are these character traits the same, according to my psychological nature, as those with which I was born? I propose that a given formation appears in response to difficulties arising in the course of adaptation to the environment. If a hearing defect did not cut this person off from his surrounding environment, and normal relations with other people continued, then there would not be anything particular about his behaviour. Although we have the right to say that this is simply a case of a response formation – suspicion and caution – it is, however, a well-known behavioural way of relating to the environment, a mode cultivated in response to those difficulties which a person confronts. But this is a fictitious condition which does not stem from reality, inasmuch as close friends and relations do not wish him evil. Further, those means of behaviour cultivated by a sick person in response to difficulties do not really overcome them. The difficulties themselves arise on the basis of ideas which are divorced from reality and on the basis of the unreal means used by the afflicted person in his struggle with these phantoms. Modern psychologists suggest that such a system of character formation be called fictitious compensation. They say that this attitude of caution, suspicion and over-anxiety arises as a form of compensation when a person tries to defend himself in some way in the face of difficulties. If we turn to the example with which I began, then we see that the two opposing lines of character development are also possible in the case of a hard-of-hearing child. The first (which we can call real compensation) occurs in response to more or less realistically accountable difficulties. Thus, if a hard-of-hearing child develops a heightened sensitivity, keenness of observation, curiosity, attentiveness and sharpness, and learns to recognise by vague signs that which other children learn by means of auditory perception, he does so because he has a healthy regard for his difficulties. He will not leave his watch post lest he miss something. This is called real compensation. We have already discussed fictitious compensation.

Finally, the last type of compensation. It may assume the most diverse forms. Here, we do not encounter the two types of compensation already identified (hallucinatory and real compensation). The third type – the most difficult to define – is so multifarious, so far removed from external unity, that it is difficult to define with one word. Here, however, is a rough explanation. Imagine that a child experiences a certain weakness. Under certain conditions, this weakness can become a strength. The child may cover up his weakness. He is weak and hears poorly. This lowers his responsiveness to other children and elicits a greater solicitude on the part of others. And he begins to cultivate an illness within himself in order to obtain the right to have more attention. He seems in devious ways to reward himself for the difficulties he experiences. Adults know what kind of advantages can be made of illness: when responsiveness on the child's part is lowered, he can place himself in an exceptional position. A child takes particular advantage of this position within the family where, because of his illness, he suddenly becomes the centre of the attention of all surrounding him. This example of withdrawal into illness for the sake of camouflaging one's weakness represents the third type of compensation. It is difficult to determine whether or not it is real. It is real in the sense that the child achieves certain advantages; it is fictitious because not only does he not rid himself of his difficulties but, on the contrary, he accentuates them even more. We have in mind the child who makes his deficit into a burden. When exposed to sound, he is apt to make his loss appear far greater than it is in reality because it is more or less advantageous for him to do so.

A reaction of a different nature can, however, occur. A child may compensate for his difficulties by exhibiting responsive, aggressive actions with respect to his social environment (his peers, his parents, the school). In other words, a child may take compensatory action of yet another kind. Allow us to illustrate with the concrete example of this deaf child. He may exhibit an increased irritability, stubbornness and aggressiveness toward other children; he will attempt to eradicate by practical means the deprivation caused by his defect. Holding last place in any game, this child will, as a consequence of his hearing loss, try to play a greater role. He will always gravitate toward younger children. Such a course of compensation is very distinctive. Here we find the cultivation of certain character traits, which we conventionally would call love of power, a tendency toward 'autocracy', stubbornness; that is, the tendency to insist without fail on one's own way, although what was suggested in no way runs counter to the child's desires. What links this last case of a child's character development with the previous example of a child who withdraws into illness and cultivates his defect? To a certain degree, this third type of compensation is real because the child achieves by other means what his defect has denied him, and at the same time, of course, it is also fictitious compensation because although he gets what he wants in a collective of younger children by stubbornness, he does not really overcome the difficulties confronting him.

Vygotsky has clear ideas, derived from his and his colleagues' extensive clinical work, about how best to diagnose the needs of children he calls 'difficult'; that is, children who may be hard to reach or have what we might call 'learning difficulties'. In doing so, he returns to his criticism of purely quantitative, 'mechanical and arithmetical' modes of analysis.

From 'The diagnostics of development and the pedological clinic for difficult children' (Vygotsky, 1993e), section 5

A researcher should remember, as he embarks on studying indications, data and symptoms, that he should be studying and determining the peculiarities and the nature of a developmental process which will not appear directly before him but which are basic to all those indications which he can observe. Thus, a researcher's task, in extensive pedological research as well as in developmental diagnosis, is not only to establish the known symptoms and to list and systemise them — nor is his task only to group events according to similar external characteristics; rather, it lies exclusively in penetrating to the deeper essentials of the developmental processes by thoughtfully analysing these external data.

Contemporary pedological research often tries to prepare final conclusions about developmental levels based on the mechanical and arithmetical analysis of external symptoms; this is what both the Binet[5] and Rossolimo[6] methods do. This research does neither more nor less than try to economise on the most important part of any scientific work — that is, on thought and reflection. A pedologue who works with the Binet or Rossolimo methods establishes certain facts; then, he analyses them using purely arithmetical methods. The result, reached in an entirely mechanical fashion, is altogether lacking in reflective analysis.

★ ★ ★

General and fundamental to compiling a scientific history of a child's development is the requirement that this educational and developmental history be a causal description of the child's life. Unlike a simple chronicle or a simple listing of individual events (such-and-such happened in such-and-such a year, something else in another year), a causal description lays out events in such a way that it puts them in cause-and-result sequence, uncovers their relationships, and examines a given period of that history as a single, intertwined, and changing entity; it tries to discover the laws, links and changes according to which that entity was built and which it follows. Usually, the pedological history of a child's development is composed of a list of separate events, not internally linked amongst themselves, connected only as in a questionnaire, and organised chronologically. Lacking, however, is a developmental history; that is, the interconnected, dynamic, unified whole. The usual descriptions remind one more of chronicles than of a true historical representation of events and their changes.

Here, Anton Chekhov's rule about the internal construction of a literary tale is entirely applicable. It discusses the need to link all parts of a story by an internal tie; for example, if the author, on the first page of the story, in describing the decor of a room, mentions that a gun hangs on the wall, then that gun must shoot on the last page of the story – or else there was no reason to have mentioned it in describing the room's decor. In a child's developmental history, every fact included must similarly serve the purpose of the whole. The gun mentioned at the beginning must, absolutely, shoot before the end. No fact at all should be included simply for its own sake. Every fact must be so interconnected with the whole that it would be impossible to discard it without destroying the whole structure.

The ideal developmental history should unfold with the same strictly logical regularity as a geometry theorem. We feel that, in the early stages of pedology, as we strive to learn and master the art of scientific developmental diagnostics, it would not be bad to borrow some logical rigour of geometry theorems, even if we were to lean a bit on the support of geometry. One should, at any rate, remember that what one wants to demonstrate at the end of a developmental history should be succinctly formulated (at least in the mind of the researcher) at the beginning; at the end, the position which was to have been proven should be clearly enunciated. This should be true not only of the developmental history as a whole, but also of the separate factors which compose that history.

From this, it should be clear that the centre of gravity in a child's developmental history must be moved from external events, which any nanny could collect as well as a pedologue could (when the child was able to sit up, speak, and so on), to the study and establishing of internal links through which the developmental process is revealed. Once more, we see the path from the superficial to the profound, from that which is obvious to that which must be sought, from a phenomenological analysis of occurrences to a determination of their deeper causes.

Vygotsky admits that, at his time of writing in the Soviet Union, professionals in pedology who were concerned with the needs of children with intellectual handicaps were still very far from being able to provide those children's teachers with the

'scientific history of a child's development', involving 'complete, specific, detailed and clear indications as to the measures to be applied to the child', which would usefully inform the teachers' practice.

From 'The diagnostics of development and the pedological clinic for difficult children' (Vygotsky, 1993e), section 6

If pedagogical recommendations are to be derived from scientific research and be the most important practical result of that research, they must be concrete, have content, and offer complete, specific, detailed and clear indications as to the measures to be applied to the child and as to the phenomena or symptoms that are to be eliminated by application of those methods. (Only this way can the pedagogical prescriptions demonstrate the entire validity of the diagnostic research.)

As we have shown, the poverty of our therapeutic pedagogy – and particularly in general practical pedagogy as it is to be applied to anomalous children – is, in part, attributable to the fact that no special methods or means of pedagogical activity have been cultivated at the centre of pedological research; these could have been built only on the scientific understanding of a child. Prescription represents a practical criterion for all pedagogical research. It is the final goal of research and it gives meaning to that enterprise. We are convinced that real cultivation of pedological prescription, derived from a rich, scientific and substantive clinical study of children, will lead to hitherto unseen flowering of all curative pedagogy, and to the whole system of individual pedagogical measures. On receiving a recommendation, a pedagogue should be able to know what it is he has to struggle with in a child's development, what means are appropriate to that purpose, and what effect they should have. Only knowing this can he evaluate the results of his activity. Otherwise, pedagogical recommendations will long rival pedagogical prognoses in their imprecision.

Notes

1. Chapter 7 is devoted to Vygotsky's writings on pedology.
2. William Stern (1871–1938) was a German psychologist, and one of the pioneers of child psychology.
3. Alfred Adler (1870–1937) was an Austrian psychotherapist and medical doctor. He founded the school of individual psychology.
4. Nikolay Shcherbina (1821–1869) was a Russian poet. He also worked at the Ministry of Public Education in St Petersburg.
5. Alfred Binet (1857–1911) was a French psychologist. He invented the first practical IQ test, intended to identify students not learning effectively through regular classroom teaching, so they could be offered remedial work.
6. Grigory Rossolimo (1860–1928) was a Russian neurologist specialising in child neuropsychology.

References

Adler, A. (1927). *Praxis und Theorie der Individualpsychologie* (*The practice and theory of individual psychology*). Munich: Bergmann.
Adler, A. (1928) *Über den nervösen Charakter* (*On the neurotic constitution*). Munich: Bergmann.
Stern, W. (1921). *Die differentielle Psychologie in ihren methodischen Grundlagen* (*The methodological foundations of differential psychology*). Leipzig: J.A. Barth.
Vygotsky, L.S. (1993). *The collected works of L.S. Vygotsky. Volume 2, The fundamentals of defectology*. Trans and intro J.R. Knox and C.B. Stevens; Rieber, R.W and Carton, A.S. (eds). New York, NY: Plenum Press.
Vygotsky, L.S. (1993a). 'Bases for working with mentally retarded and physically handicapped children' [1928], in Vygotsky, L.S. (1993), *The collected works of L.S. Vygotsky. Volume 2, The fundamentals of defectology*, pp. 178–183.
Vygotsky, L.S. (1993b). 'The collective as a factor in the development of the abnormal child' [1931], in Vygotsky, L.S. (1993), *The collected works of L.S. Vygotsky. Volume 2, The fundamentals of defectology*, pp. 191–208.
Vygotsky, L.S. (1993c). 'Defect and compensation' [1927], in Vygotsky, L.S. (1993), *The collected works of L.S. Vygotsky. Volume 2, The fundamentals of defectology*, pp. 52–64.
Vygotsky, L.S. (1993d). 'Defectology and the study of the development and education of abnormal children' [n.d.], in Vygotsky, L.S. (1993), *The collected works of L.S. Vygotsky. Volume 2, The fundamentals of defectology*, pp. 164–170.
Vygotsky, L.S. (1993e). 'The diagnostics of development and the pedological clinic for difficult children' [1936], in Vygotsky, L.S. (1993), *The collected works of L.S. Vygotsky. Volume 2, The fundamentals of defectology*, pp. 241–291.
Vygotsky, L.S. (1993f). 'The difficult child' [1928], in Vygotsky, L.S. (1993), *The collected works of L.S. Vygotsky. Volume 2, The fundamentals of defectology*, pp. 139–149.
Vygotsky, L.S. (1993g). 'Introduction: The fundamental problems of defectology' [1929], in Vygotsky, L.S. (1993), *The collected works of L.S. Vygotsky. Volume 2, The fundamentals of defectology*, pp. 29–51.
Vygotsky, L.S. (1993h). 'The psychology and pedagogy of children's handicaps' [1924], in Vygotsky, L.S. (1993). *The collected works of L.S. Vygotsky. Volume 2, The fundamentals of defectology*, pp. 76–93.

Chapter 4

On the crisis in psychology

A preoccupation throughout Vygotsky's career was his desire to forge a unity between the diverse and often contradictory 'psychologies' which all existed in that still relatively new discipline. The two extremes in this field were known as 'behaviourism', or in Russia 'reflexology' – materialistic and scientifically rigorous – and what was known as 'idealism', a more subjective and descriptive approach to psychology, derived from philosophy. Reflexology, which relied on the observation of the conditional reflex in animals, seemed to Vygotsky incapable of offering a way of understanding human psychology, for at least two reasons: it ignored human consciousness – the invisible activity of the mind – and did not take account of the essentially social nature of human experience. Meanwhile, idealistic philosophical psychology seemed to Vygotsky to lack rigour; it was 'spiritual', advancing its propositions largely on the basis of speculation.

Vygotsky wanted the best of both worlds: the scientific discipline associated with behaviourism, but transformed by a determination to understand the uniqueness of human experience, an experience in which social interactions and consciousness are central.

This chapter draws on two of Vygotsky's major works: his article 'Consciousness as a problem in the psychology of behaviour' (Vygotsky, 1997a) and his book *The historical meaning of the crisis in psychology* (Vygotsky, 1997b).

From 'Consciousness as a problem in the psychology of behaviour', section 1

The denial of consciousness and the aspiration to create a psychological system without this concept, as a 'psychology without consciousness' in the words of Blonsky[1] [1921], brings with it the fact that our methods lack a most necessary means to investigate reactions that are non-manifest and cannot be observed with the naked eye, such as internal movements, internal speech, somatic reactions, etc. The study only of those reactions that can be observed with the naked eye is utterly powerless and invalid for even the most simple problems of human behaviour.

DOI: 10.4324/9781003448938-4

Meanwhile, the behaviour of man is organised in such a way that precisely the internal movements that are difficult to detect direct and guide his behaviour. When we create a conditional reflex in a dog we, as a preliminary, organise his behaviour in a well-known way – otherwise the experiment would not succeed. We put the dog on the stand, tie it with straps, etc. And when these internal movements suddenly change in the course of the experiment the whole picture of the behaviour changes abruptly. Thus, we always use inhibited reflexes. We know that they continually take place in the organism and that they exert an influential regulatory role in behaviour – insofar as it is conscious. But we lack any means to investigate these internal reactions.

To put it more simply: man always thinks to himself. This will always influence his behaviour. A sudden change of thought during the experiment will always have immediate repercussions for the whole of the subject's behaviour (suddenly a thought: I will not look into the apparatus). But we have no idea how to take this influence into account.

* * *

Reflexology's basic assumption that it is possible to fully explain all of man's behaviour without resorting to subjective phenomena (to build a psychology without a mind) is the dualism of subjective psychology turned inside out. It is the counterpart of subjective psychology's attempt to study the pure, abstract mind. It is the other half of the previous dualism: there mind without behaviour, here behaviour without mind. Both here and there mind and behaviour are not one but two.

Vygotsky viewed animal behaviour and human behaviour as essentially different. Whereas animal behaviour can be described as the interaction of two kinds of reflex, human behaviour draws on historical, social and 'doubled' experience, this last referring to humans' ability to imagine the work they are to do before doing it, so allowing 'man to develop active forms of adaptation which the animal does not have'.

From 'Consciousness as a problem in the psychology of behaviour', sections 1 and 2

Scientific psychology must not ignore the facts of consciousness but materialise them, translate them into the objective language of the objectively existing. It must forever unmask and bury fictions, phantasmagorias, etc. Without this all work is utterly impossible – both teaching, critique and research.

It is not difficult to understand that from the biological, physiological and psychological viewpoint consciousness should not be viewed as *a second series* of phenomena. We must find a place for it and interpret it in one and the same series of phenomena with all the reactions of the organism. This is the first requirement our working hypothesis should meet. Consciousness is the problem of the structure of behaviour.

Another requirement is that the hypothesis must provide an uncontrived explanation of the basic problems connected with consciousness: the problem of the conservation of energy; self-consciousness; the psychological possibility of knowing other persons' consciousness; the conscious awareness of the three main spheres of empirical psychology – thinking, feeling and will; the concept of the unconscious; the evolution of consciousness and its identity and unity.

Here, in this short and cursory essay, we have merely stated the most preliminary, most general and most basic ideas. It seems to us that a future working hypothesis about consciousness in the psychology of behaviour will originate at their intersection.

Let us approach the question from the outside, not from within psychology.

The main forms of all animal behaviour consist of two groups of reactions: inborn or unconditional reflexes and acquired or conditional reflexes. The inborn reactions constitute, as it were, the biological extract of the inherited collective experience of the whole species, and acquired reactions evolve on the basis of this inherited experience by establishing new connections encountered in the personal experience of the individual. Thus, we can provisionally describe all animal behaviour as inherited experience plus inherited experience multiplied by personal experience. The origin of inherited experience has on the whole been clarified by Darwin. The mechanism of the multiplication of this experience by personal experience is the mechanism of the conditional reflex established by Academician Pavlov.[2]

With this formula, animal behaviour can in general be exhaustively described.

The case is different with man. Here, in order to understand behaviour more or less completely, we must introduce new members into the formula. Here we must first of all point to the quite extended inherited experience of man in comparison to animals. Man does not only make use of physically inherited experience. Our whole life, work and behaviour are based on the tremendously broad use of the experience of previous generations which is not transmitted from father to son through birth. Let us provisionally call it historical experience.

Next to this we must put social experience, the experience of other people, which forms a very significant component in human behaviour. I do not only have available the connections formed in my personal experience between various unconditional reflexes and various elements of the environment, but also a multitude of connections established in the experience of other people. If I know the Sahara and Mars although I have never left my own country and never looked through a telescope, then it is obvious that the origin of this experience is due to the experience of other people who have travelled to the Sahara and who have looked through a telescope. It is equally obvious that animals usually do not have such experience. Let us call this the social component of our behaviour.

Finally, what is also essentially new for human behaviour is that his adaptation and the behaviour connected with it takes new forms in comparison to animals. In animals we have passive adaptation to the environment, in humans active adaptation of the environment to oneself. It is true that in animals as well we encounter rudimentary forms of active adaptation in instinctive behaviour (nest building, the building of a dwelling, etc.), but in the animal kingdom these forms, first, are not predominant, of fundamental importance and, second, still remain passive in their essence and in the mechanism of their realisation.

Spiders that spin their web and bees that build cells out of wax do this because of an inherited instinct and in a machine-like manner, always in the same way. They do not display more activity than in all their other adaptive activities. It is different with a weaver or an architect. As Marx said, they first build their creation in their imagination. The result of the labour process existed in an ideal form before beginning of this work.[3]

This perfectly indisputable explanation by Marx refers to nothing other than *doubling of experience* that is unavoidable in human labour. In the movements of the hands and the transformations of the material, labour repeats what was first, as it were, done in the worker's imagination with models of these movements and this same material. Such *doubled experience* allows man to develop active forms of adaptation which the animal does not have. Let us provisionally call this new type of behaviour doubled experience.

Now the new part of the formula of human behaviour looks like this: historical experience, social experience and doubled experience.

In the pursuit of his understanding of the role of consciousness in human behaviour, Vygotsky saw that consciousness begins in the physical. 'The capacity of our body to be a stimulus (through its own acts) for itself (for new acts) is the basis of consciousness' (Vygotsky, 1997a, p.71). In developing this thought, Vygotsky cites the work of other psychologists, including Sherrington's[4] work on the 'proprioceptive field' – the mechanisms that enable us to monitor our physical movements constantly. Our proprioceptive field is always helping us to monitor and adjust our muscular reactions so that we can, for instance, keep our balance.

From 'Consciousness as a problem in the psychology of behaviour', sections 4 and 5

We must evidently conceive of awareness itself or the possibility of becoming conscious of our acts and mental states first of all as a system of transmission mechanisms from some reflexes to others, which functions properly in each conscious moment. The more correctly each internal reflex, as a stimulus, elicits a whole series of other reflexes from other systems and is transmitted to other systems, the better we are capable of accounting for ourselves and others for what is experienced, the more consciously it is experienced (felt, fixed in words, etc.).

'To account for' means to translate some reflexes into others. The psychological unconscious stands for reflexes that are not transmitted to other systems. There can be endlessly varied degrees of awareness, i.e. of cooperation between the systems included in the mechanism of the acting reflex. To be conscious of one's experiences is nothing other than to have them as object (stimulus) for other experiences. Consciousness is the experience of experiences just like experiences are simply experiences of objects. But precisely this capacity of the reflex (the experience of an object) to be a stimulus (the object of an experience) for a new reflex (a new experience) – this mechanism of conscious awareness – is the mechanism of the transmission of reflexes from one system to another.

★ ★ ★

Psychology must state and solve the problem of consciousness by saying that it is interaction, the mutual influence and stimulation of various systems of reflexes. Consciousness is what is transmitted in the form of a stimulus to other systems and elicits a response in them. Consciousness is always an echo, a response apparatus.

★ ★ ★

Sherrington distinguishes between the exteroceptive field as the field of the external surface of the body and the interoceptive field as the internal surface of certain organs to which 'a certain part of the external environment is led'. Elsewhere he talks about the proprioceptive field that is stimulated by the organism itself, by changes that take place in the muscles, tendons, joints, blood vessels, etc.

> The excitation of the receptors of the proprioceptive field, in contradistinction from those of the exteroceptive, is related only secondarily to the agencies of the environment. The proprioceptive receive their stimulation by some action, e.g. a muscular contraction, which was itself a primary reaction to excitation of a surface receptor by the environment. Reflexes arising from proprioceptive organs come to be habitually attached to reflexes excited by exteroceptive organs.
>
> (Sherrington, 1904)

Moreover, the combination of these secondary reflexes with the primary reactions, this 'secondary connection', can combine, as research demonstrates, reflexes of both the allied and the antagonistic type. In other words, the secondary reaction can both strengthen and terminate the primary one. And this is the mechanism of consciousness.

* * *

In this way we have solved the problem of the mind without expense of energy. Consciousness is fully and completely reduced to transmitting mechanisms of reflexes that work according to general laws, i.e. no processes other than reactions can be accepted to exist in the organism.

The solution of the problem of self-consciousness and self-observation now becomes possible as well. Inner perception or introspection is only possible owing to the existence of the proprioceptive field and the secondary reflexes connected to it. It is always, as it were, an echo of a reaction.

This exhaustively explains self-consciousness as the 'perception of what goes on in man's soul', in Locke's[5] expression. Moreover, it becomes clear why this experience is only accessible to one person – the one who is experiencing this experience. Only I and I alone can observe and perceive my own secondary reactions, because only for me do my reflexes serve as new stimuli for the proprioceptive field.

This being so, one can easily explain the split nature of experience: the mental is unlike anything else precisely because it is dealing with stimuli *sui generis* which are met *nowhere else but in my own body*. The movement of my hand perceived by the eye can be a stimulation for my eye as well as for someone else's eye. But the conscious awareness of this movement, [and] the proprioceptive excitation which emerges in that process and which elicits secondary reactions, exist only for myself. They have nothing in common with the first stimulation of the eye. Here we have completely different nervous paths, different mechanisms, and different stimuli.

* * *

Taking into account the enormous and primary role that the mind, i.e. the non-manifest group of reflexes, plays in the system of behaviour, it would be suicidal to refrain from its exposure through the indirect path of its reflection on other systems of reflexes. After all, we are studying reflexes to stimuli that are internal and hidden from us.

* * *

The behaviour of man and the formation of new conditional reactions in man are not only determined by the manifest, complete, fully exposed reactions, but also by reactions which do not manifest their external part and are invisible to the naked eye. Why can we study complete speech reflexes and not take account of the thought reflexes … although there can be no doubt that the latter, too, are reactions that really and indisputably exist?

When in free association I pronounce aloud, audible for the experimenter, the word 'evening', then this word that comes to my mind is taken into account as a verbal reaction, a conditional reflex. But when I pronounce it inaudibly, for myself, when I *think it*, does it really stop being a reflex and change its nature? And where is the boundary between the pronounced and the unpronounced word? When my lips started moving, when I whispered but still inaudibly for the experimenter – what then? Can he ask me to repeat this word aloud or will that be a subjective method that can be practised only on oneself? If he can (and almost everybody will, probably, agree about this), then why cannot he ask me to pronounce aloud a word that was pronounced *in thought*, i.e. without the movement of the lips and the whispering? After all, it still was and now remains a speech motor reaction, a conditional reaction without which there would be no thought. But this is already an interrogation, an utterance of the subject, his verbal account of reactions that undoubtedly objectively existed but were not manifest and *not perceived by the experimenter's ear* (here we have the sole difference between thoughts and speech). We can convince ourselves by many means that they [non-manifest reflexes] existed, existed objectively with all the signs of material being. The elaboration of these means is one of the most important tasks of psychological methods. Psychoanalysis is one of these means.

But what is most important is that they [non-manifest reflexes] themselves will take care to convince us of their existence. They will *express themselves* with such a force and vividness in the further course of the reaction that they *force* the experimenter to take them into account, or to fully refrain from the study of such streams of reactions in which they pop up. And are there many such behavioural processes in which non-manifest reflexes would not pop up? Thus, either we refrain from the study of human behaviour in its most essential forms, or we introduce the obligatory registration of these internal movements in our experiment.

Vygotsky equates 'the mechanism of social behaviour and the mechanism of consciousness', and sees speech as the source of both.

From 'Consciousness as a problem in the psychology of behaviour', section 6

In man, a group of reflexes easily stands out, which we should call the system of reversible reflexes. These are reflexes to stimuli that in turn can be created by man. The word that is heard is a stimulus. The word that is pronounced is a reflex that creates the same stimulus. Here the reflex is reversible, because the stimulus can become a reaction and vice versa. These reversible reflexes create the basis for social behaviour and serve the collective coordination of behaviour. In the whole multitude of stimuli one group clearly stands out for me, the group of social stimuli coming from people. It stands out because I can reconstruct these stimuli, because they very soon become reversible for me and thus determine my behaviour *in another way* from all others. They make me comparable to another, identical to myself. The source of social behaviour and consciousness also lies in speech in the broad sense of the word.

It is extremely important to state the idea here, albeit in passing, that if this is really so, then the mechanism of social behaviour and the mechanism of consciousness are one and the same. Speech is, on the one hand, the system of the 'reflexes of social contact' and, on the other hand, the system of the reflexes of consciousness par excellence, i.e. an apparatus for the reflection of other systems.

The key to the problem of another person's ego, of the knowledge of another person's mind, lies here. The mechanism of knowledge of the self (self-consciousness) and knowledge of others is the same. The usual theories about the knowledge of another person's mind either accept that it cannot be known, or they try to build a plausible mechanism with the help of various hypotheses. In the theory of *Einfühlung* [empathy] and in the theory from analogy the essence of such a mechanism is the same: we know others insofar as we know ourselves. When I know another person's anger, I reproduce my own anger.

In reality it would be more correct to put it the other way around. We are conscious of ourselves because we are conscious of others and by the same method as we are conscious of others, because we are the same vis-à-vis ourselves as others are vis-à-vis us. I am conscious of myself only to the extent that I am another to myself, i.e. to the extent that I can again perceive my own reflexes as stimuli. In principle there is no difference in mechanism whatsoever between the fact that I can repeat aloud a word spoken silently and the fact that I can repeat a word spoken by another: both are reversible reflex-stimuli.

That is why the acceptance of the hypothesis proposed will lead directly to the sociologising of all consciousness, to the acceptance that the social moment in consciousness is primary in time as well as in fact. The individual aspect is constructed as a derived and secondary aspect on the basis of the social aspect and exactly according to its model.

The core of Vygotsky's book *The historical meaning of the crisis in psychology: a methodological investigation* (Vygotsky, 1997b) is the recognition that there was as yet no definition of the general discipline of psychology. Meanwhile, several schools of psychology were vying for this status. Powered by his conviction 'that psychology really should rest upon universal laws', Vygotsky discusses four of these schools, analysing their strengths and weaknesses, and insisting that the partial truths they represent are inadequate materials for the building of a general psychology.

From *The historical meaning of the crisis in psychology*, section 4

These four ideas are: psychoanalysis, reflexology, Gestalt psychology, and personalism.

The idea of psychoanalysis sprang from particular discoveries in the area of neuroses. The unconscious determination of a number of mental phenomena and the hidden sexuality of a number of activities and forms, until then not included in the field of erotic phenomena, were established beyond doubt. Gradually this discovery, corroborated by the success of therapeutic measures based on this conception, i.e. sanctioned by practice, was transferred to a number of adjacent areas – the psychopathology of everyday life and child psychology – and it conquered the whole field of the theory of neuroses. In the struggle between the disciplines this idea brought the most remote branches of psychology under its sway. It has been shown that on the basis of this idea a psychology of art and an ethnic psychology can be developed. But psychoanalysis at the same time transcended the boundaries of psychology: sexuality became a metaphysical principle amidst all other metaphysical ideas, psychoanalysis became a world view, psychology a metapsychology. Psychoanalysis has its own theory of knowledge and its own metaphysics, its own sociology and mathematics. Communism and totem, the church and Dostoyevsky's creative work, occultism and advertising, myth and Leonardo da Vinci's inventions – it is all disguised and masked sex and sexuality, and that is all there is to it.

The idea of the conditional reflex followed a similar course. Everybody knows that it originated in the study of mental salivation in dogs. But then it was extended to a number of other phenomena as well. It conquered animal psychology. In Bekhterev's[6] system it is applied and used in all domains of psychology and reigns over them. Everything – sleep, thought, work, and creativity – turns out to be a reflex. It ended up dominating all psychological disciplines: the collective psychology of art, industrial psychology and pedology, psychopathology, even subjective psychology. And at the moment reflexology only rubs shoulders with universal principles, universal laws, first principles of mechanics. Just as psychoanalysis grew into a metapsychology via biology, reflexology via biology grows into a world view based on energy. The table of contents of a textbook in reflexology is a universal catalogue of global laws. And again, just as with psychoanalysis, it turned out that everything in the world is a reflex. Anna Karenina and kleptomania, the class struggle and a landscape, language and dream are all reflexes (Bekhterev, 1921, 1923).

Gestalt psychology also originally arose in the concrete psychological investigation of the processes of form perception. There it received its practical christening; it passed the truth test. But, as it was born at the same time as psychoanalysis and reflexology, it covered the same path with amazing uniformity. It conquered animal psychology, and it turned out that the thinking of apes is also a Gestalt process. It conquered the psychology of art and ethnic psychology, and it turned out that the primitive conception of the world and the creation of art are *Gestalten* as well. It conquered child psychology and psychopathology, and both child development and mental disease were covered by the Gestalt. Finally, having turned into a world view, Gestalt psychology discovered the Gestalt in physics and chemistry, in physiology and biology, and the Gestalt, withered to a logical formula, appeared to be the basis of the world. When God created the world he said: let there be Gestalt – and there was Gestalt everywhere (Koffka, 1925; Köhler, 1917, 1920; Wertheimer, 1925).

Finally, personalism[7] ... extended the concept of personality not only to man, but to animals and plants as well ... everything in the world is personality. The philosophy which began by contrasting the personality with the thing, by rescuing the personality from the power of things, ended up by accepting all things as personalities. The things disappeared altogether. A thing is only a part of the personality: it does not matter whether we are dealing with the leg of a person or the leg of a table. But as this part again consists of parts, etc., and so on to infinity, it – the leg of a person or a table – again turns out to be a personality in relation to its parts and a part only in relation to the whole. The solar system and the ant, the tram driver and Hindenburg, a table and a panther – they are all personalities (Stern, 1924a).

These fates, similar as four drops of the same rain, drag the ideas along one and the same path. The extension of the concept grows and reaches for infinity and according to the well-known logical law, its content falls just as impetuously to zero. Each of these four ideas is extremely rich, full of meaning and sense, full of value and fruitful in its own place. But elevated to the rank of universal laws they are worthy of each other, they are absolutely equal to each other, like round and empty zeros. Stern's personality is a complex of reflexes according to Bekhterev, a Gestalt according to Wertheimer,[8] sexuality according to Freud.

★ ★ ★

Doesn't this tendency of each new idea in psychology to turn into a universal law show that psychology really should rest upon universal laws, that all these ideas wait for a master-idea which comes and puts each different, particular idea in its place and indicates its importance? The regularity of the path covered with amazing constancy by the most diverse ideas testifies, of course, to the fact that this path is predetermined by the objective need for an explanatory principle and it is precisely because such a principle is needed and not available that various special principles occupy its place. Psychology, realising that it is a matter of life or death to find a general explanatory principle, grabs for any idea, albeit an unreliable one.

Spinoza[9] [1677] in his 'Treatise on the improvement of the understanding' describes a similar state of knowledge:

> A sick man struggling with a deadly disease, when he sees that death will surely be upon him unless a remedy is found, is compelled to seek such a remedy with all his strength, inasmuch as his whole hope lies therein.

Earlier in this chapter, we saw the clarity of Vygotsky's conviction that consciousness is central to any adequate understanding of the human mind. This conviction led him to argue that psychological investigations which confine themselves to what can be 'seen', to immediate experience, are inadequate. Here, he pursues his argument.

From *The historical meaning of the crisis in psychology,* section 8

... it is a gross mistake to suppose that science can only study what is given in immediate experience. How does the psychologist study the unconscious; the historian and the geologist, the past; the physicist-optician, invisible beams; and the philologist, ancient languages? The study of traces, influences, the method of interpretation and reconstruction, the method of critique and the finding of meaning have been no less fruitful than the method of direct 'empirical' observation. Ivanovsky[10] used precisely the example of psychology to explain this for the methodology of science. Even in the experimental sciences the role of immediate experience becomes smaller and smaller. Planck[11] says that the unification of the whole system of theoretical physics is reached due to the liberation from anthropomorphic elements, in particular from specific sense perceptions. Planck (1970, p. 118) remarks that in the theory of light and in the theory of radiant energy in general, physics works with such methods that

> the human eye is totally excluded, it plays the role of an accidental, admittedly highly sensitive but very limited reagent; for it only perceives the light beams within a small area of the spectrum which hardly attains the breadth of one octave. For the rest of the spectrum the place of the eye is taken by other perceiving and measuring instruments, such as, for example, the wave detector, the thermo-element, the bolometer, the radiometer, the photographic plate, the ionisation chamber. The separation of the basic physical concept from the specific sensory sensation was accomplished, therefore, in exactly the same way as in mechanics where the concept of force has long since lost its original link with muscular sensations.

Thus, physics studies precisely what cannot be seen with the eye. For if we, like the author, agree with Stern [1924b, p. 36] that childhood is for us 'paradise lost', that 'we grown-ups can never again come to a complete and absolute understanding of the special nature and construction of the child-soul',[12] as it is not given in direct experience, we must admit that the light beams which cannot be directly perceived by the eye are a paradise lost for ever as well, the Spanish inquisition a hell lost for ever, etc., etc. But the whole point is that scientific knowledge and immediate perception do not coincide at all. We can neither experience the child's impressions, nor witness the French Revolution, but the child who experiences his paradise with all directness and the contemporary who saw the major episodes of the revolution with his own eyes are, despite that, farther from the scientific knowledge of these facts than we are. Not only the humanities, but the natural sciences as well, build their concepts in principle independently from immediate experience. We are reminded of Engels' words about the ants and the limitations of our eye.

★ ★ ★

For psychology, the need to fundamentally transcend the boundaries of immediate experience is a matter of life and death. The demarcation, separation of the scientific concept from the specific perception can take place only on the basis of the indirect method. The reply that the indirect method is inferior to the direct one is in scientific terms utterly false. Precisely because it does not shed light upon the plentitude of experience, but only on one aspect, it accomplishes scientific work: it isolates, analyses, separates, abstracts a single feature. After all, in immediate experience as well we isolate the part that is the subject of our observation. Anyone who deplores the fact that we do not share the ant's immediate experience of chemical beams is beyond help, says Engels, for on the other hand we know the nature of these beams better than ants do. The task of science is not to reduce everything to experience. If that were the case it would suffice to replace science with the registration of our perceptions. Psychology's real problem resides also in the fact that our immediate experience is limited, because the whole mind is built like an instrument which selects and isolates certain aspects of phenomena. An eye that would see everything would for this very reason see nothing. A consciousness that was aware of everything would be aware of nothing, and knowledge of the self, were it aware of everything, would be aware of nothing. Our knowledge is confined between two thresholds; we see but a tiny part of the world.

Vygotsky returns to his discussion of the two opposing poles in contemporary psychology.

From *The historical meaning of the crisis in psychology*, section 11

Two psychologies exist – a natural scientific, materialistic one and a spiritualistic one. This thesis expresses the meaning of the crisis more correctly than the thesis about the existence of *many* psychologies. For *psychologies* we have *two*, i.e. two different, irreconcilable types of science, two fundamentally different constructions of systems of knowledge. All the rest is a difference in views, schools, hypotheses: individual, very complex, confused, mixed, blind, chaotic combinations which are at times very difficult to understand. But the real struggle only takes place between two tendencies which lie and operate behind all the struggling currents.

That this is so, that two psychologies, and not many psychologies, make up the meaning of the crisis, that all the rest is a struggle *within* each of these two psychologies, a struggle which has quite another meaning and operational field, that the creation of a general psychology is not a matter of agreement, but of a rupture – all this methodology realised long ago and *nobody contests it* ... Nobody contests that the general psychology will not be a third psychology added to the two struggling parties, but one of them.

Having identified the two poles of psychology, Vygotsky argues that applied psychology represents the best hope for the science's future. Applied psychology has inverted the conventional understanding of the relationship between theory and practice.

From *The historical meaning of the crisis in psychology*, section 12

Let us say right away that *the main driving force of the crisis in its final phase is the development of applied psychology as a whole.*

The attitude of academic psychology toward applied psychology has up until now remained somewhat disdainful, as if it had to do with a semi-exact science. Not everything is well in this area of psychology, there is no doubt about that, but nevertheless there can be no doubt for an observer who takes a bird's-eye view, i.e. the methodologist, that the leading role in the development of our science belongs to applied psychology. It represents everything of psychology which is progressive, sound, which contains a germ of the future. It provides the best methodological works. It is only by studying this area that one can come to an understanding of the meaning of what is going on and the possibility of a genuine psychology.

The centre has shifted in the history of science: what was at the periphery became the centre of the circle ... 'the stone which the builders rejected is become the head stone of the corner'.

★ ★ ★

A psychology which is called upon to confirm the truth of its thinking in practice, which attempts not so much to explain the mind but to understand and master it, gives the practical disciplines a fundamentally different place in the whole structure of the science than the former psychology did. There, practice was the colony of theory, dependent in all its aspects on the metropolis. Theory was in no way dependent on practice. Practice was the conclusion, the application, an excursion beyond the boundaries of science, an operation which lay outside science and came after science, which began after the scientific operation was considered completed. Success or failure had practically no effect on the fate of the theory. Now the situation is the opposite. Practice pervades the deepest foundations of the scientific operation and reforms it from beginning to end. Practice sets the tasks and serves as the supreme judge of theory, as its truth criterion. It dictates how to construct the concepts and how to formulate the laws.

Vygotsky is convinced that, in scientific investigation, a general principle may be abstracted from the study of a single phenomenon, *a unit of analysis* – as long as that single phenomenon is adequate for the task.

From *The historical meaning of the crisis in psychology*, section 13

The method of analysis in the natural sciences and in causal psychology consists of the study of a *single* phenomenon, a typical representative of a whole series.

★ ★ ★

When our Marxists explain the Hegelian principle[13] in Marxist methodology, they rightly claim that each thing can be examined as a microcosm, as a universal measure in which the whole big world is reflected. On this basis they say that to study one single thing, one subject, one phenomenon until the end, exhaustively, means to know the world in all its connections. In this sense it can be said that each person is to some degree a measure of the society, or rather class, to which he belongs, for the whole totality of social relationships is reflected in him.

From this alone we see that knowledge gained on the path from the special to the general is the key to all social psychology. We must reconquer the right for psychology to examine what is special, the individual as a social microcosm, as a type, as an expression or measure of the society.

★ ★ ★

… analysis is in principle not opposed to induction, but related to it. It is its highest form which contradicts its essence (repetition). It rests on induction and guides it. It states the question. It *lies at the basis of each experiment*. Each *experiment is an analysis in action, as each analysis is an experiment in thought*. That is why it would be correct to call it an experimental method. Indeed, when I am experimenting, I am studying A, B, C …, i.e. a number of concrete phenomena, and I assign the conclusions to different groups: to all people, to school-aged children, to activity, etc. The analysis suggests to what extent the conclusions may be generalised, i.e. it distinguishes in A, B, C ... the characteristics that a given group has in common. But even more: in the experiment I always observe just one feature of a phenomenon, and this is again the result of analysis.

Let us now turn to the inductive method in order to clarify the analysis. Let us examine a number of applications of this method.

Pavlov is studying the activity of *the salivary gland in dogs*. What gives him the right to call his experiments the study of the higher nervous activity of *animals*? Perhaps he should have verified his experiments on horses, crows, etc., on all, or at least the majority, of animals, in order to have the right to draw these conclusions? Or perhaps he should have called his experiments 'a study of salivation in dogs'? But it is precisely the salivation of dogs per se which Pavlov did not study and his experiments have not for one bit increased our knowledge of dogs as such and of salivation as such. In the dogs he did not study the dog, but *an animal in general*, and in salivation *a reflex in general*, i.e. in this animal and in this phenomenon he distinguished what they have in common with all homogeneous phenomena. That is why his conclusions do not just concern all animals, but the whole of biology as well. The established fact that Pavlov's dogs salivated to signals given by Pavlov immediately became a general biological principle – the principle of the transformation of inherited experience into personal experience. This proved possible because Pavlov *maximally abstracted* the phenomenon he studied from the specific conditions of the particular phenomenon. He brilliantly *perceived the general in the particular*.

What did the extension of his conclusions rest upon? Naturally, on the following: we extend our conclusions to something which has to do *with the same elements* and we rely upon similarities established in advance (the class of hereditary reflexes in all animals, the nervous system, etc.). Pavlov discovered a general biological law while studying dogs. But in the dog he studied what forms the basis of any animal.

This is the methodological path of any explanatory principle. In essence, Pavlov did not extend his conclusions, and the degree of their extension was determined in advance. It was implied in the very statement of the problem. The same is true for Ukhtomsky.[14] He studied several preparations of frogs. If he had generalised his conclusions to all frogs this would have been induction. But he talks about the dominant as a principle of psychology applicable to the heroes of *War and Peace*, and this he owes to analysis. Sherrington studied the scratching and flexive reflexes of the hind leg in many cats and dogs, but he established the principle of the struggle for the motor path which lies at the basis of the personality. But neither Ukhtomsky nor Sherrington added anything to the study of frogs or cats as such.

★ ★ ★

It may seem that analysis, like experiment, distorts reality by creating artificial conditions for observation. Hence the demand that the experiment should be realistic and natural. If this idea goes further than a technical demand – not to scare off what we are searching for – it leads to absurdity. The strength of analysis is in abstraction, just as the strength of experiment is in its artificiality. Pavlov's experiments are the best specimen: for the dogs it is a *natural* experiment – they are fed, etc.; for the scientist it is the summit of artificiality – salivation takes place when a specific area is scratched, which is an unnatural combination. Likewise, we need destruction in the analysis of a machine, mental or real damage to the mechanism, and in the [analysis of the] aesthetic form we need deformation.

If we remember what was said above about the indirect method, then it is easy to observe that analysis and experiment presuppose *indirect* study. From the analysis of the stimuli we infer the mechanism of the reaction, from the command, the movements of the soldiers, and from the form of the fable, the reactions to it.

Marx says essentially the same when he compares abstraction with a microscope and chemical reactions in the natural sciences. The whole of *Das Kapital* is written according to this method. Marx analyses the 'cell' of bourgeois society – the form of the commodity value – and shows that a mature body can be more easily studied than a cell. He discerns the structure of the whole social order and all economical formations in this cell. He says that 'to the uninitiated its analysis may seem the hair-splitting of details. We are indeed dealing with details, but such details as microscopic anatomy is also dealing with' [Marx, 1867, p. 6].[15] He who can decipher the meaning of the cell of psychology, the mechanism of one reaction, has found the key to all psychology.

Vygotsky had insisted that there could only be one psychology. Science could no longer allow philosophical idealistic psychology to coexist tolerantly with materialist experimental psychology, with a blurred boundary between them. Only the second qualifies as a real science. He uses a dramatic analogy to state the need for scientific materialist psychology to rid itself of idealistic psychology.

From *The historical meaning of the crisis in psychology*, section 13

Following Spinoza [see page 47 above], we have compared our science to a mortally ill patient who looks for an unreliable medicine. Now we see that it is only the surgeon's knife which can save the situation. A bloody operation is imminent. Many textbooks we will have to rend in twain, like the veil in the temple, many phrases will lose their head or legs, other theories will be slit in the belly. We are only interested in the border, the line of the rupture, the line which will be described by the future knife.

In the last chapter of the book, Vygotsky considers the problem of what to call the unified psychology he believes must survive the 'bloody operation'. He rejects a variety of compound possibilities – 'objective psychology', 'the psychology of behaviour', 'Marxist psychology', 'scientific psychology' – and opts for a single, inclusive term.

From *The historical meaning of the crisis in psychology*, section 13

It remains for us to accept this name. It perfectly well stresses what we want – the size and the content of our task. And it does not reside in the creation of a school next to other schools; it does not cover some part or aspect, or problem, or method of interpretation of psychology alongside analogous parts, schools, etc. We are talking about all of psychology, in its full capacity; about the only psychology which does not admit of another one. We are talking about the realisation of psychology as a science.

That is why we will simply say: psychology.

Notes

1. Pavel Blonsky (1884–1941) was a Russian philosopher and behaviourist psychologist, and a theorist of Soviet pedology.
2. Ivan Pavlov (1849–1936) was a Russian neurologist, physiologist and psychologist, best known for his discovery of conditioning through experiments with dogs.
3. See the reference list to Chapter 1 for the source of the quotation from Marx.
4. Charles Sherrington (1857–1952) was an English neurophysiologist. 'Synapse' – the connection between two neurons – is a word he coined, as is the word 'proprioceptive'.
5. John Locke (1632–1704) was an English philosopher and physician. He was one of the first British empiricists.
6. Vladimir Bekhterev (1857–1927) was a Russian neurologist. His research revealed that there are zones within the brain, each of which has a specific function.
7. William Stern (see Chapter 3, note 2) was 'founder of the philosophy of personalism, which included the idea that rocks, plants, animals, and humans are born with free will' (Vygotsky, 2021, translators' notes, note 3).
8. Max Wertheimer (1880–1943) was a Czech-born psychologist. Together with Kurt Koffka and Wolfgang Köhler, he founded Gestalt psychology.
9. Baruch Spinoza (1632–1677) was a Dutch philosopher of Portuguese-Jewish origin. He was Vygotsky's favourite philosopher.
10. Dmitri Ivanovsky (1864–1920) was a Russian botanist who discovered viruses and was one of the founders of virology.
11. Max Planck (1858–1947) was a German theoretical physicist, most famous as the originator of quantum theory.
12. This version of the translation is from the 1924 English translation of Stern's book (Stern 1924b).
13. Georg Hegel (1770–1831) was a German philosopher. The Hegelian principle states that ideas develop in a threefold manner: from abstract, to negative, to concrete. Marx, while admiring the dynamic nature of Hegel's principle, said that it was idealist and mystical. Turning it 'right side up', 'the ideal is nothing else than the material world reflected by the human mind, and translated into forms of thought' (Marx, 1873).

14. Alexei Ukhtomsky (1875–1942) was a Russian physiologist. He proposed the theory of the dominant focus in nerve centres.
15. The reference in the reference list below (Marx, 1867) is to an online version of Marx's work. This translation uses slightly different wording from, but with a similar sense to, the wording in the text.

References

Bekhterev, V.M. (1921). *Kollektivaja refleksologija*. St Petersburg: n.p.
Bekhterev, V.M. (1923). *Obshchie osnovy refleksologii cheloveka*. St Petersburg: n.p.
Blonsky, P.P. (1921). *An essay in scientific psychology*. Moscow: Gosizdat.
Koffka, K. (1925). *Die Grundlagen der psychischen Entwicklung (The foundations of mental development)*. Osterwieck am Harz: A.W. Zickfeldt (Russian translation 1934).
Köhler, W. (1917). *Intelligenzprüfungen an Anthropoiden (The mentality of anthropoids)*. Berlin: Julius Springer (Russian translation 1930).
Köhler W. (1920). *Die physischen Gestalten in Ruhe und im stationären Zustand: Eine naturphilosophische Untersuchung (Physical form at rest and in the stationary condition: a natural-philosophical investigation)*. Erlangen: Verlag der philosophischen Akademie.
Marx, K. (1867). *Das Kapital. Volume 1, Preface to the first German edition*. Available online in the Marxist Archive at www.marxists.org/archive/marx/works/download/pdf/Capital-Volume-I.pdf
Marx, K. (1873). *Das Kapital. Volume 1, Afterword to the second German edition*. Available online in the Marxist Archive at www.marxists.org/archive/marx/works/1867-c1/p3.htm
Planck, M. (1970). *Das Wesen des Lichts (The essence of light)* [1919], in Plank, M., *Vortrage und Erinnerungen*. Darmstadt: Wissenschaftliche Buchgesellschaft, pp. 112–124.
Sherrington, C.S. (1904). 'The correlation of cerebrospinal reflexes and the principle of the common path', in *Nature*, 8 September, pp. 460–466 (Russian translation 1912).
Spinoza, B. (1677). *Tractatus de intellectus emendatione (Treatise on the improvement of the understanding)* [Unfinished].
Stern, W. (1924a) *Person und Sache (Person and thing). Volume 3. Wertphilosophie*. Leipzig: J.A. Barth.
Stern, W. (1924b) *Psychology of early childhood up to the sixth year of age* [1914]. Trans. A. Barwell. London: George Allen and Unwin.
Vygotsky, L.S. (1997). *The collected works of L.S. Vygotsky. Volume 3, Problems of the theory and history of psychology*, trans. and intro. R. Van der Veer; Rieber, R.W. and Wollock, J. (eds). New York, NY: Plenum Press.
Vygotsky, L.S. (1997a). 'Consciousness as a problem in the psychology of behaviour' [1925], in Vygotsky, L.S. (1997), *The collected works of L.S. Vygotsky. Volume 3, Problems of the theory and history of psychology*, pp. 63–79.
Vygotsky, L.S. (1997b). *The historical meaning of the crisis in psychology: a methodological investigation* [1926–7], in Vygotsky, L.S. (1997), *The collected works of L.S. Vygotsky. Volume 3, Problems of the theory and history of psychology*, pp. 233–343.
Vygotsky, L.S. (2021). 'The problem of age periodisation in child development' [1932–4], in Vygotsky, L.S. (2021), *L.S. Vygotsky's pedological works. Volume 2, The problem of age*. Trans. and notes D. Kellogg and N. Veresov. Singapore: Springer, pp. 15–38.
Wertheimer, M. (1925). *Drei Abhandlungen zur Gestalttheorie (Three treatises on Gestalt theory)*. Erlangen: Verlag der philosophischen Akademie.

Chapter 5

Discovering the power of the sign

Extracts from *Tool and symbol in child development*

Tool and symbol in child development (Vygotsky and Luria, 1994) was probably written in 1930.[1] The book is a discussion of child development, comparing children's development with that of young primates, commenting on the role of language in development, and reporting on a series of experiments with children conducted from 1928 to 1930 by the authors and their collaborators at the Moscow Institute of Psychology. Vygotsky called the technique used in these experiments 'the instrumental method' or 'the method of double [or twofold] stimulation'. The game-like experiments set out to provoke and stimulate development in children, often by presenting them with tasks beyond their immediate capabilities. The main conclusion which Vygotsky and his colleague Alexander Luria draw from the experiments is that, while children's early practical intelligence, as shown in tool use, is similar to that of young apes, it is when language enters the picture and is combined with action that their problem-solving behaviour becomes qualitatively different. Human development is an essentially social process, in which speech plays a central role.

In the first extract, Vygotsky and Luria criticise and dismiss a position held by many researchers at the time: that there was no connection between a child's developing use of tools and her developing powers of speech. To the contrary, their experiments had revealed a 'newly born unity of perception, speech and action'. They admire the work of Wolfgang Köhler,[2] who conducted a long series of experiments with apes, but argue that the limitation in apes' behaviour which Köhler identified is proof that the unity of the two systems of 'practical intellect and symbolic activity' is unique to humans.

From *Tool and symbol in child development*, part 1, 'The problem of the practical intelligence in animal and child', section entitled 'The function of speech in tool use: the problem of practical and verbal intelligence'

For many long years scientific opinion held that practical intelligent action connected to the use of tools had no basic relation to the development of sign or symbolic operations, such as, for instance, speech. Psychological literature almost ignored the question of the structural and genetic relations of these two functions.

All the information that could be obtained by modern science led rather to the treatment of these two psychological processes as two quite independent lines of development which, although they might come into contact, basically had nothing in common.

In the classic work on the use of tools by apes, Köhler [1921] obtained what one might call the pure culture of practical intellect, developed to a fairly high degree, but having no ties with the application of symbols. Having described brilliantly examples of the use of tools by anthropoids, he went on to demonstrate how futile it was to attempt to develop even the most elementary sign and symbolic operations in animals. The practical intellectual behaviour of the ape proved to be absolutely independent from symbolic activity. Further attempts to cultivate speech in the ape (see works by Yerkes and Learned [1925]) also gave negative results, thus showing once more that the practical 'ideational' behaviour of the animal is completely autonomous and isolated from speech-symbol activity, and that, notwithstanding the similarity of both man's and the ape's vocal apparatus, speech remains beyond the ape's grasp.

The acceptance of the fact that the beginning of practical intellect may be observed to almost its full extent in the pre-human and pre-speech period led psychologists to the assumption that the use of tools, which originates as a natural operation, remained the same in the child. A number of authors, engaged in the study of practical operations of children of different ages, attempted to define as exactly as possible the age period during which child behaviour resembles in all respects that of the chimpanzee. The addition of speech in the child's case was regarded by those authors as exogenous, secondary and independent of practical operations. Speech, at the most, was looked on as an element accompanying operations just as harmony assists the main melody. The tendency to ignore speech while studying the laws of practical intellect was a normal development; the analysis of the child's practical action boiled down to the simple mechanical subtraction of speech from the integral system of child activity.

The isolated examination of the use of tools and of symbolic activity was a common tendency in the research work of authors who studied the natural history of practical intellect: psychologists, studying the development of symbolic processes in the child, followed the same principle.

The origin and development of speech, and of all other symbolic action, was treated as a factor having no ties with the organisation of the child's practical activity, the child being regarded as purely *res agitans*.[3] Such an approach could not but lead to the proclamation of pure intellectualism; psychologists, preferring to study the development of symbolic activity as the spiritual, as opposed to the natural, history of the child, often attributed this activity to the spontaneous discovery by the child of the relationship between signs and their meaning. This happy moment, according to the well-known expression of W. Stern,[4] constitutes 'the greatest discovery in the child's life'. A number of authors fix this moment at the borderline between the child's first and second year, and regard it as the result of the child's conscientious activity. The problems of the *development* of speech and other forms of symbolic activity were thus erased, being supplanted by a purely logical process projected into early childhood, and containing in complete form all the stages of future development.

From the examination of symbolic speech activities on the one hand, and practical intellect on the other, as isolated phenomena, it followed that not only the genetic analysis of these functions led to their being regarded as having completely different origins, but also to their participation in a common operation being considered as accidental and of no basic psychological importance. Even in cases when speech and the use of tools were closely linked in one operation, they were still studied as separate processes belonging to two completely different classes of independent phenomena. At the most, the reason for their mutual appearance was defined as exterior.

If authors, studying practical intellect in its natural history, concluded that its natural forms were not in the slightest degree connected to symbolic activity, child psychologists who studied speech made the similar assumption, albeit from the opposite side. Observing psychological development of the child, they established the fact that, during the whole period of development, symbolic activity, accompanying the general activity of the child, discloses its egocentric nature but, being in essence separated from action, does not co-act but merely runs parallel to it. In his description of the egocentric speech of the child, Piaget held this viewpoint. He did not attribute any important role to speech in organising the child; nor did he admit its communicative functions, although he was obliged to admit its practical importance.

A series of observations leads us to assume that such an isolated examination of practical intellect and symbolic activity is absolutely wrong. If the one could exist without the other in the case of higher animals, then one must logically conclude that the unity of these two systems is the very thing to be regarded as specific to the complex behaviour of man. For this results in symbolic activity's beginning to play a specific organising part, penetrating into the process of tool use and giving birth to principally new forms of behaviour.

We arrived at this conclusion after the most careful study of child behaviour and new research which helped to establish the functional features strictly pertaining to the child as opposed to animals, while simultaneously defining the child's specific behaviour as a human being.

★ ★ ★

Speech and action in child behaviour

Our research leads us not only to the conviction of the fallacy of this approach, but also to the positive conclusion that *the great genetic moment of all intellectual* development, from which grew the purely human forms of practical and gnostic intellect, is realised in the unification of these two previously completely independent lines of development.

The child's use of tools is comparable to that of an ape's only during the former's pre-speech period. As soon as speech and the use of symbolic signs are included in this operation, it transforms itself along entirely new lines, overcoming the former natural laws and for the first time giving birth to authentically human use of implements.

From the moment the child begins to *master the situation with the help of speech, after mastering his own behaviour,* a radically new organisation of behaviour appears, as well as new relations with the environment. We are witnessing the birth of those specifically human forms of behaviour that, breaking away from animal forms of behaviour, later create intellect and go on to become the base of labour: the specifically human form of the use of tools.

This unification appears with the greatest clarity in our experimental genetic research.

The very first observations of a child in an experimental situation similar to that in which Köhler observed the practical use of tools by apes, show that the child not only acts endeavouring to achieve its goal, but at the same time also *speaks*. This speech as a rule arises spontaneously in the child and continues almost without interruption throughout the experiment. It increases and is of a more persistent character every time the situation becomes more difficult and the goal more difficult to attain. Attempts to block it (as the experiments of our collaborator R.E. Levina have shown) are either futile or lead to the termination of all action, 'freezing' as it were the child's behaviour, something quite apparent and easily observed in the experiment.

In this situation, it thus seems both natural and necessary for the child to speak while it acts, and experimenters are under the impression that speech does not simply follow in the wake of practical activity, but plays some kind of specific role of no little importance. The impressions we are left with as the result of similar experiments place the observer face to face with the following two facts, both of capital importance:

1. A child's speech is an inalienable and internally necessary part of the operation, its role being as important as that of action in the attaining of a goal. The experimenter's impression is that the child not only speaks about what he is doing, but that for him speech and action are in this case *one and the same complex psychological function,* directed toward the solution of the given problem.
2. The more complex the action demanded by the situation and the less direct its solution, the greater the importance played by speech in the operation as a whole. Sometimes speech becomes of such vital importance that without it the child proves to be positively unable to accomplish the given task.

These observations lead us to the conclusion that *the child does a practical task with the help of not only eyes and hands, but also speech*. This newly born unity of perception, speech and action, which leads to the inculcation of the laws of the visual field, constitutes the real and vital object of analysis aimed at studying the origin of specifically human forms of behaviour.

In the course of the experiments which Vygotsky and Luria and their colleagues undertook with children, the experimenters found that children's 'examined activity' changed, which required that the focus of the research should change accordingly. The research team recognised that the children were construing the experiments as social situations with the experimenter as a participant. Their relationship with the experimenter became a source of development in the children.

From *Tool and symbol in child development*, part 1, 'The problem of the practical intelligence in animal and child', sections entitled 'The development of the child's higher forms of practical activity' and 'Development in the light of facts'

We observed a child's activity in a number of experiments, analogous in structure, but drawn out in time and representing series of situations, each following one more difficult than the preceding. We established one most important point ignored by psychologists, which permits us to characterise with certainty the difference between the behaviour of an ape and that of a child in the genetic plane, while former observations allowed us to do the same with regard to the structure of activity. The fact is that over the course of a series of experiments, the examined activity of the child changes, not only perfecting itself as is the case in the process of teaching/learning,[5] but undergoing such great qualitative changes as can only be regarded in their totality as development in the literal meaning of the word.

... in a series of experiments drawn out in time, we immediately found ourselves faced with a cardinal fact: that, actually, we were not studying one and the same activity each time in its new concrete expressions, but that, over a series of experiments, the object [the aim] of research itself changed. Thus, in the process of development, we acquired forms of activity that were completely different in structure. This represented an unpleasant complication for all psychologists who at any cost endeavour to preserve the invariability of the examined activity; but for us it at once became central, and we concentrated all our attention on its study. This study led us to the conclusion that the activity of the child differs in organisation, structure and methods from the ape's behaviour, does not appear in a ready-made form, but arises out of the *consecutive changes of genetically interrelated psychological structures* and, thus, forms an *integral historical process of development of the higher psychological functions.*

★ ★ ★

The entire history of the child's psychological development shows us that, from the very first days of development, its adaptation to the environment is achieved by social means, through the people surrounding him. The road from object to child and from child to object lies through another person.

The extracts which follow show Vygotsky and Luria discussing, on the basis of their experiments, the dynamic relationship between children's egocentric speech (speech for oneself) and their social speech (speech for and with others). Here too is the insight, to be further developed in *Thinking and speech* (Vygotsky, 1987a, and see Chapters 10 and 11), that social speech can become internalised, can become a new kind of speech for and within oneself.

From *Tool and symbol in child development*, part I, 'The problem of the practical intelligence in animal and child', section entitled 'The function of socialised and egocentric speech'

The first of the processes we study here is connected with the formation of 'speech for oneself', which, as we noted earlier, regulates the child's actions and permits him to achieve a given task in an organised way, through preliminary control of himself and his activity.

If we study carefully the records of our experiments with small children, we find that, along with the appeals to the experimentalist for help, there is a wealth of manifestations of egocentric speech by the child.

We already know that difficult situations evoke excessive egocentric speech and that, under conditions of hyper-difficulties, the coefficient of egocentric speech is almost doubled in comparison to uncomplicated situations.

★ ★ ★

For a correct understanding of the nature of egocentric speech and for the clarification of its genetic functions in the process of the socialisation of the child's practical intellect, it is important to remember that egocentric speech is linked to the child's social speech by thousands of transitional stages, a fact both experimentally proven and emphasised by us. Very frequently these transitional forms were not clear enough for us to determine to what form of speech one or another of the child's expressions could be related. This resemblance and mutual relation of both forms of speech is reflected in the close ties of those of the child's functions which are carried out by both forms of the child's verbal activity. It would be a mistake to think that his social speech consists solely of appeals to the experimentalist for help: it always consists of emotional and expressive elements, communications as to what he intends to do, and so on. It sufficed to obstruct his social speech during the experiment (for instance, by the experimentalist leaving the room, or by not answering the child's questions, etc.) for egocentric speech to increase immediately.

If at the earliest stages of a child's development egocentric speech does not yet indicate the method of solution, this is first expressed by speech addressed to the adult. The child, hopeless of attaining his end directly, turns to the adult and describes verbally the method, which he himself is unable to use in a direct way. The greatest change in child development occurs when this socialised speech, previously addressed to the adult, *is turned to himself*, when, instead of appealing to the experimentalist with a plan for the solution of the problem, the child appeals to himself. In this latter case the speech, participating in the solution, *from an inter-psychological category now becomes an intra-psychological function*.

The child applies to itself the method of behaviour that it previously applied to another, thus *organising its own behaviour according to a social type*. The source of intelligent action and control over his own behaviour in the solution of a complex practical problem is, consequently, not an invention of some purely logical act, but the application of *a social attitude to itself*, the transfer of a social form of behaviour into its own psychological organisation.

A series of observations permits us to trace this complex path followed by the child in his transition to the interiorisation of social speech. The cases we described in which the experimenter, to whom the child formerly appealed for help, left the scene of the experiment, throw this climax into bold relief. It is in such a case when the child is deprived of the possibility of appealing to an adult that this socially organised function switches over to egocentric speech, and suggestions as to the ways of solving the problem gradually lead to their independent realisation.

Another development revealed by the experiments concerns the changing relationship between speech and action. At an early stage in the experiments, children's speech was merely an accompaniment to action; later, it preceded action and took on a planning role.

From *Tool and symbol in child development*, part I, 'The problem of the practical intelligence in animal and child', section entitled 'The change of the function of speech in practical operation'

We would like to emphasise the second, and no less important, transformation which the child's speech undergoes in the series of experiments described.

Tracing the child's speech–action relation in time and studying that dynamic structure, displayed in time and arising from that relation, we were able to establish the following fact: this structure does not remain permanent over the entire course of the experiments; speech and action change in relation to each other, forming a mobile system of functions with a changing character of interrelations ... This change consists in the fact that *the child's speech, which previously accompanied its activity and reflected its chief vicissitudes* in a disrupted and chaotic form, *moves more and more to the turning and starting points of the process, beginning thus to precede action and throw light on the conceived of but as yet unrealised action.* In the development of practical intellect we observed a process analogous to that occurring in another mobile system of functions – speech–drawing. Just as the child first draws and, only *post factum* seeing the results of its work, recognises and states the drawing's theme in words, so in the practical operation the child begins by verbally describing the operation's result or its individual elements. At best, the child does not state the result but conveys the preceding moment of action. In our experiments the 'scheme of action' begins to be verbally described by the child directly prior to its beginning (just like in the development of drawing the naming of the theme of the drawing moves closer to the beginning of the process), thus anticipating its further development.

This displacement signifies not only the temporary transfer of speech as related to action, but also the transfer of the entire system's functional centre. In the first stage speech, following action, reflecting it and strengthening its results, remains structurally subject to action and provoked by it, while at the second stage speech, transferred towards the starting point of the process, begins to dominate over action, guides it and determines its subject and development. Therefore the second stage gives birth to speech's real function of planning, and thus speech begins to fix the direction of future operations.

This next extract reports on the findings of one of Vygotsky and Luria's colleagues, Natalia Morozova. She conducted a series of 'choice experiments' with small children, initially requiring them to press one of five keys on a keyboard in response to specific stimuli.

Luria (1979, p. 47) describes the experiments in his autobiography *The making of mind*: 'In her experiments a three- or four-year-old child would be presented with a simple task: "Press the button when you see a red card." Then two or three cards were shown to the child simultaneously and three keys were made available for pressing. When these complications were introduced, the systematic flow of the child's responding disintegrated.'

As we shall see from the extract, the children's tentative movements, their 'mass of diffused gropings and trials', showed how difficult they were finding the tasks. But when the researcher marked each key with an additional corresponding sign, 'as early as five or six the child fulfils this task with the greatest ease'. This method of 'double stimulation' shows the importance of cultural symbols in enabling children to gain more control over their own behaviour.

From *Tool and symbol in child development*, part 2, 'The function of signs in the development of higher psychological processes', section entitled 'The separation of the primary unity of the sensori-motor functions'

Studying the movements of the child during the complex reactions of choice in experimental conditions, we were able to establish that these movements did not remain absolutely the same at all the stages but, on the contrary, underwent a complex evolution, the central and crucial moment of which consisted in a fundamental change in the relations between the sensory and motor parts of the reactive process.

★ ★ ★

A concrete experimental situation gives us the opportunity to follow this. We pose before a small child, aged four or five, a problem, i.e. to press one of five keys of a keyboard when identifying a given stimulus. The task exceeds the natural capabilities of the child and, therefore, causes intensive difficulties and still more intensive efforts aimed at solving the problem.

★ ★ ★

The child's choice resembles ... a somewhat delayed selection of its own movements; vacillations in the structure of perception find here their direct reflection in the structure of movement, and the mass of diffused gropings and trials delayed in the very motoric process, interrupting and succeeding one another, are in reality the child's process of selection itself: it suffices to glance at the cyclographic curve[6] recorded by us, to become convinced of the motor nature of the reactive process both in child and adult, as well as to grasp the basic difference between this act as standing at the source of all the complex forms of human behaviour and representing them in their completed aspects.

We cannot better express the main point of this difference in the process of selection in a child and in an adult than by saying that, in the former, a series of trial movements are substituted for selection. The child does not choose the *stimulus* (the necessary key) as the starting point for the consequent movement, but selects the *movement*, checking its result by the instructions. Thus, the child solves its problem of selection not in perception, but in movement, hesitating between two stimuli, its fingers hovering above and moving from one key to another, going halfway and then coming back; when the child transfers its attention to a new point, creating a new centre in the dynamic structure of perception, which is also *shaken by selection*, the child's hand obediently moves towards this new centre, forming one whole with the eye. In short, its movement is not separated from its perception: the dynamic curve of both processes coincides almost exactly in both one and the other case.

And yet this primitive diffusive structure of the reactive process undergoes a fundamental change as soon as a complex psychological function enters the process of direct selection, transforming the natural process, fully apparent in animals, into a higher psychological operation characteristic of man.

Directly upon having observed in the child a diffusive impulsive process, organically fused with perception of selection of movement, we attempted to simplify the task of selection by marking each key with a corresponding sign, which would serve as an additional stimulus, directing and organising the process of selection. As early as age five or six, the child fulfils this task with the greatest ease, marking the key that it must press, upon the appearance of a certain stimulus, with that stimulus's corresponding sign. The use of this auxiliary sign does not, however, remain a secondary and additional fact only slightly complicating the nature of the operation of choice; the structure of the psychological process is radically changed under the influence of the new ingredient applied to it, and the primitive natural operation is replaced here by a new and cultured one. When the child turns to the auxiliary sign in order to find the key corresponding to the given stimulus, it no longer has those motor impulses, arising directly from perception, those uncertain groping movements in the air, which we observed in the primitive reaction of choice. The use of auxiliary signs destroys the fusion of the sensory field with the motor system, it places a sort of 'functional barrier' between the primary and final moments of reactions, replacing the direct switching over of the reaction to the motor sphere of preliminary circuits, achieved with the aid of the higher psychological systems. The child that formerly solved the problem impulsively now solves it through the internal re-establishment of the connection between the stimulus and the corresponding auxiliary sign, while the movement which previously made the choice now serves only as a system fulfilling the prepared operation. The system of symbols reconstructs the whole psychological process, and the speaking child masters its movement on a totally new foundation.

Alexei Leontiev, at this time one of Vygotsky and Luria's closest colleagues, conducted a series of experiments involving a game of 'forbidden colours', which also showed how auxiliary signs transformed children's ability to perform tasks which otherwise were beyond them.

From *Tool and symbol in child development*, part 4, 'The analysis of sign operations in the child', section entitled 'The structure of sign operation'

... new psychological structures are created which were formerly non-existent and, probably, impossible without such sign operations. We shall illustrate this with the example of a genetic study of the activity of the child's voluntary attention.

A child of seven or eight years was placed in conditions calling for a high degree of constant and concentrated attention (for instance, asking the child to name the colour of a number of objects without repeating the same colour or naming two 'forbidden' colours). A direct attempt to solve the task led to a total inability to achieve a correct solution. However, as soon as the child switches over to an indirect organisation of the process by using certain auxiliary signs, the task becomes easy to solve.

In the experiments carried out in our laboratories by Leontiev, the child was given a number of coloured cards to be used for the simplification of the task. In cases when the child did not use them in its activities (as, for instance, putting 'forbidden' colours aside and removing them from the fixed field), the task proved to be unsolvable. It was easily carried out, however, when instead of naming the colours, the child used a complex structure of replies based on the auxiliary signs given him: placing the two 'forbidden' colours inside the fixed field and adding each newly named colour, the child thus formed an auxiliary control group, and the task was easily fulfilled. Replying each time *with the aid* of these auxiliary stimulus signs, the child organised its *active attention* from without, thus becoming adapted to a task that could not be solved by direct, elementary forms of behaviour.

The experimenters observed how, in the course of the experiments, children moved from the external use of auxiliary signs to the internalisation of those signs. The move from external to internal use of signs parallels the move from external to inner speech.

From *Tool and symbol in child development*, part 4, 'The analysis of sign operations in the child', section entitled 'The further development of sign operations'

We are present at what is actually a process of the greatest psychological importance: what was an outward sign operation, i.e. a certain cultural method of self-control from without, is now *transformed into a new intra-psychological layer* and gives birth to a new psychological system, incomparably superior in content, and cultural-psychological in genesis.

The process of 'interiorisation' of cultural forms of behaviour, which we have just touched upon, is related to radical changes in the activity of the most important psychological functions, to the reconstruction of psychological activity on the basis of sign operations. On the one hand, natural psychological processes as we see them in animals actually cease to exist as such, being incorporated in this system of behaviour, now reconstructed on a cultural-psychological basis so as to form a new entity. This new entity must by definition include these former elementary functions which, however, continue to exist in subordinate forms acting now according to new laws characteristic of this whole system. On the other hand, the operation per se of the use of external signs is also radically reconstructed. Formerly a decisively important operation in young children, it is replaced here by essentially different forms. The inwardly instrumented process begins to make use of entirely new connections and methods unlike those that were characteristic of the outward sign operation. The process here undergoes alterations analogous to those observed in the child's transition from 'outward' speech to 'inward'. As a result of the process of interiorisation of the higher psychological operation, we have a new structure, a new function of formerly applied methods and an entirely new composition of psychological processes.

At the end of the fifth part of *Tool and symbol*, Vygotsky and Luria criticise as inadequate the methods of investigation of the behaviourist or reflexological school, which relied entirely on tightly controlled experiments, and those of the idealist school, whose 'comparative-genetic method was usually detached from the experiment'. Combining 'both these lines of research', they discuss the 'experimental-genetic method' of 'two-fold [or double] stimulation' which they and their colleagues have employed, involving – as we have seen – the introduction of challenges at or beyond the limit of a child's competence, and the use (initially external but later interiorised) of auxiliary cultural signs or symbols of various kinds. Crucially, Vygotsky and Luria return to their insistence on the central role of speech as 'a system of auxiliary symbols'.

From *Tool and symbol in child development*, part 5, 'Methods for the study of higher psychological functions'

In one respect the method we applied differs sharply from those that prevailed in contemporary child psychology. Whereas the experiment was usually isolated from the comparative-genetic method of study, focusing only on the relatively stable forms of behaviour, while the comparative-genetic method was usually detached from the experiment, we follow a reverse course combining both these lines of research in an integral *experimental-genetic* method. By employing the method of twofold stimulation, we are able to offer the subject tasks geared to differing phases of development and to provoke in reduced form those processes of mastering tasks which allow us to trace, in the experiment, consecutive stages of psychological development. By shifting the difficulty of our requirements, exposing the methods by which the task is mastered, and by prolonging our experiment over a number of consecutive series, we find ourselves capable of tracing in laboratory conditions *the process of development in all its basic features* and, hence, of arriving at an analysis of the factors that take part in it. By including and excluding speech from the operation, by giving the subject signs and means which he previously never used, by depriving the already developed subject of these signs, we obtained a sufficiently comprehensive idea of separate stages of development, their typical peculiarities, sequence, and also the main structural laws of the higher psychological systems.

With the application of a series of experimental-genetic methods, the psychology of childhood for the first time poses a number of concrete questions pertaining to the genesis of the higher psychological structures and to the structure of their genesis itself.

In our experimental researches there is no mandatory need to proceed each time by presenting our subject with ready-made external means with the help of which he must solve a given problem. The basic outline of our tests does not suffer in the least if, instead of giving the child ready-made external means, we wait until it applies spontaneously some kind of auxiliary method, incorporating in its operation some kind of auxiliary system of symbols.

A considerable part of our experiments was carried out following the above method. When asking our subject to memorise something (stimulus), we suggest that he draw something to make the subject to be memorised more easily kept in mind (auxiliary symbol). We thus created conditions for the reconstruction of the psychological process of memorising and the application of given auxiliary means. Without furnishing the child with ready-made symbols, we were able to follow, in the spontaneous unfolding of the methods applied, how all the essential mechanisms of the child's complex symbolic activities were manifested.

In the final part of *Tool and symbol*, Vygotsky and Luria discuss the dynamic and changing relationship between word and action in the child's mind. Their conclusions as to what children become able to do as this relationship develops are partly drawn from observations of what some children – those suffering from aphasia (difficulties with speech) – are unable to do.

From *Tool and symbol in child development*, part 6, 'Conclusions', sections entitled 'The use of tools in animal and human behaviour' and 'Word and action'

... the phylogenetic [evolutionary] history of man's practical intellect is closely tied, not only to mastering nature, but also to mastering himself. The history of labour and that of speech can scarcely be understood without each other.

Man not only invented tools, by means of which he conquered nature, but he invented also stimuli that motivated and regulated his own behaviour and by means of which he subjugated his own forces to his will. This becomes apparent at the earliest stages of the development of man.

★ ★ ★

... there are two types of activity between which the psychologist must discriminate in principle: one is the behaviour of animals, the other that of man; activity as a product of biological evolution and activity originating in the process of man's historical development.

The temporality of life, cultural development, work – in short, everything that distinguishes man from animals in the psychological field: all this is intimately related to the fact that, parallel to his conquest of nature over the course of his historical development, man also mastered his own self, his own behaviour.

★ ★ ★

... we were able to observe on a factual basis how, in the process of development, the child's action becomes social, and how, in losing speech because of aphasia, its practical action falls to the level of its elementary zoopsychological form.

He who pays no attention to these facts inevitably presents the psychological nature of speech and of action in a false light, for the source of their changes rests in their functional junction. Anyone who ignores this fundamental fact and who, having the purity of concept classification as his purpose, tries to represent speech and action as two never-meeting parallels, willy-nilly limits the real scope of both concepts because this scope of content is rooted first and foremost in the ties of both of them.

Gutzmann[7] limits speech to expressive functions, communication of inner states, communicative activity. The entire individual-psychological aspect of speech, all the word's reformative inner activity, are simply ignored. If this parallel and independent relation between speech and act were preserved throughout the entire process of development, speech would be powerless to change anything in behaviour. The affective aspect of the word is mechanically excluded, therefore there inevitably arises an underestimation of volitional action, action in its highest forms, that is, action tied to the word.

The essence of the matter, as demonstrated in investigations of these ties between word and action in child-age and in cases of aphasia, lies in the fact that speech lifts action to its highest stage, action that was previously independent of it. Both the development and the disintegration of higher forms of activity corroborate this fact ... The disorder of higher forms of action tied to the word, the disintegration of these higher forms, coupled to a cutting off of the action and its functioning according to independent primitive laws; in fact, the reversion to a more primitive organisation of action during aphasia and its fundamentally important sinking to a lower genetic level, something we were able to observe in all our experiments – all this shows that the pathological disintegration of action and speech, as in their genetic construction, does not proceed along two independent, never-meeting parallel lines.

We have, it seems, dwelt sufficiently on this problem in the previous treatment of our topic; as a matter of fact, our entire article was devoted to this problem. Now it is only a question of concentrating its contents into one concise formula which would express with the greatest possible exactness the essence of everything we have found in our clinical and experimental investigations of higher psychological functions in their development and disintegration, and, in particular, in investigations of practical intellect.

★ ★ ★

In [this article] we have tried to show how the *word*, becoming intellectualised and developing on the basis of *action*, lifts this action to a supreme level, subjects the child to its power, stamps it with the seal of will. But since we wanted to express all this in one short formula, in one sentence, we might put it thus: if *at the beginning* of development there stands the act, independent of the word, then at the end of it there stands the word which becomes the act, the word which makes man's action free.

Notes

1. The unusual history of the text from which we have taken extracts is described by Elkonon Goldberg in his book *The wisdom paradox* (2005, p.99):

    [Vygotsky and Luria's] 'historical-cultural psychology' was first presented in a paper titled *The Tool and the Symbol* [sic], an intellectual manifesto of sorts. Co-authored by Vygotsky and Luria in the late 1920s [probably 1930], it could not be published because it did not adhere to the increasingly oppressive dogma in the Soviet Union. The original Russian text was lost and only the English translation remained, prepared for a conference in the United States but never actually delivered. Forty years later, in the late sixties, the political climate thawed and their early ideas were exonerated. It was then that Luria discovered, to his dismay, the loss of the Russian original. Not one to be stymied by a challenge and always a practical man, he told me to translate *The Tool and the Symbol* from English 'back' into Russian and make it sound like the original text. With a mixture of awe and amusement, I did just that, and our benign forgery was passed for the real thing. Today, it graces the opening volume of Vygotsky's writings [in the Russian *Collected works*, not the English], without an explanation of what had actually happened.

2. Wolfgang Köhler (1887–1967) was a German psychologist. He and Max Wertheimer and Kurt Koffka created Gestalt psychology. He worked in the Canary Islands for six years, studying the behaviour of apes, during which he wrote his book *The mentality of apes* (1921).
3. *Res agitans* – a driving or driven thing, as opposed to Descartes's *res cogitans* – a thinking thing.

4. See Chapter 3, note 2.
5. The Russian word *obuchenie* means 'the combination and interaction of teaching and learning'.
6. Morozova used a cyclograph, which enabled her to keep a graphic record of these 'gropings' by showing the details of the children's motor reactions.
7. Hermann Gutzmann (1865–1922) was a German physician. He founded the medical discipline of phoniatrics: the study and treatment of the organs of speech production.

References

Goldberg, E. (2005). *The wisdom paradox*. London: Simon and Schuster.
Köhler, W. (1921). *Intelligenzprufugen an Menschenaffen (The mentality of apes)*. Berlin: Springer.
Luria, A.R. (1979). *The making of mind: a personal account of Soviet psychology*. Cole, M. and Cole, S. (eds). Cambridge, MA: Harvard University Press.
Van der Veer, R. and Valsiner, J. (eds) (1994). *The Vygotsky reader*. Oxford, UK and Cambridge, MA: Blackwell.
Vygotsky, L.S. (1987). *The collected works of L.S. Vygotsky. Volume 1, Problems of general psychology*. Trans. and intro. N. Minick; Rieber, R.W. and Carton, A.S. (eds). New York, NY: Plenum Press.
Vygotsky, L.S. (1987a). *Thinking and speech* [1934], in Vygotsky, L.S. (1987), *The collected works of L.S. Vygotsky. Volume 1, Problems of general psychology*, pp. 37–285.
Vygotsky, L.S. and Luria, A.R. (1994). *Tool and symbol in child development* [1930], in *The Vygotsky reader* (1994). Van der Veer, R. and Valsiner, J. (eds), pp. 99–174.
Yerkes, R.M. and Learned, B.W. (1925). *Chimpanzee intelligence and its vocal expressions*. Baltimore, MD: Williams and Wilkins.

Chapter 6

In pursuit of a unified psychological structure

Extracts from *The history of the development of higher mental functions*

The history of the development of higher mental functions (Vygotsky, 1997a) was written in about 1931, but not published in Vygotsky's lifetime. In this very long book, Vygotsky summarises much of his recent work in psychology, including the picture of the development of higher mental functions he and Luria advanced in *Tool and symbol in child development* (Vygotsky and Luria, 1994; see Chapter 5). We will not revisit the clear model of mental development arrived at in that book. Here we shall focus on the much more complex model of mental development that *The history of the development of higher mental functions* introduces.

A key difference between this book and *Tool and symbol*, where the evidence was drawn from laboratory research, is the focus on development in normal life, where the relationship between lower and higher mental functions is seen as more fluid, with the lower functions always present as a subsidiary stratum – not cancelled out by the process of transformation but instead 'sublated' or 'superseded and saved'. The whole book is an in-depth exploration of mental development, presented as a revolutionary process of contradiction, challenge and struggle, rather than a smooth evolutionary unfolding.

Vygotsky sets out his thinking in the context of existing psychological research on child development, using conventional psychological terms, and frequently using the language of reflexology (the book seems to assume a readership of psychologists).

Early in the book, Vygotsky lays out the 'three basic concepts of our research: [i] *the concept of higher mental function,* [ii] *the concept of cultural development of behaviour,* and [iii] *the concept of mastery of behaviour by internal processes*'. None of this trio of intimately interrelated concepts has been properly attended to, he says.

From *The history of the development of higher mental functions*, chapter 1, 'The problem of the development of higher mental functions' – the three basic concepts

The history of the development of will in the child has not yet been written. In one of the concluding chapters of our monograph, we will try to show that, in essence, this is tantamount to an assertion that the history of the development of all higher mental functions has not yet been written or that the history of the cultural development of the child has not yet been written. In essence, all three statements are equivalent – they express one and the same idea. But now we will use this indisputable position as an example which, owing to the factual similarity of the scientific fate of many related problems, can be extended also to the remaining higher functions, leaving aside for the time being the complex course of further thought that would bring to our attention three basic concepts of our research: *the concept of higher mental function; the concept of cultural development of behaviour; and the concept of mastery of behaviour by internal processes.* Just as the history of the development of child volition has not yet been written, the history of the development of the remaining higher functions has not yet been written: of voluntary attention, logical memory, etc. This is a fundamental fact which we must not bypass. In essence, we know nothing about the development of these processes. Except for fragmentary observations frequently found in two or three lines of text, we may say that child psychology passes over these questions in silence.

In the book's second chapter, Vygotsky discusses humans' use of signs and tools. He draws a parallel between the use of signs and the use of tools as mediating activities, but also points to the differences between them. Signs, which are a key element in cultural development, are *inwardly* directed: '... a means of psychological action on behaviour, one's own or another's, a means of internal activity directed towards mastering man himself; the sign is directed inward'. Tools are directed *outward*: '... the means for man's external activity toward subjugating nature' (Vygotsky, 1997a, p. 62).

From *The history of the development of higher mental functions*, chapter 2, 'Research method' – tools and signs

... as a point of departure, we can establish three points that seem to us ... sufficiently important for the understanding of the research method we have chosen. The first point pertains to the analogy and points of contiguity between both types of activity [the use of the sign and the use of the tool], the second elucidates the basic points of divergence, and the third attempts to indicate the real psychological connection between the one and the other, or at least to suggest it.

As has already been said, the basis for the analogy between the sign and the tool is the mediating function of the one and the other. From the psychological aspect, they may, for this reason, be classified in the same category. In [Figure 6.1],

74 The history of the development of higher mental functions

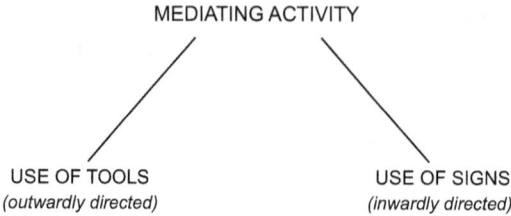

Figure 6.1 The relationship between tool and sign.
Source: Vygotsky (1997a, fig. 1, p. 62).

we present a diagram attempting to show the relation between the use of signs and the use of tools; from the logical aspect, both may be considered as coordinative concepts included in a more general concept – mediating activity.

With full justification, Hegel[1] used the concept of mediation in its most general meaning, seeing in it the most characteristic property of the mind. He said that the mind is as resourceful as it is powerful. In general, resourcefulness consists in mediating activity that, while it lets objects act on each other according to their nature and exhaust themselves in that activity, does not at the same time intervene in the process, but fulfils only *its own proper role*. Marx [1867] refers to this definition when he speaks of the tools of work and indicates that man 'makes use of mechanical, physical, chemical properties of things in order to change them into tools to act on other things according to his purpose.'[2]

It seems to us that on this basis the use of signs should be classified as a mediating activity, since the essence of this is that man acts on behaviour through signs, that is, stimuli, letting them act according to their psychological nature. In both cases, the mediating function is of the first order. We shall not define the relation of these coordinative concepts to each other or to the common generic concept [mediating activity] any more precisely. We should like only to note that neither can in any case be considered equivalent in meaning nor of equal value in fulfilling functions, nor, finally, in exhausting the *whole* range of the concept of mediating activity. Together with these, we might have enumerated quite a few mediating activities, since the activity of the mind is not exhausted by the use of tools and signs.

We must emphasise also that our diagram is intended to present the logical relation of the concepts, but not the genetic or functional (on the whole, real) relations of the phenomena. We would like to point to the relation of the concepts, but not in any way to their origin or real root. So conditionally, but at the same time in a purely logical scheme of relations of the concepts, our diagram presents both types of devices as *diverging* lines of mediating activity. The second point we have developed consists of this. A more substantial difference of the sign from the tool, and the basis of the real divergence of the two, lies in the different purpose of the one and the other. The tool serves for conveying man's activity to the object of his activity, it is directed outward, it must result in one change or another in the object, it is the means for man's external activity directed toward subjugating nature. The sign changes nothing in the object of the psychological operation, it is a means of psychological action on behaviour, one's own or another's, a means of internal activity directed towards mastering man himself; the sign is directed inward. These activities are so different that even the nature of the devices used cannot be one and the same in both cases.

Finally, the third point, which like the first two, we will develop further, having in view the real connection of these activities and, of course, the real connection of their development in phylogenesis [evolutionary development] and ontogenesis [the development of an individual]. Mastery of nature and mastery of behaviour are mutually connected because when man changes nature he changes the nature of man himself. In phylogenesis, we can restore the connection according to separate, fragmentary, documentary traces that do not leave room for doubt; in ontogenesis, we can trace it experimentally.

The extracts in the rest of this chapter focus on Vygotsky's 'three basic concepts'. The first two deal with the first concept: higher mental functions. Vygotsky criticises inadequate models of the development of these functions. Neither a model which likens their development to plant growth, nor one which likens it to the development of an embryo, will do. Darwin's discovery of 'the true origin of species', in which '[s]pecies arose and died out, species changed and developed in the struggle for survival', is a better analogy for the development of higher mental functions in the child. And, in this development, the higher mental functions, such as 'voluntary attention, logical memory, formation of concepts', replace the lower functions through a dialectical process in which conscious processes gain ascendancy over natural ones (for example, voluntary as opposed to involuntary attention).

From *The history of the development of higher mental functions*, chapter 5, 'Genesis of higher mental functions' – the genesis of higher psychological processes

Now the problem that confronts psychology is to detect the true uniqueness of child behaviour in all the fullness and richness of its actual expression and to present a positive picture of the child personality. But a positive picture is possible only if we radically change our representation of child development and take into account that it is a complex dialectical process that is characterised by complex periodicity, disproportion in the development of separate functions, metamorphoses or qualitative transformation of certain forms into others, a complex merging of the process of evolution and involution, a complex crossing of external and internal factors, a complex process of overcoming difficulties and adapting.

Another thing that must be overcome to clear the road for contemporary genetic research is cryptic evolutionism, which thus far dominates child psychology.

Evolution or development by gradual and slow accumulation of separate changes continues to be regarded as the only form of child development which exhausts all the processes we know that make up this general concept. In essence, in discussions of child development, an analogy to processes of plant growth shows through.

Child psychology wants to know nothing about the critical, spasmodic and revolutionary changes with which the history of child development is replete and which are found so often in the history of cultural development. To the naïve consciousness, revolution and evolution seem incompatible. For the naïve, historical development continues only as long as it proceeds along a straight line. Where a turn, a break of the historical tissue, a jump occurs, the naïve consciousness sees only catastrophe, a failure, a break. For the naïve, history stops at this point for the whole period until it again enters on a direct and smooth road.

Scientific consciousness, on the other hand, considers revolution and evolution as two mutually connected and closely interrelated forms of development. Scientific consciousness considers the leap itself that is made in the development of the child during such changes as a certain point in the entire line of development as a whole.

This position has an especially important significance for the history of cultural development because, as we shall see, the history of cultural development consists to a great extent of these kinds of crucial and spasmodic changes that occur in the development of the child. The very essence of cultural development consists in a confrontation of developed cultural forms of behaviour which confront the child and primitive forms that characterise his own behaviour.

The most obvious consequence of what has been said is the change in the generally accepted point of view of the processes of mental development of the child and the representation of the nature of the structure and flow of these processes. Usually all processes of child development are presented as stereotypically occurring processes. The image of development, seemingly the model with which all other forms are compared, is considered as embryonal development. This type of development depends least on the environment, and the word 'development' can be applied to it quite justifiably in the literal sense, that is, as an unfolding of possibilities that are contained in the embryo in a convoluted form. Also, embryonal development cannot be considered as a model of any process of development in the strict sense of the word. Rather, it can be represented as its result, its outcome. It is a process that has already stopped, that is concluded and proceeds more or less stereotypically.

We need only to compare the process of embryonal development with the process of the evolution of animal species, the true origin of species as disclosed by Darwin, in order to see the radical difference between the one type of development and the other. Species arose and died out, species changed and developed in the struggle for survival, in the process of adaptation to the environment. If we should want to draw an analogy between the process of child development and any other kind of process of development, we would have to select the evolution of animal species rather than embryonal development.

Least of all does child development resemble a stereotypic process protected from external influence; the development of the child occurs in an active adaptation to the environment. Ever newer forms arise in this process and not simply stereotypically produced links of a chain assembled earlier. Every new stage in the development of the embryo already present in a potential form in a preceding stage occurs due to the unfolding of internal potentials; it is not so much a process of development as a process of growth and maturation. This form, this type is also represented in the mental development of the child; but in the history of cultural development another form, another type has a much greater place; this consists in the new stage arising not out of unfolding potentials contained in the preceding stage, but out of an actual confrontation between the organism and the environment and an active adaptation to the environment.

From *The history of the development of higher mental functions*, chapter 3, 'Analysis of higher mental functions' – interaction between higher and lower psychological functions

It seems to us that … the relation between higher and lower forms may be best expressed by admitting what in dialectics is usually termed 'removal'. We can say that the lower, elementary processes and patterns that direct them represent a removed category. Hegel indicates that we must remember the dual meaning of the German expression 'to remove'. In this word, we understand, first, 'removal', 'rejection', and according to this we say that the laws are revoked, 'cancelled', but the same word also means 'preserved', and we say that we will 'save' something. The dual meaning of the term 'remove' is usually translated well into Russian by the word '*skhoronit*' [to bury], which also has a positive and a negative sense – destruction and preservation [sublation].

Using this work, we could say that the elementary processes and the patterns that govern them are buried in the higher form of behaviour, that is, they appear in it in a subordinate and cryptic form.

---

78 The history of the development of higher mental functions

The next group of extracts is concerned with Vygotsky's second concept: the cultural development of behaviour. The first extract asserts that the developing mastery of cultural forms (or cultural languages – e.g. written language or the language of mathematics) combines with the development of higher mental functions in 'the development of higher forms of the child's behaviour'. This is a major revision of the theory and gives a central place to these cultural languages in mental development. The second extract, using the young child's pointing gesture as an example, emphasises the essentially social nature of cultural development: 'through others we become ourselves'. The third extract is from Vygotsky's famous discussion of the essential roles of gesture, scribbling, drawing, play and speech in the development of the child's competence in writing. In the fourth extract, on arithmetic, Vygotsky describes a three-stage process of development, from direct to mediated to internalised or abstracted competence in the use of arithmetical symbols.

From *The history of the development of higher mental functions*, chapter 1, 'The problem of the development of higher mental functions' – two streams 'inseparably connected, but never merging into one'

The concept 'development of higher mental functions' and the subject of our research encompass two groups of phenomena that seem, at first glance, to be completely unrelated, but in fact represent two basic branches, two streams of the development of higher forms of behaviour inseparably connected, but never merging into one. These are, first, the processes of mastering external materials of cultural development and thinking: language, writing, arithmetic, drawing; second, the processes of development of special higher mental functions not delimited and not determined with any degree of precision and in traditional psychology termed voluntary attention, logical memory, formation of concepts, etc. Both of these taken together also form that which we conditionally call the process of development of higher forms of the child's behaviour.

From *The history of the development of higher mental functions*, chapter 5, 'Genesis of higher mental functions' – the social nature of cultural development

All cultural development of the child passes through three basic stages that can be described in the following way, using Hegel's analysis.

As an example, we will consider the history of the development of the pointing gesture; as we shall see, it plays an exceptionally important role in the development of speech in the child and is, to a significant degree, the ancient basis for all higher forms of behaviour. Initially, the pointing gesture represents a simply unsuccessful grasping movement directed toward an object and denoting a future action. The child attempts to grasp an object that is somewhat too far away, his hands stretched toward the object are left hanging in the air, the fingers make pointing movements. This situation is the point of departure for further development. Here the pointing movement, which we may arbitrarily term a pointing gesture, appears for the first time. This is movement of the child objectively indicating an object and only an object.

When the mother comes to help the child and recognises his movement as pointing, the situation changes substantially. The pointing gesture becomes a gesture for others. In response to the unsuccessful grasping movement of the child, there arises a reaction not on the part of the object, but on the part of another person. In this way, others carry out the initial idea of the unsuccessful grasping movement. And only subsequently, on the basis of the fact that the unsuccessful grasping movement is connected by the child with the whole objective situation, does he himself begin to regard this movement as a direction.

★ ★ ★

In this way, the child is the last one to recognise his gesture. Its significance and function are initially made up of an objective situation and then by the people around the child. The pointing gesture most likely begins to indicate by movement what is understood by others and only later becomes a direction for the child himself.

Thus we might say that through others we become ourselves, and this rule refers not only to the individual as a whole, but also to the history of each separate function. This also comprises the essence of the process of cultural development expressed in a purely logical form. The individual becomes for himself what he is in himself through what he manifests for others. This is also the process of forming the individual. In psychology, the problem of the relation of external and internal mental functions is posed here for the first time in all its significance. Here, as has been said, it becomes clear why everything internal in higher forms was of necessity external, that is, was for others what it is now for oneself. Every higher mental function necessarily passes through an external stage of development because function is primarily social. This is the centre of the whole problem of internal and external behaviour. Many authors have long since pointed to the problem of interiorisation, internalising behaviour. Kretschmer[3] sees in this a law of nervous activity. Bühler[4] reduces the whole evolution of behaviour to the fact that the field of selection of positive actions is transferred inward from outside.

But we have something else in mind when we speak of the external stage in the history of the cultural development of the child. For us, to call a process 'external' means to call it 'social'. Every higher mental function was external because it was social before it became an internal, strictly mental function; it was formerly a social relation of two people. The means of acting on oneself is initially a means of acting on others or a means of action of others on the individual.

The shift in the three basic forms of development in the functions of speech can be traced step by step in the child. More than anything, the word must have meaning, that is, it must relate to a thing, there must be an objective connection between the word and what it signifies. If there is not, further development of the word is impossible. Further, the objective connection between the word and the thing must be functionally used by adults as a means of socialising with the child. Only then will the word have meaning for the child also. Thus, the meaning of the word exists objectively first for others and only later begins to exist for the child himself. All basic forms of social intercourse between the adult and the child later become mental functions.

We can formulate the general genetic law of cultural development as follows: every function in the cultural development of the child appears on the stage twice in two planes; first, the social, then the psychological, first between people as an intermental category, then within the child as an intramental category. This pertains equally to voluntary attention, to logical memory, to the formation of concepts, and to the development of will. We are justified in considering the thesis presented as a law, but it is understood that the transition from outside inward transforms the process itself, changes its structure and functions. Genetically, social relations, real relations of people, stand behind all the higher functions and their relations. From this, one of the basic principles of our will is the principle of division of functions among people, the division into two of what is now merged into one, the experimental unfolding of a higher mental process into the drama that occurs among people.

For this reason, we might term the basic result to which the history of the cultural development of the child leads us as sociogenesis of higher forms of behaviour.

The word 'social', as applied to our subject, has a broad meaning. First of all, in the broadest sense, it means that everything cultural is social. Culture is both a product of social life and of the social activity of man, and for this reason the very formulation of the problem of cultural development of behaviour already leads us directly to the social plane of development. Further, we could indicate the fact that the sign found outside the organism, like a tool, is separated from the individual and serves essentially as a social organ or social means.

Going further, we might say that all higher functions were formed not in biology, not in the history of pure phylogenesis, but that the mechanism itself that is the basis of higher mental functions is a copy from the social. All higher mental functions are the essence of internalised relations of a social order, a basis for the social structure of the individual. Their composition, genetic structure, method of action – in a word, their entire nature – is social; even in being transformed into mental processes, they remain quasi-social. Man as an individual maintains the actions of socialising.

From *The history of the development of higher mental functions*, chapter 7, 'Prehistory of the development of written language' – the connections between speech, play, drawing and writing

The history of the development of the written language of the child presents great difficulties for research. To the extent that this can be judged by extant materials, the development of written language does not proceed along a single line preserving a continuity of forms. The history of the development of the written language of the child contains the most unexpected metamorphoses, that is, conversion of some forms of written language into other forms. In the beautiful expression of Baldwin,[5] there is as much involution as there is evolution. This means that together with processes of development, movement forward and the birth of new forms, we must at each step detect processes of reduction, dying off, reverse development of the old forms.

Here, as in the history of cultural development of the child, we frequently encounter characteristics of spasmodic changes and disruptions or breaks in the line of development. The line of development of written language in the child sometimes stops almost completely, then suddenly, as if completely out of nowhere, from outside, a new line begins and at first glance it seems that between the broken-off past and the beginning new there is absolutely no continuous connection. But only a naïve representation of development as a purely evolutionary process accomplished exclusively by gradual accumulation of separate small changes, an unnoticeable transition of one form into another, can conceal from our eyes the true essence of the processes that are occurring. Only someone who is inclined to imagine all processes of development as processes of germination will deny that the history of written language of the child is fully entitled to be represented by a single line of development regardless of the breaks, dying off, and metamorphoses of which we spoke above.

We already know that every process of cultural development of the child, like every other process of his mental development, is a model of revolutionary development. We have seen above that the type of cultural development of human behaviour arising from a complex interaction between the organic maturing of the child and the cultural environment must of necessity present for us at each step an example of this revolutionary development. In general, for science, the type of revolutionary development is nothing new; it is new only for child psychology, and for this reason, regardless of individual, sometimes boldly conceived studies, in child psychology we still have no coherent attempt to present the history of the development of written language as a historical process, as a single process of development.

★ ★ ★

The history of the development of writing begins with the appearance of the first visual signs in the child and is based on the same natural history of emergence of signs from which speech was derived. A gesture is specifically the initial visual sign in which the future writing of the child is contained, as the future oak is contained in the seed. The gesture is a writing in the air and the written sign is very frequently simply a fixed gesture.

★ ★ ★

Now we would like to note two points that genetically connect the gesture with the written sign. The first point is the scribbles that a child makes. As we have often observed during experiments, when a child draws, he very often makes a transition to dramatisation, showing by a gesture what he wants to picture, and the line made by the pencil only supplements what has been depicted by the gesture. In psychological literature, we know of only a single indication of this. We think that the paucity of similar observations can be explained simply by the absence of attention to this phenomenon which is very important in the genetic respect.

Stern[6] made a remarkable observation that pointed out the distant relationship between drawing and the gesture. A child of four sometimes added meaning to a picture by the movement of his hand. This was several months after his scribbles were replaced by ordinary, immature drawing. For example, once, the sting of a mosquito was symbolised by a stinging motion of the hand and by the point of the pencil. Another time, the child wanted to show in a drawing how it gets dark when the curtains are closed and he made a forceful line down on the board as if he was drawing a window shade. The drawing movement did not signify a cord, but expressed specifically the movement of drawing a curtain.

★ ★ ★

The second point that forms a genetic connection between the gesture and written language brings us to child's play. As we know, in play some objects can very easily represent others, replace them and become their signs. We also know that in this case the similarity that exists between the toy and the object that it represents is not important. Most important is its functional use, the possibility of using it to produce the representing gesture. In our opinion, this is the only key to explaining the whole symbolic function of child's play. In play, a lump of rag or wood becomes a small child because the child makes gestures that imitate carrying a small child in his arms or feeding it. The child's own movement, his own gesture is what ascribes the function of a sign to a suitable object, and this imparts meaning to it. All symbolic graphic activity is full of such indicating gestures. Thus, a stick becomes a horse for the child because it can be placed between the legs, and a gesture can be applied to it that will indicate that the stick in this case represents a horse.

In this way, a child's symbolic play may, from this point of view, be understood as a very complex system of speech aided by gestures that supplement and indicate the meaning of individual toys. Only on the basis of indicating gestures does the toy gradually acquire its meaning precisely as drawing, supported at first by a gesture, becomes an independent sign.

★ ★ ★

G. Gettser,[7] wishing to study how mentally mature a school-age child must be to learn to write, was the first to develop a broad formulation of this problem. She tried to study how the child's function of symbolic representation of things, which is so important for learning to write, develops. To do this, Gettser had to elucidate experimentally the development of the symbolic function in children aged three to six years. The experiments consisted of four basic series. The symbolic function of play was studied in the first series. The child in play had to represent the father or mother and do what they do during a day. In the process of play, arbitrary interpretation of the objects involved in playing occurred and the researcher could trace the symbolic function assigned to the objects in play. Construction material was used to represent the mother or father, which was then coloured with coloured pencils. In the second and third series, special attention was given to the moment the appropriate meaning was assigned. Finally in the fourth series, in a game of postman, the researcher was able to observe to what extent the child is able to perceive a purely arbitrary combining of signs since the blocks coloured with different colours served as signs of different letters delivered by the postman: telegrams, newspapers, remittances, packages, letters, postcards, etc.

Thus, experimental study placed in one order the various kinds of activities, united only by the fact that each of them was based on the symbolic function, and the study tried to establish a genetic connection between all of these types of activity and the development of written language.

In Gettser's experiments, we can see quite clearly how the symbolic meaning in play develops with the help of a graphic gesture and with the help of a word. Here the child's egocentric speech was very apparent. While in some children everything is represented with the help of movement, and mimicking and speech are not involved as symbolic means, in other children speech accompanies action: the child talks and acts. In a third group, purely verbal expression begins to dominate unsupported by any other kind of activity. Finally, the fourth group of children hardly played at all and speech was the only means of representation, while mimicking and gesture were relegated to the background.

The experiment demonstrated that with years, the percentage of purely play actions gradually diminishes and that speech begins to dominate. The most essential conclusion from this genetic study, as Gettser says, is the fact that the difference in play between three-year-old and six-year-old children is not in the perception of symbols, but in the method by which the various forms of representation are used. It seems to us that this is the most important conclusion showing that symbolic representation in play and at a very early age is, in essence, a unique form of speech that leads directly to written language.

★ ★ ★

Experiments have shown that the child who knows letters and can, with help, isolate their individual sounds in words, does not at all immediately come to a full mastery of the mechanism of writing. However, even here ... we do not find the most important moment that characterises the real transition to written language. It is easy to note that everywhere written signs represent symbols of the first order directly signifying objects or actions, and the child at the stage we are describing does not approach symbolism of the second order, which consists of using written signs for oral symbols of words.

For this, the child must make a special discovery – specifically, not only things, but speech also, can be drawn. Only this discovery brought humanity to the brilliant method of writing with words and letters; it also brings the child to literate writing and, from the psychological point of view, must be constructed like the transition from drawing things to drawing speech. However, it is difficult to trace how this transition is accomplished because the appropriate research has not yet resulted in definite results and the generally accepted methods of teaching writing do not allow a thorough observation of the transition process. One thing is not subject to doubt: in all probability, real written language of the child (not mastery of the habit of writing) develops in a similar way – the way the transition is made from drawing things to drawing words. Various methods of teaching writing confirm this in different ways. Many methods use auxiliary gestures as a means of uniting the written and the oral symbol; others use drawing depicting the corresponding object, and the whole secret in teaching written language consists in preparing and organising this natural transition properly. As soon as this is done, the child masters the mechanics of written language and he only needs to perfect this method subsequently.

With the present state of psychological information, many will think the idea extremely forced that all the stages we have considered – play, drawing and writing – may be presented as different moments of an essentially single process of developing written language. The breaks and jumps in the transition from one device to another are somewhat large for the connection between the separate moments to be sufficiently obvious and clear. But experiments and psychological analysis lead us specifically to this conclusion and show that no matter how complex the process of development of written language seems to us, no matter how zig-zag, broken and confused its course might seem at a superficial glance, actually we have before us a single line of the history of writing that leads to higher forms of written language. The higher form, which we touch in passing, consists in the fact that the written language of symbolism of the second order becomes again symbolism of the first order. The initial written symbols serve as a sign of verbal symbols. Understanding written language is done through oral speech, but gradually this path is shortened, the intermediate link in the form of oral speech drops away, and written language becomes direct symbol just as understandable as oral speech. One only has to imagine what an enormous break occurs in the whole cultural development of the child due to the mastery of written language, due to the possibility of reading and consequently to being enriched by everything that human genius has created in the sphere of the written word in order to understand the decisive moment experienced by the child in the discovery of writing.

From *The history of the development of higher mental functions*, chapter 8, 'Development of arithmetic operations' – from direct to mediated means of solving arithmetical challenges, and thence to the use of conventional arithmetical symbols

... we must indicate the final stage through which [the] development [of preschool arithmetic] passes. Quite soon, the older child is confronted with the fact that the method of dividing with the help of 'tractors' and 'clocks'[8] distracts energy, attention and time from the non-mediated task before him. The child is confronted with arithmetical difficulties, one of which is that the remainder exceeds the divisor. Then the child makes a transition to another, simpler form of operation. He begins to use as a basic auxiliary means not such concrete forms as 'tractors' or 'clocks', but certain spatial, abstract forms that correspond to the number and may be divided according to units.

As far as we could trace this, it is evidently the last stage in the development of preschool arithmetic. We cannot say which paths further development would take if the child were left to himself, if he would not find himself in school and was not taught our method of counting, if he were to continue to develop along the natural, innate path. In practice, we cannot observe this. Almost always there are exceptionally crucial points in the development of the child, there is always a collision between his arithmetic and another form of arithmetic that adults teach him. The pedagogue and the psychologist should know that the child's learning cultural arithmetic produces a conflict.

In other words, development here consists of a certain break, a certain collision, a collision between the forms of operating with numbers that the child developed himself and those that adults teach him. Up to this time, psychologists and mathematicians are divided into two camps. Some say that the process of learning arithmetic proceeds more or less along a straight line, that preschool arithmetic prepares one for school arithmetic completely naturally the way the prattling of a child prepares for his speaking. The schoolteacher only corrects the child and pushes him further in the same direction. Other methodologists say that the process occurs in a completely different way. Between the preschool stage and the school stage there is a certain break, a transition from one path to another. This displacement marks a turning point in the arithmetical development of the child.

The child makes a transition from direct perception of number to mediated perception by experience, that is, to mastery of signs and ciphers and their correct meaning, to those rules that we use which consist of replacing operation with objects by operation with number systems. If we want to divide a certain number of objects among a certain number of participants, then at the beginning we count the objects and the participants. Then we carry out the arithmetical operation of division. The point at which the child makes the transition from direct reaction to number to abstract operations with signs is the point of conflict. It creates a collision between the former line of development with that which begins with the learning of school signs.

We cannot imagine that development goes along a completely straight line. There are many breaks, leaps and turns.

This extract is concerned with Vygotsky's third concept: self-control or 'the mastery of behaviour by internal processes'. In the first extract in this chapter, Vygotsky writes:

> The history of the development of will in the child has not yet been written. In one of the concluding chapters of our monograph, we will try to show that, in essence, this is tantamount to an assertion that the history of the development of all higher mental functions has not yet been written or that the history of the cultural development of the child has not yet been written.
>
> (Vygotsky, 1997a, p. 7)

This bold statement of Vygotsky's is not entirely borne out by the chapter on self-control at the end of his book, in that this chapter does not focus on the growth of self-control in a way that parallels the development of other higher forms of mental function such as attention, choice and memory. For much of the chapter, Vygotsky is concerned with negative aspects of will – 'hypobulia or resistance': the will *not* to cooperate.

However, Vygotsky does see the development of will, self-control, as being basic to the development of self and the development of social man. Here he quotes Engels, who sees control of nature and control of self as one.

From *The history of the development of higher mental functions*, chapter 12, 'Self-control' – control of nature and control of self placed 'in one order'

Perhaps the most remarkable thing that the psychologist can now say about will is the following: will develops and is the product of the cultural development of the child. Self-control and the principles and means of this control do not differ basically from control over the environment. Man is part of nature, his behaviour is a natural process, and controlling it forms [develops] like all control of nature, according to Bacon's[9] principle that 'nature is overcome by subjection'. Not in vain does Bacon place control of nature and control of intellect in one order; he says that the bare hand and the mind taken in themselves do not mean much – the deed is done with tools and auxiliary means.

But no one expressed with such clarity the general idea that freedom of will is derived from and develops in the process of the historical development of humanity as did Engels. He says [1877]:[10] 'Not in the imaginary independence of laws of nature does freedom lie, but in recognising these laws and, based on this, knowing the possibilities of systematically making the laws of nature work toward certain goals. This refers both to laws of external nature and to laws that govern the bodily and mental existence of man himself – that there are two classes of laws that can be separated from each other is the most important thing in our concept which is by no means far from reality. Consequently, freedom of will means nothing other than the ability to make a decision with knowledge of the matter.' In other words, Engels places in one order the control of nature and control of self. Freedom of will with respect to one and the other is, for him as for Hegel, understanding necessity.

Engels says: 'Consequently, freedom is based on recognising the needs of nature (*Naturnotwendigheiten*), control of ourselves and of external nature; for this reason, it is an indispensable product of historical development. The first humans coming out of the animal kingdom were in all essentials as lacking in freedom as the animals; but each step forward on the path of culture was a step toward freedom' [ibid.].

Therefore, the psychologist-geneticist is confronted with the most important task of finding in the development of the child the lines along which maturation of freedom of the will occurs. We are confronted with the task of presenting the gradual growth of this freedom, of disclosing its mechanisms and showing it as a product of development.

Throughout *The history of the development of higher mental functions*, Vygotsky's focus is on how human beings are constantly engaged in the process of changing and controlling their behaviour and themselves.

Notes

1. See Chapter 4, note 13.
2. The reference in the reference list below (Marx, 1867) is to an online version of Marx's work. This translation uses slightly different wording from, but with a similar sense to, the wording in the text.
3. Ernst Kretschmer (1888–1964) was a German psychiatrist. He proposed that there are connections between a person's physical constitution and the characteristics of their personality, including their tendency to mental illness.

4. Karl Bühler (1879–1963) was a German psychologist and linguist, known for his work in Gestalt psychology.
5. James Mark Baldwin (1861–1934) was an American psychologist and philosopher.
6. See Chapter 3, note 2.
7. G. Gettser was a colleague of Charlotte Bühler (1893–1974), a German developmental and humanistic psychologist.
8. Tractors and clocks were aids which Vygotsky and his colleagues introduced to help children with their calculations.
9. Francis Bacon (1561–1626) was an English philosopher and statesman. He is one of the founders of empiricism.
10. The reference in the reference list below (Engels, 1877) is to an online version of Engels' work. This translation uses slightly different wording from, but with a similar sense to, the wording in the text.

References

Engels, F. (1877) *Anti-Dühring, Part One, Chapter XI*. Available online in the Marxist Archive: www.marxists.org/archive/marx/works/1877/anti-duhring/ch09.htm.

Marx, K. (1867). *Das Kapital. Volume 1, Part 3, Chapter 7, Section 1*. Available online in the Marxist Archive: www.marxists.org/archive/marx/works/1867-c1/ch07.htm.

Van der Veer, R. and Valsiner, J. (eds) (1994). *The Vygotsky reader*. Oxford, UK and Cambridge, MA: Blackwell.

Vygotsky, L.S. (1997). *The collected works of L.S. Vygotsky. Volume 4, The history of the development of higher mental functions*. Rieber, R.W. (ed.). New York, NY: Plenum Press.

Vygotsky, L.S. (1997a). *The history of the development of higher mental functions* [1931], in Vygotsky, L.S. (1997), *The collected works of L.S. Vygotsky. Volume 4, The history of the development of higher mental functions*, pp. 1–251.

Vygotsky, L.S. and Luria, A.R. (1994). *Tool and symbol in child development* [1930], in *The Vygotsky reader* (1994). Van der Veer, R. and Valsiner, J. (eds), pp. 99–174.

Chapter 7

Vygotsky the pedologist

Pedology, or child science, was an international movement which arose in Europe and America in the late nineteenth century. It was cross-disciplinary, advocating the study of the whole child. Vygotsky was a practising pedologist. He was intensely committed to pedology and wrote many pedological works, extracts from some of which appear in this chapter.

The chapter begins with extracts from Vygotsky's seminal talk 'On psychological systems' (Vygotsky, 1997a), which he gave in October 1930 at the Moscow State University Clinic of Nervous Diseases. In this talk, he moves beyond the account of higher mental functions he had expounded at length in *The history of the development of higher mental functions* (Vygotsky,1997c; see Chapter 6). In that book, with the inclusion of 'cultural languages', he had identified a wider range of these functions. In 'On psychological systems' he now explores the way that functions may interact and change in the process of interaction.

From 'On psychological systems'

From Introduction

When I called my talk 'On psychological systems', I was thinking of the complex connections that develop between different functions in the process of development and that dissolve or undergo pathological change in the process of dissolution.

When we studied thinking and speech in childhood we saw that the process of development of these functions does not amount to a change within each function. What is changed is chiefly the original link between these functions, the link which is characteristic of phylogenesis [evolutionary development] in the zoological plane and of child development in the earliest stage. This link and this relation do not remain the same in the further development of the child. Therefore, one of the fundamental ideas in the area of the development of thinking and speech is that there can be no fixed formula which determines the relationship between thinking and speech and which is suitable for all stages of development and forms of loss. In each stage of development and in each form of loss we see a unique and changing set of relations. My report is dedicated to this very theme. Its main (and extremely simple) idea is that in the process of development, and in the historical development of behaviour in particular, it is not so much the functions which change (these we mistakenly studied before). Their structure and the system of their development remain the same. What is changed and modified are rather the relationships, the links between the functions. New constellations emerge which were unknown in the preceding stage. That is why intra-functional change is often not essential in the transition from one stage to another. It is inter-functional changes, the changes of inter-functional connections and the inter-functional structure, which matter.

The development of such new flexible relationships between functions we will call *a psychological system*, giving it all the content that is usually attached to this unfortunately too broad concept.

A few words about the arrangement of my material ... I do not yet have a general theoretical view that encompasses all the material and I would consider it a mistake to theorise prematurely. I will simply present a certain ladder of facts in a systematic manner, proceeding from below upwards. I confess beforehand that I am still unable to encompass the whole ladder of facts with a real theoretical conception and cannot yet logically arrange the facts and the links between them.

From part 1

When we go up one step and pay attention to the results of other investigations, we see still another regularity in the formation of new psychological systems. It brings us *au courant* and sheds light on the central question of my talk of today – the relationship of these new systems to the brain, to their physiological substrate.

When we studied the processes of the higher functions in children we came to the following staggering conclusion: each higher form of behaviour enters the scene twice in its development – first as a collective form of behaviour, as an inter-psychological function, then as an intra-psychological function, as a certain way of behaving. We do not notice this fact, because it is too commonplace and we are therefore blind to it. The most striking example is speech. Speech is at first a means of contact between the child and the surrounding people, but when the child begins to speak to himself, this can be regarded as the transference of a collective form of behaviour into the practice of personal behaviour.

According to the beautiful formula of one psychologist,[1] speech is not only a means to understand others, but also a means to understand oneself.

From part 2

When we go up yet another step in the study of those complex systems and relationships that are unknown in the early stages of development and develop relatively late, we arrive at a very complex system of changes of connections and the development of new ones. These changes take place on the path toward the development and formation of a new person in adolescence. Until now the shortcoming of our investigations was that we confined ourselves to early childhood and took little interest in adolescents. When I was faced with the necessity of studying the psychology of adolescence from the viewpoint of our investigations I was surprised at the extent to which this stage contrasts with childhood. Here the essence of psychological development is not that the connections increase in number, but that they change.

The tremendous difficulty connected with the psychology of adolescence was caused by the investigation of the adolescent's thinking. Indeed, there is little in the speech of the 14- to 16-year-old adolescent that changes in the sense of the appearance of fundamentally new forms compared to what a child of 12 years old has at his disposal. We do not notice anything that might explain what goes on in the adolescent's thinking. Thus, memory and attention in adolescence hardly show anything new compared to school age. But when you take, in particular, the material worked upon by Leontiev (1931), then you will see that characteristic of the adolescent age is the transition of these functions inward. What is external in the area of logical memory, voluntary attention and thinking in the school child becomes internal in the adolescent. Research confirms that here a new aspect emerges. We see that the transition inward takes place because these external operations enter into a complex alloy and synthesis with a number of internal processes. Because of its internal logic the process cannot remain external. Its relation to all other functions becomes different, a new system is formed, strengthened and becomes internal.

I will give a very simple example: memory and thinking in adolescence. We can notice (I simplify somewhat) the following interesting rearrangement here. You know what a colossal role memory plays in the thinking of the child before adolescence. For him to think means to a significant degree to rely on memory.

★ ★ ★

Now take adolescence. You will see that for the adolescent to remember means to think. Whereas the thinking of the pre-adolescent child rested on memory and to think meant to remember, for the adolescent memory rests mainly on thinking: to remember is first of all to search for what is needed in a certain logical order. This rearrangement of functions, the change of their relationships, the leading role of thinking in absolutely all functions as a result of which thinking turns out to be not just one function among a number of others, but a function which restructures and changes other psychological processes, we observe in adolescence.

From part 3

Preserving the same order of exposition and proceeding from lower psychological systems to the formation of systems of an ever higher order, we arrive at the systems which form the key to all processes of development and loss: concept formation, a function which fully ripens and takes shape first in adolescence.

★ ★ ★

Only in adolescence does this function finally take shape. The child turns to thinking in concepts from another system of thinking, from the complex-like connections. We may ask ourselves: what distinguishes the child's complex? First of all, the system of a complex is a system of ordered concrete connections and relationships to the object that rest mainly on memory. A concept is a system of judgements which involves a relation to the entire, broader system. Adolescence is the age when world view and personality take shape, when self-consciousness and coherent notions of the world develop. Thinking in concepts is at its basis. For us the whole experience of contemporary civilised mankind, the external world, the external reality and our internal reality are represented in a certain system of concepts. In concepts we find that unity of form and content which I mentioned above.

To think in concepts means to possess a certain ready-made system, a certain form of thinking which in no way predetermines the further content at which we arrive. Both Bergson[2] and the materialist think in concepts, both use the same form of thinking, although they reach diametrically opposed conclusions.

It is exactly in adolescence that the formation of all the systems is finished.

From part 4

Nothing can be isolated from the brain. The whole question is what it is in the brain which physiologically corresponds to thinking in concepts.

In order to explain its development in the brain it suffices to assume that the brain contains the conditions and possibilities for a combination of functions, a new synthesis, new systems which do not at all have to be structurally engraved beforehand. I think that all of contemporary neurology leads us to this assumption. More and more we see the infinite diversity and incompleteness of brain functions. It is much more correct to assume that the brain contains enormous possibilities for the development of new systems.

★ ★ ★

In actual fact, it seems to me that by introducing the concept of psychological system in the form we discussed, we get a splendid possibility of conceiving the real connections, the real complex relationships that exist.

To a certain degree this also holds true for one of the most difficult problems – the localisation of higher psychological systems. So far they have been localised in two ways. The first viewpoint considered the brain as a homogeneous mass and rejected the idea that the different parts are not equivalent and play different roles in the formation of psychological functions. This viewpoint is manifestly untenable. Therefore, henceforth it was tried to deduce the functions from different brain parts, distinguishing, for example, a practical area, etc. The areas are mutually connected, and what we observe in mental processes is the joint activity of separate areas. This conception is undoubtedly more correct. What we have is a complex collaboration of a number of separate zones. The brain substrate of the mental processes [does not consist of] isolated parts but complex systems of the whole brain apparatus. But the problem is the following: if this system is given in the very structure of the brain in advance, i.e. if it is fully determined by connections that exist in the brain between its various parts, then we must assume that those connections from which the concept develops are given beforehand in the structure of the brain. But if we assume that it is possible to have more complex systems which are not given in advance, a new perspective on this problem results.[3]

Allow me to clarify this with an admittedly very rough schema. Forms of behaviour that earlier were shared by two persons are now combined in the person: the order and its execution. Before, they took place in two brains. One brain acted upon the other with, say, a word. When they are combined in one brain we get the following picture: point A in the brain cannot reach point B through a direct combination. It has no natural connection with it. The possible connections between different parts of the brain are established through the peripheral nervous system, from outside.

Proceeding from such ideas, we can understand a number of facts of pathology. These include, first of all, patients with a lesion of the brain systems who are not capable of doing something directly, but can carry it out when they tell themselves to do so. Such a clinically clear picture is observed in Parkinsonian patients. The Parkinsonian patient cannot take a step. But if you tell him to take a step or if you put a piece of paper on the floor, he will take this step ... Why can the Parkinsonian patient walk when pieces paper are spread out on the floor?

★ ★ ★

Each of the systems I mentioned goes through three stages. First, an interpsychological stage – I order, you execute. Then an extra-psychological stage – I begin to speak to myself. Then an intra-psychological stage – two points of the brain which are excited from outside have the tendency to work in a unified system and turn into an intra-cortical point.

★ ★ ★

I would like to end by pointing out once more that I have presented a ladder of facts which, although it is still incoherent, nevertheless goes from below upwards. I skipped almost all theoretical considerations. It seems to me that this viewpoint sheds light on our investigations and gives them their proper place. I do not have enough theoretical strength to combine all this. I presented a very big ladder, but as the idea that comprehends all this I proposed a general idea. Today I wanted to elucidate whether this main idea, which I nourished during a number of years but hesitated to express fully, is confirmed by the facts. And our next task is to clarify this in the most business-like and detailed manner. Relying on the above-mentioned facts, I would like to express my fundamental conviction that the entire issue resides not just in the changes within the functions, but in the changes in the connections and in the infinitely diverse forms of development that develop from this. It resides in the development of new syntheses in a certain stage of development, new central functions and new forms of connections between them. We must take interest in systems and their fate. Systems and their fate – it seems to me that for us the alpha and omega of our next work must reside in these four words.

As we have seen, Vygotsky several times discusses adolescence in 'On psychological systems'. *Pedology of the adolescent* (Vygotsky, 1998a), published in 1931, from which the following extracts are taken, is the longest of Vygotsky's works to appear in print in his lifetime. It was a handbook for teachers across the Soviet Union. It draws on the research Vygotsky and his colleagues had been doing using the 'comparative-genetic method', which compared in broad terms the thinking of children and young people at different stages of development, and made detailed observations of the same child as he or she grew older, providing a unique longitudinal picture of growth. In the first two chapters of the book, Vygotsky explores the essential psychological nature of this transitional and turbulent period between childhood and adulthood. He argues that *the development of interests* is the key to understanding the psychological development of the adolescent; he identifies an essential difference between childhood and adolescence – that the adolescent has begun to think in concepts: 'Thinking in concepts leads to discovery of the deep connections that lie at the base of reality.' He also emphasises the central importance of speech in the formation of concepts: speech is 'a powerful means of analysis and classification of phenomena'.

From *Pedology of the adolescent*, chapter 1, 'Development of interests at the transitional age', section 1

The key to the whole problem of the psychological development of the adolescent is the *problem of interests* during the transitional age. All human psychological functions at each stage of development function not without a system and not automatically, but within a certain system, directed by certain tendencies, trends and interests established in the personality.

These driving forces of our behaviour change at each age level, and their evolution is the base for change in behaviour itself. It would, therefore, be incorrect, as has frequently been done, to consider the development of separate psychological functions and processes only from the formal aspect, in an isolated form, without regard for their direction and independently of the driving forces that these psycho-physiological mechanisms bring into play. A purely formal consideration of psychological development is essentially anti-genetic since it ignores the fact that with a move to a new age level, not only the mechanisms of behaviour themselves change and develop, but also its driving forces. Lack of attention to this circumstance can also explain the lack of results of many psychological studies, especially those pertaining to the transitional age. These studies frequently vainly tried to establish some kind of substantial qualitative differences in the activity of separate behavioural mechanisms: for example, of attention or memory of the adolescent in comparison with the younger, school-age child and the very young child. If such features were established, they usually were limited to purely quantitative description that demonstrated the growth of a function and an increase in its numerical index, but not a change in its internal structure.

★ ★ ★

The key to the understanding of the psychology of age, as has been said, is based in the problem of direction, in the problem of driving forces, in the structure of *tendencies and aspirations of the child*. The same habits, the same psycho-physiological mechanisms of behaviour that, from the formal aspect, frequently show no substantial difference at different age levels or at different stages of childhood are included in a completely different *system of tendencies and inclinations* in a completely different force field of direction, and from this arises the deep *uniqueness of their structure, their activity*, and their changes at a *given* definite phase of childhood.

Specifically because of this failure to take into account the indicated circumstances, for many decades child psychology was not able to find even one essential trait that would distinguish the child's perception from the adult's perception and would indicate the content of the processes of development in this area. For this reason, a serious turning point in the history of the study of child behaviour was the realisation that formal consideration alone was inadequate and there was a need to study those basic points of *direction, points with a unique configuration whose structure we find at each given stage, within which all mechanisms of behaviour find their place and their significance.*

A point of departure for scientific study in this area is admitting that not just the child's habits and psychological functions (attention, memory, thinking, etc.) are developing – at the base of mental development lies, first of all, an evolution of the child's behaviour and interests, a change in the structure of the direction of his behaviour.

From *Pedology of the adolescent,* chapter 1, 'Development of interests at the transitional age', sections 6 and 7

For us, this phase [the adolescent phase] is characterised by the fact that it contains two basic points: first, the unfolding and dying off of formerly established systems of interests (the basis for the negative, protesting, rejecting character), and, second, the processes of maturation and appearance of the first organic tendencies that signify the onset of sexual maturation. Specifically, the combination of both points taken together characterises what at first glance is a strange fact, that in the adolescent we can see as if a common general decrease, and sometimes even a complete absence, of interests. The disruptive, devastating phase, during which the adolescent finally concludes his childhood, caused L.N. Tolstoy [1854] to term this period the 'desert of adolescence'.[4]

Thus, the period as a whole is characterised by two basic traits: first, this is a period of a breaking away from and demise of old interests and, second, a period of maturing of a new biological base on which new interests develop later.

From *Pedology of the adolescent,* chapter 2, 'Development of thinking and formation of concepts in the adolescent', section 26

What we would like to bring to the forefront are the deep and fundamental changes in the content of the thinking of the adolescent. Without overstating, we could say that the whole content of thinking is reformed and reconstructed in conjunction with the formation of concepts. The content and form of thinking do not relate to each other as water does to a glass. The content and form are in an indissoluble relationship and mutual dependence.

If we understand content of thinking to be not simply the external data that comprise the subject of thinking at any given moment, but the actual content, we will see how, in the process of the child's development, it constantly moves inward, becomes an organic component part of the personality itself and of separate systems of its behaviour. Convictions, interests, world view, ethical norms and rules of behaviour, inclinations, ideals, certain patterns of thought – all of this is initially external, and becomes internal specifically because as the adolescent develops, in conjunction with his maturation and the change in his environment, he is confronted by the task of mastering new content, and strong stimuli are created that nudge him along the path of developing the formal mechanisms of his thinking as well.

The new content, which confronts the adolescent with a series of problems, leads to new forms of activity, to new forms of combining elementary functions, and to new methods of thinking. As we shall see, specifically during the transitional period, the new content itself creates new forms of behaviour, mechanisms of a special type about which we shall speak in a later chapter. Together with the transition to thinking in concepts, the adolescent is confronted by a world of objective, societal consciousness, a world of societal ideology.

Cognition in the true sense of that word – science, art, various spheres of cultural life – may be adequately assimilated only in concepts. True, even the child assimilates scientific facts, and the child is imbued with a certain ideology, and the child grows into separate spheres of cultural life. But an inadequate, incomplete mastery of all of this is characteristic for the child, and for this reason the child, perceiving the established cultural material, does not yet actively participate in its creation.

On the contrary, the adolescent, making the transition to an adequate assimilation of this content which can be presented in all its completeness and depth only in concepts, begins actively and creatively to participate in various spheres of cultural life that open before him. Without thinking in concepts there is no understanding of relations that underlie the phenomena. The whole world of deep connections that underlie external, outward appearances, the world of complex interdependencies and relations within every sphere of activity and among its separate spheres, can only be disclosed to one who approaches it with the key of the concept.

Volume 5 of the English edition of Vygotsky's *Collected works* contains only a small selection from Vygotsky's voluminous writings on the topic of pedology. Fortunately, David Kellogg and Nikolai Veresov have, since 2019, been giving full attention to Vygotsky's pedological writings in their series of volumes entitled *L.S. Vygotsky's pedological works*. Extracts from three of Vygotsky's pedological works, included in the first two volumes (Vygotsky, 2019, 2021), follow here.

The first is from one of a series of lectures which Vygotsky gave under the title *Foundations of pedology* at the Herzen Institute in Leningrad from 1932 until 1934, just before his death. The key concept here is *perezhivanie*, best translated in English as 'lived-through experience'. The term 'environment' refers to the social rather than the physical environment. In the course of this lecture, Vygotsky takes as an example of the difference between different people's 'lived-through experiences' the case of three children who had been brought to his Pedological Clinic. They have an alcoholic, mentally ill mother who regularly beats them, but their *perezhivanie* of this situation is different in each case.

From 'The problem of the environment in pedology' (Vygotsky, 2019a) – the concept of *perezhivanie*

Concerning those examples that we saw with various children, we may say, more precisely and more exactly, that the substantial moments for identifying the influence of the environment on the psychological development of the child, on the development of his conscious personality, are those of *perezhivanie* [lived-through experience]. The *perezhivanie* of any situation, the *perezhivanie* of any part of the environment, defines what will be the effect of this situation or this environment on the child. In this way, it is not in itself this moment or that moment, taken without regard to the child, but that moment, refracted through the *perezhivanie* of the child, which is able to define how that moment will affect the course of future development.

Let us consider a simple example from the cases in our clinic. We are faced with three children brought to us from one and the same family. The external environment of this family has been identical for all three children. The substance of this situation is simple. The mother drinks and, apparently, suffers several nervous and psychological disorders as a result. There arises an extremely serious situation for the children. When intoxicated, the mother once tried to throw a child from the window, and she often beats them or throws them to the floor. In a word, the children live in a situation of terror and fear in connection with these conditions.

The three children are brought to us. Each of these children presents a completely different picture of developmental disorder due to the same situation. One and the same setting presents to these three children completely different pictures.

With the youngest child, we find the picture that is most frequent for young children in this case. He reacts to it with a series of neurotic symptoms, i.e. symptoms of defence. He is overwhelmed by the horror of what is happening to him. As a result, he develops terrors; enuresis develops; a stammer develops; sometimes he is simply silent, and he loses his voice. In other words, the child reacts as though completely overwhelmed and helpless in this situation.

With the second child, a state of acute torment developed (an example of which we saw when we examined one of our children),[5] a state which can be called inner conflict. This is frequently encountered in such cases, whenever a child has opposing affective relations with the mother or – you remember that we spoke of it – an ambivalent relationship. On one side, the mother of the child – the object of great affection; on the other hand, the mother of the child – the source of every fear, of the most difficult impressions that the child undergoes. German authors call such an affective complex that a child undergoes the *'Mutter-Hexkomplex'*, i.e. the 'mother-witch complex', where the love of the mother and the horror of the witch are united. The second child was brought to us with this very pronounced conflict, a sharp contradiction in the form of a positive and a negative relation to the mother, dire attachment to her and desperate hatred for her, along with acutely contradictory behaviour. He wanted to be sent home immediately, and yet expressed horror whenever being sent home was spoken of.

Finally, the third and eldest child at first sight gave us a completely unanticipated impression. He appeared a dull, unintelligent child, rather timid, but nevertheless displaying some traits of early maturity, early seriousness, early considerateness. He already understood the situation. He understood that his mother was ill and pitied her. He had seen the younger children at risk when the mother was raging. And this accounts for his special role. He had to calm the mother and to watch over her so that no harm was done to the younger ones, and to console the younger ones. He was, after all, the elder of the family, the one who had to take care of the rest. As a result, the entire course of his development had changed drastically. This was not a lively child with normal, lively, simple interests and lively activities corresponding to his age. This was a child who had changed drastically in development into a child of a different type. And when you take such an example into account – and any research which deals with concrete material is replete with such examples – we can easily see that the same environmental situation, the same events for different people at different age levels, can have different influences upon their development.

What determines the fact that the same environmental conditions have three different effects on three different children? This is due to the fact that the attitude of each of these children to an event is different. Or, as we might say, each of these children has undergone the experience of this situation differently. One of them underwent the experience as a meaningless, incomprehensible horror which plunged him into a state of helplessness. Another underwent the experience as meaningful, as a clash of acute affection with a no less acute sense of fear, hatred and anger. And the third underwent the experience, to the extent which it is possible for a boy of ten or eleven to surmount such experience, as a misfortune befalling his family which required him to put everything aside and somehow try to alleviate the unhappiness, to help the sick mother and children. And so, depending on the three different *perezhivaniya* [lived-through experiences] of one and the same situation, the impact that the situation has upon their development turns out to be different.

This next extract was written at some point in the years 1932–1934 as a chapter for a book that Vygotsky was preparing on developmental psychology in the last years of his life. It is about 'periodicity': the characteristics of the different stages in a child's and young person's life. Vygotsky's model of development aims to identify the new developments – 'neoformations' – that characterise the essence of new levels. In this model, development consists of a series of long stable periods with minor changes, interrupted by crises, which involve abrupt shifts, major changes and discontinuities in behaviour. These are turning points in development.

From 'The problem of age periodisation in child development' (Vygotsky, 2021b)

In reality, the factual study of child development and the observation of its course inevitably lead to the conclusion that development in different periods takes on different characteristics. In not a few epochs or ages, development is characterised by a slow, incrementally evolutionary, diffuse course. These ages are predominantly those of smooth, gradual, often imperceptible, and internal changes in the child's personality, brought about by way of accumulating apparently insignificant 'molecular' motions. Here over a more or less extended period of time usually lasting several years, no fundamental or catastrophic shifts or alterations reconstruct the whole personality of the child. More or less significant changes in the child's personality occur in these ages only through or as a result of an extended course of a 'molecular' development process. They emerge and become accessible to direct observation only as the conclusion of an extended process of latent development. 'As this process takes place entirely in a hidden form, the moment of detection often produces impressions full of surprise for the observer. The child can do something which does not yet, apparently, fall within the circle of his interests; it simply occurs to him' (Stern).[6]

In these ages, which could be called, due to the inherent character of their development, relatively steady or stable ages, development takes place in the main due to microscopic changes occurring daily in the personality of the child which accumulate to a certain point, and then, in a single leap, appear as a given age neoformation. These ages take up, if we judge purely chronologically, the major part of childhood. This is the age of maturation in the sense that it is in these ages that the child acquires the aspects and properties of his personality that bring him to maturity. If, then, within these ages development goes on as if by some underground path, it is no wonder that when we compare the child at the beginning and at the end of these clearly stable ages, the vast change that has taken place in the personality, the significant progress in its maturation, clearly stands out and even strikes the eye.

These ages and this type of child development have been studied more completely than ages characterised by a different course of child development. These latter were discovered by empirical paths, one by one, in a haphazard manner, and many have still not been shown by the majority of investigators in systems and are not included in the general periodisation of child development. Many authors have even doubted the inner necessity of their existence. Many are inclined to take them as 'maladies' of development, as deviations of the process from the normal path, rather than as internally necessary periods of child development. Almost none of the bourgeois investigators have realised their theoretical significance, and the attempt in our book at their systematisation, at their theoretical interpretation, and at their inclusion in the general scheme of child development for this reason should be seen as perhaps the first attempt of this kind.

However, no researcher can deny the fact of the existence of these unique periods in child development and even the most non-dialectically oriented authors acknowledge the necessity of allowing, at least as a hypothesis, the presence of crises in the development of the child, even in early childhood (Stern).

These ages are characterised by a purely factual aspect of the matter, the inverse of the relationship we have just described as steady or stable age. Here, in these periods, in a relatively short time of several months, years, or at most two years, there are sharply concentrated changes and alterations, shifts and breaks in the personality of the child of capital importance. The child changes the main features of his personality as a whole before our very eyes and in a very short period of time. Development takes rapid, speedy alterations of its course that are sometimes catastrophic in character. There occurs in a short period a radical and fundamental restructuring of the whole interior aspect of the personality of the child and the whole system of its relationship with the surrounding environment. Development in these periods resembles a revolutionary rather than evolutionary course of events, both in the tempo of changes taking place and in the significance of the events that occur. This – the age of fractures and ruptures – takes place at turning points in the history of child development. The flow of development takes the form of acute crisis.

These ages, which are usually called, because of the intrinsic character of development, critical ages, in contrast to the stable ages, have a series of features that make the correct theoretical understanding of them extremely problematic.

The first of these features consists in this: that the borders separating the beginning and the end of the crisis from the ages that are adjacent are delineated in a manner that is vague to the highest degree. The crisis grows imperceptibly; it is difficult to define the precise moment of its beginning and its ending. It simply flows imperceptibly forth or shades into the subsequent age as it did from the preceding one. On the other hand, it is characterised by a sharp intensification of the crisis usually occurring around the middle of the age period. Such a culminating point, at which the critical course of development reaches its apogee, characterises all critical ages without exception and sharply distinguishes them from the stable epochs of child development.

Next, the second feature of these ages consists in what is the starting point for their empirical study. A significant number of children, undergoing critical periods of development, appear to be difficult to teach. Children are apt to drop out of the system of pedagogical influence which up to now has provided the normal course of enculturation and teaching-and-learning. At the age of schooling, during critical periods, a decline in school performance is apparent, alongside a slackening of interest in school tasks and generally decreased work productivity. With all critical ages, development is often accompanied by more or less sharp conflicts with the milieu. With all critical ages, the inner life of the child is often linked with disorders and painful experiences, with internal conflicts, and with the overcoming of previously unencountered problems. As with teething, crises of child development are often accompanied by pain and not a few general disorders in the life activities of the child.

★ ★ ★

Thirdly, and this is perhaps the feature of the critical ages that is most important in relation to theory – the most obscure, the most unclear, and therefore the most difficult for the correct understanding of the nature of child development during these periods – there is the negative character of the development which distinguishes these ages. All who write about these unique periods of child development have noted in the first place as their most striking and most eye-catching feature the circumstance that development in this period, in contrast to the stable ages, accomplishes more destructive than constructive work. The progressive direction of development, pushing forward the formation of the child's personality, pushing him up the ladder of development, the continuous and unbroken construction of the new which was so distinctly carried forward in all of the stable ages as the basic content of child development, now, in the period of crisis, seems to fade away and be shut off, temporarily suspended, quitting the stage, and disappearing from the sight of the observer. In place of these constructive processes of development in the first plane are processes of dying away, withering, and decay of what was formed in the preceding stage and which distinguished a child of that age. The child in these periods does not so much acquire as discard much of what was previously acquired.

★ ★ ★

… the conception of the separate critical ages has been introduced into science in an empirical way, at random, or, rather, in disarray, in isolation from general development and in one form or another. Before all of the others came the discovery and description of *the crisis at 7–8* years. It was noted in practical work and in scientific observation that the seventh year of life in the child consists of a transition between the preschool and juvenile periods. A child of 7–8 years of age is already no longer a preschooler but is not yet a youngster. The seven-year-old is an utterly unique being, distinct from a preschooler and from a school child. In view of this, the seven-year-old is difficult, in relation to enculturation.

The negative content of this age is manifest first of all with respect to a disruption in psychological equilibrium, with respect to volatility in volition, and in a reduced ability to defer, and instability of mood (Vasileysky).[7]

Later came the discovery and description of *the crisis at three*, referred to by many authors as the phase of obstinacy and stubbornness. In this period, the child's personality undergoes abrupt and drastic changes in a limited period of time. The child becomes difficult to teach. He displays obstinacy, stubbornness, capriciousness, and wilfulness. Internal and external conflicts often accompany this whole period. A strong emphasis on his own 'I' leads to an almost asocial character to this child, and the child may consciously set himself apart from other people and be antagonistic to them (Stern).

Still later, the crisis at *thirteen years*, which was described as the negative phase of the age of sexual maturation, was discovered and studied. As indicated by the very name, the negative content of this crisis appears in this period in the first plane and due to a superficial observation seems to exhaust the sense of development in this period. Achievement decreases, efficiency drops, disharmony in the internal structure of the personality, collapse and death of the established system of interests, negative, protesting character of the whole of behavior – all this was characterised by Kroh[8] as an entire period of disorientation in the internal and external relationships, leading to this: hardly ever in the entire process of development is the human 'I' and the world more separated than in this period. This is what gave rise to Tolstoy calling this period 'the desert of adolescence'.

Finally, what has been theoretically acknowledged comparatively recently is the proposition, which for a long time has been well studied from the factual aspect, that the transition from infancy to early childhood age that occurs around one year of life is, in essence, also a critical period of development characterised by all of the distinguishing features which are familiar to us in the general description of this particular form of development.

★ ★ ★

In this way, we have revealed a completely regular, profoundly meaningful, and clear picture. Critical ages are interleaved with stable ages. They constitute watersheds, turning points, once again confirming that the development of the child is a dialectical process in which the transition from one state to another is carried out not in an evolutionary but in a revolutionary way.

The last extract in this chapter is a transcript of another in the series of lectures Vygotsky gave at the Herzen Pedagogical Institute in Leningrad. This was given during the academic year 1933–1934. In 'The crisis at three years of age' (Vygotsky, 2021a), Vygotsky identifies seven symptoms, four major and three minor, of what in a modern euphemism we might call 'challenging behaviour'. In this extract, Vygotsky discusses the first major symptom.

From 'The crisis at three years of age'

In considering the crisis at three years of age, we cannot approach it with a theoretical scheme alone. For us there can be no other path than the path of analysing factual material, so as to understand, in the process of analysis, the basic theories which have been put forward to explain this material. In order to make sense of what goes on in the period of three years of age, it is necessary first of all to consider the situation of development – internal and external – in which the crisis happens. Consideration ought to commence with the symptoms of the age. Those symptoms of the crisis which have been advanced to the first plane in the literature have been referred to as the first belt of symptoms, or the seven stars of the crisis at the age of three. All of them have been written of as folk concepts and they need to be analysed in order to acquire a precise scientific meaning.

The first symptom by which the onset of the crisis is characterised: the emergence of negativism. It is necessary to conceive clearly what we are talking about here. When people talk about child negativism, it must be distinguished from ordinary disobedience. In negativism, all the child's behavior goes contrary to that required of him by adults. If the child does not want to do what displeases him (if, for example, he is playing, and he is required to go and sleep but he does not want to sleep), this will not be negativism. The child wants to do what pleases him, that which he desires but which is forbidden to him; if he still does it, this will not be negativism. This will be a reaction in opposition to an adult demand, a reaction which is motivated by strong wishes in the child.

We will term negativism only those manifestations of behaviour of the child when he does not wish to do something merely because it is the proposal of some adult, that is, this reaction is not to the content of the action, but to the proposition of the adult. Negativism includes in itself, as a trait that distinguishes it from normal disobedience, that the child *does not do something because it was proposed to him*. A child playing in the yard does not want to go into the house. He is sleepy but he does not obey and disregards his mother's request. And if he is asked for something different, he would do whatever was pleasant to him. The negativist reaction of the child is to not do something simply because it is requested. Here there is a specific shift in motivation.

Let me give you a typical example of behaviour, selected from observations made in our clinic. A girl in her fourth year of life, with a prolonged crisis of three years and with clearly expressed negativism, wishes to be taken to the conference at which we evaluate the children. The girl has even gotten ready to go. I invite her. But since I have called her, she will not go. She keeps struggling. 'Well, then go all by yourself.' She will not go. 'Well, then come with me' – she does not come. When we leave her alone, she begins to weep. She is sad that we did not take her. In this way, negativism forces the child to act contrary to her affective wish. The girl wanted to go, but because we proposed it, she would never agree.

In its most drastic form, negativism produces an opposite response to any proposal made in an authoritative tone. A number of authors beautifully describe similar experiments. For example, an adult approaches a child and says, in an authoritative tone, 'This dress is black,' and receives the answer: 'No, it is white.' When one says, 'It is white,' the child answers: 'No, black.' The will to contradict, the will to perform the opposite of whatever he is told, this is negativism in the true sense of the word.

Negative reactions differ from ordinary disobedience in two substantial moments. Firstly, they place the social relation, the relationship to other people, in the front of the stage. In a given case, the reaction of the child is not motivated by the content of the situation itself, whether or not the child wants to do what he is asked. Negativism is an act of a social character: it is first of all addressed to a person, not to the content that has been requested of the child. The second essential moment – a new relation of the child to his own affect. The child does not act directly under the influence of affect but proceeds contrary to his own inclinations. Concerning these relations with affect, let me remind you of early childhood just before the crisis at three. The most characteristic of early childhood, from the point of view of all of research, is the complete unity of affect and activity. The whole child is in the grip of affect; he is completely inside the situation. During preschool age, motives also appear in relation to other people, which follow immediately from those effects which are linked to other situations. If the motivation for the refusal of the child lies within the situation, if he does not do something because he does not wish to or because he wishes to act otherwise, this is not negativism. Negativism – such a reaction, such a tendency – is where the motive lies outside the given situation.

Vygotsky goes on to discuss the six other symptoms of the crisis at age three: stubbornness, recalcitrance (he refers to the German word '*Trotz*' for this symptom), wilfulness, protest and revolt, deprecation and despotic wishes.

Vygotsky died in June 1934. Kellogg and Veresov (Vygotsky, 2021, p. vi) tell us that 'the problem of age caught Vygotsky's attention and held his interest even as his own health disintegrated, the professional position of pedology deteriorated, and the revolutionary reconstruction of his country turned to bloody and famished shambles'. One effect of Stalin's tyranny, and of the fearful and cowardly intellectual obedience it caused, was to brand pedology 'reactionary bourgeois science ... [One article] called pedology "the servant of the capitalists"' (Minkova, 2012, p. 92). Pedology was banned on 4 July 1936 by a decree of the Communist Party's Central Committee. So, for many years after Vygotsky's death, his works on pedology were banned or censored.

Notes

1. Vygotsky is quoting from *Thought and language* (1862) by the Ukrainian linguist and philosopher Alexander Potebnya (1835–1891).
2. Henri Bergson (1859–1941) was a French philosopher. Vygotsky mentions him here as a proponent of an idealist philosophical perspective.
3. Tatiana Akhutina, a student of Luria's, writes (2003, p. 168): 'Vygotsky developed two principles of neuropsychology: social genesis and the systemic structure of psychological functions. He also outlined the initial contours of the principle of dynamic localisation of functions.' Akhutina sees Vygotsky as having arrived gradually at a 'comprehensive development of the principles of neuropsychology' (ibid., p. 159).
4. In chapter 20 of *Boyhood*, the second novel in his autobiographical trilogy *Childhood, Boyhood, Youth*, Tolstoy writes: 'I involuntarily want to get through the desert of boyhood and reach that happy time when again a truly tender, noble feeling of friendship will illuminate the end of this age…' The reference in the reference list below is to an online version of the novel, which uses a slightly different form of words.
5. 'This seems to refer to one of the clinical visits between Vygotsky's lectures, when Vygotsky allowed his students to examine patients in the clinic' (translators' note).
6. The editors have not been able to identify this quotation from Stern, nor the passages from his writings to which Vygotsky twice refers later in the chapter.
7. 'Serafim Mikhailovich Vasileysky (1888–1961) was a student of Wilhelm Wundt and the philosopher Johannes Vokelt … [He returned] to Russia from Germany during the war and the revolution … In the 1920s, he worked in "psycho-technical selection" (that is, looking for gifted children) and thus became involved in pedology …' (translators' note).
8. Oswald Kroh (1887–1955) was a German educationist and psychologist.

References

Akhutina, T. (2003). 'L.S. Vygotsky and A.R. Luria: Foundations of neuropsychology'. *Journal of Russian and East European Psychology*, 41(3/4), pp. 159–190.

Leontiev, A. (1931). *Razvitie pamjati (The development of memory)*. Moscow-Leningrad: Uchpedgiz.

Minkova, E. (2012). 'Pedology as a complex science devoted to the study of children in Russia: the history of its origin and elimination'. *Psychological Thought*, 5(2), pp. 83–98. doi: 10.5964/psyct.v5i2.23

Stern, W. (1924). *Psychology of early childhood up to the sixth year of age* [1914]. Trans. A. Barwell. London: George Allen and Unwin.

Tolstoy, L. (1854). *Boyhood*. Available online at https://gutenberg.org/cache/epub/2450/pg2450-images.html#chap20.

Vygotsky, L.S. (1997). *The collected works of L.S. Vygotsky. Volume 3, Problems of the theory and history of psychology*. Trans. and intro. R. Van der Veer; Rieber, R.W. and Wollock, J. (eds). New York, NY: Plenum Press.

Vygotsky, L.S. (1997a). 'On psychological systems' [1930], in Vygotsky, L.S. (1997), *The collected works of L.S. Vygotsky. Volume 3, Problems of the theory and history of psychology*, pp. 91–107. Also available online in the Marxist Archive: www.marxists.org/archive/vygotsky/works/1930/psychological-systems.htm

Vygotsky, L.S. (1997b). *The collected works of L.S. Vygotsky. Volume 4, The history of the development of higher mental functions*. Rieber, R.W. (ed.). New York, NY: Plenum Press.

Vygotsky, L.S. (1997c). *The history of the development of higher mental functions* [1931], in Vygotsky, L.S. (1997b), *The collected works of L.S. Vygotsky. Volume 4, The history of the development of higher mental functions*, pp. 1–251.

Vygotsky, L.S. (1998). *The collected works of L.S. Vygotsky. Volume 5, Child psychology*. Rieber, R.W. (ed.). New York, NY: Plenum Press.

Vygotsky, L.S. (1998a). *Pedology of the adolescent* [1930–31], in Vygotsky, L.S. (1998), *The collected works of L.S. Vygotsky. Volume 5, Child psychology*, pp. 3–184.

Vygotsky, L.S. (2019). *L.S. Vygotsky's pedological works. Volume 1, Foundations of pedology*. Trans. and notes D. Kellogg and N. Veresov. Singapore: Springer.

Vygotsky, L.S. (2019a). 'The problem of the environment in pedology' [1935], in Vygotsky, L.S. (2019), *L.S. Vygotsky's pedological works. Volume 1, Foundations of pedology*, pp. 23–42.

Vygotsky, L.S. (2021). *L.S. Vygotsky's pedological works. Volume 2, The problem of age*. Trans. and notes D. Kellogg and N. Veresov. Singapore: Springer.

Vygotsky, L.S. (2021a). 'The crisis at three years of age' [1932–4], in Vygotsky, L.S. (2021), *L.S. Vygotsky's pedological works. Volume 2, The problem of age*, pp. 191–199.

Vygotsky, L.S. (2021b). 'The problem of age periodisation in child development' [1932–4], in Vygotsky, L.S. (2021), *L.S. Vygotsky's pedological works. Volume 2, The problem of age*, pp. 15–38.

Chapter 8

Play, imagination and creativity

Vygotsky's work in pedology had enabled him to take a much wider view of child development, giving greater weight to children's emotional experiences and their response to their social environment in addition to their mental development. In the period 1930–1933, as well as several pedological publications, Vygotsky wrote four texts which give us a very full picture of his interest in play and the imagination …

(Barrs, 2022)

This chapter presents extracts from three of them.

This first text was originally given as a lecture at the Herzen Pedagogical Institute in Leningrad in 1933. It is thanks to a stenographic record of the lecture that the text has survived. It has since become a key influence on research on play, and on practice in early-years settings. The extracts which follow are from a translation by Nikolai Veresov and Myra Barrs.

(Vygotsky uses two words to signify two kinds of meaning. '*Znachenie*' is the denotative meaning of a word. '*Smysl*' is a word's connotative meaning, closer to 'sense'. In this translation, both words are rendered by 'meaning'; in most cases one or other Russian word appears here in square brackets after the English word.)

From 'Play and its role in the mental development of the child' (Vygotsky, 2016)

At preschool age special needs and incentives arise which are very important for the whole of the child's development and which directly lead to play. In essence, there arise in the child of this age a large number of unrealisable tendencies and immediately unrealisable desires. Any delay in fulfilling them is difficult for the early-years child and is acceptable only within certain narrow limits; no one has met a child under three who wanted to do something a few days hence. Ordinarily, the interval between the motive and its realisation is extremely short. I think that if there were no maturing in preschool years of needs that cannot be realised immediately, there would be no play. Experiments show that the development of play is arrested both in intellectually underdeveloped children and in those who are emotionally immature.

From the viewpoint of the affective sphere, it seems to me that play is invented at the point in development where unrealistic tendencies begin to appear. This is the way a very young child behaves: he wants a thing and he must have it at once. If he cannot have it, either he throws a temper tantrum, lies on the floor and kicks his legs, or he is refused, pacified, and does not get it. His unsatisfied desires have their own particular modes of substitution, rejection, etc. Toward the beginning of the preschool age, unsatisfied desires and tendencies that cannot be realised immediately make their appearance, while on the other hand the tendency to immediate fulfilment of desires, characteristic of the preceding age, is retained. For example, the child wants to be in his mother's place, or wants to be a rider on a horse. This desire cannot be fulfilled right now. What does the very young child do if he sees a passing cab and wants to ride in it, no matter what may happen? If he is a spoilt and capricious child, he will demand that his mother put him in the cab at any cost, or he may throw himself on the ground right there in the street, etc. If he is an obedient child, used to renouncing his desires, he will turn away, or his mother will offer him some candy, or simply distract him with some stronger affect, and he will renounce his immediate desire.

In contrast to this, a child over three clearly shows his own particular conflicting tendencies. On the one hand, a large number of long-lasting needs and desires appear that cannot be met at once but that nevertheless are not passed over like whims; on the other hand, the urge towards the immediate realisation of desires is almost completely retained.

Henceforth play appears which – in answer to the question of why the child plays – must always be understood as the imaginary, illusory realisation of unrealisable desires.

★ ★ ★

It is at preschool age that we first find a divergence between the field of meaning [*smyslovoye pole,* 'field of sense'] and the visual field. It seems to me that we would do well to restate the notion of one of the investigators who said that in play thought is separated from objects, and action arises from thoughts rather than from objects.

Thought is separated from objects because a piece of wood begins to play the role of a doll and a stick becomes a horse. Action according to rules begins to be determined by thought, not by objects themselves. This is such a reversal of the child's relationship to the real, immediate, concrete situation that it is hard to evaluate its full significance. The child does not do this all at once. It is terribly difficult for a child to split off thought (the meaning of a word) [*znachenie slova,* the denotative meaning of a word] from its object. Play is a transitional stage in this direction. At that critical moment when a stick – i.e. an object – becomes a pivot for severing the meaning [*znachenie*] of horse from a real horse, one of the basic psychological structures determining the child's relationship to reality is radically altered.

★ ★ ★

Nevertheless, properties of things as such are still significant: any stick can be a horse, but, for example, a postcard can never be a horse for a child. Goethe's contention that in play any thing can be anything for a child is incorrect. Of course, for adults who can make conscious use of symbols, a postcard can be a horse. If I want to show the location of something, I can put down a match and say, 'This is a horse.' And that would be enough. For a child a match cannot stand for a horse; there has to be a stick. Therefore, play is not symbolism. A symbol is a sign, but the stick is not the sign of a horse. Properties of things are retained, but their meaning is inverted, i.e. the thought becomes the central point. It can be said that in this structure objects are moved from a dominating to a subordinate position.

Thus, in play the child creates the structure: meaning [*smysl*]/object, where the semantic aspect – the meaning of the word, the meaning of the thing – dominates and determines his behaviour.

To a certain extent meaning [*znachenie*] is freed from the object with which it was directly fused before. I would say that in play a child operates with meaning severed from objects, but that meaning is not severed in real action with real objects.

Therefore an extremely interesting contradiction arises in which, in play, the child operates with meanings [*znacheniya*] severed from their original objects and actions – and yet operates with these meanings inseparably attached to other real objects and real actions. This is the transitional nature of play, which makes it an intermediate between the purely situational constraints of early childhood and thought that is totally free of real situations.

In play a child operates with things as having meanings [*smýsly*], he operates with word meanings [*znacheniya*], which replace objects, and thus an emancipation of word from object occurs (a behaviourist would describe play and its characteristic properties in the following terms: the child gives ordinary objects unusual names and ordinary actions unusual designations, despite the fact that he knows the real ones).

Separating words from things requires a pivot in the form of another thing. The child cannot sever meaning from an object, or a word from an object, except by finding a pivot in something else, i.e. by the power of one object to steal another's name. From the moment the stick – i.e. the 'other thing' – becomes the pivot for severing the meaning of 'horse' from a real horse, the child makes one thing influence another in the semantic sphere. Transfer of meanings [*znacheniya*] is facilitated by the fact that the child accepts a word as the property of a thing; he does not see the word, but the thing it designates. So for a child the word 'horse' applied to the stick means 'There is a horse there', i.e. mentally he sees the object standing behind the word.

At school age play is converted to internal processes, becoming part of inner speech, logical memory, and abstract thought. In play a child operates with meanings[1] separated from their real referents (e.g. the horse). But at the same time, these meanings can only be separated through real actions with real things (the stick). To separate the meaning of 'horse' from a real horse, and to transfer it to a stick (which is the necessary material pivot to keep the meaning from evaporating), and then to act with the stick as if it really were a horse, is a vital transitional stage to operating with meanings alone. A child first acts with meanings as with objects and later realises them consciously and begins to think, just as a child, before he has acquired grammatical and written speech, knows how to do things but is not aware that he knows, i.e. he does not realise or master them consciously. In play a child unconsciously and spontaneously makes use of the fact that he can separate meaning from an object, without knowing he is doing it – just as he talks without paying attention to the words and does not know that he is speaking in prose.

★ ★ ★

I do not think that play is the predominant type of child activity. In fundamental, everyday situations a child behaves in a manner diametrically opposed to his behaviour in play. In play, action is subordinated to meaning [*smysl*]; but in real life, of course, action dominates over meaning [*smysl*].

Thus we find in play – if you will – the negative of a child's general, everyday behaviour. Therefore, to consider play as the prototype of his everyday activity and its predominant form is completely without foundation ... Koffka[2] considers play as the child's other world. According to Koffka, everything that concerns a child is play reality, while everything that concerns an adult is serious reality. A given object has one meaning [*smysl*] in play, and another outside it. In a child's world the logic of wishes and of satisfying urges dominates, not real logic. The illusory nature of play is transferred to life. This would be true if play were indeed the predominant form of a child's activity. But the child would look like a patient in a mental hospital if the form of activity we have been speaking of were to become the predominant form of his everyday activity – or even if it were only partially transferred to real life.

Koffka gives a number of examples to show how a child transfers a situation from play into life. But the real transference of play behaviour to real life can be regarded only as an unhealthy symptom. To behave in a real situation as in an illusory one is the first sign of delirium.

As research has shown, play behaviour in real life is normally seen only in the type of game in which sisters play at 'sisters', i.e. when children sitting at dinner can play at having dinner, or (as in Katz's[3] example) when children who do not want to go to bed say, 'Let's play that it's night time and we have to go to sleep.'

112 Play, imagination and creativity

They begin to play at what they are in fact doing; evidently they are creating connections that facilitate the execution of an unpleasant action.

Thus, it seems to me that play is not the predominant type of activity at preschool age. Only theories maintaining that a child does not have to satisfy the basic requirements of life, but can live in search of pleasure, could possibly suggest that a child's world is a play world.

Is it possible to suppose that a child's behaviour is always guided by meaning [*smysl*], that a preschooler's behaviour is so arid that he never behaves with candy as he wants to, simply because he thinks he should behave otherwise? This kind of subordination to rules is quite impossible in life, but in play it does become possible; thus, play creates the zone of proximal development of the child. In play a child is always above his average age, above his daily behaviour; in play it is as though he were a head taller than himself. As in the focus of a magnifying glass, play contains all developmental tendencies in a condensed form; in play it is as though the child is trying to jump above the level of his normal behaviour.

The play-development relationship can be compared with the instruction-development relationship, but play provides changes in needs and in consciousness of a much wider nature. Play is the source of development and creates the zone of proximal development. Action in the imaginative field, in an imaginary situation, the creation of voluntary intentions and the formation of real-life plans and volitional motives – all appear in play and make it the highest level of preschool development.

The child moves forward essentially through play activity. It is in this way that play can be termed a leading activity that determines the child's development.

The extracts that follow are also taken from the text of a lecture: one of a series of six lectures in psychology which Vygotsky gave at the Herzen Pedagogical Institute in 1932. Here, Vygotsky rejects theories of the imagination which see it either as an associative process – that is, an aspect of memory – or (the idealistic view) as a separate, free-standing characteristic of mind. Neither of these theories is sufficiently developmental. Vygotsky is interested in the relationship between the development of the child's speech and the development of his imagination. (He notes that the development of the imagination is delayed in deaf and speech-retarded children.) Vygotsky accepts that thinking (or, sometimes, 'realistic thinking') and the imagination are two distinct processes in the child's mind; they are not the same thing. On the other hand, they are intimately connected: 'we must emphasise the extraordinary kinship that exists between thinking and imagination'. And the key bond which establishes and maintains this 'extraordinary kinship' is speech: 'The key transition point in the development of both thinking and imagination corresponds with the appearance of speech …'

From 'Imagination and its development in childhood' (Vygotsky, 1987a)

Bleuler[4] and his school have ... shown why the development of speech is such a powerful impetus for the development of imagination. Speech frees the child from the immediate impression of an object. It gives the child the power to represent and think about an object that he has not seen. Speech gives the child the power to free himself from the force of immediate impressions and go beyond their limits. The child can express in words something that does not coincide with the precise arrangement of objects or representations. This provides him with the power to move with extraordinary freedom in the sphere of impressions, designating them with words.

Studies have shown that not only speech but the further development of the child's life serves the development of his imagination. Such a role is played, for example, by school. Here the child can meditate on some imagined form before he acts on it. This is why it is during the school age that we find the first forms of true daydreaming, the potential and capacity to consciously surrender oneself to a certain intellectual construction independent of its function in realistic thinking.

Finally, the formation of concepts that signals the onset of the transitional age is an extremely important factor in the development of the most varied and complex combinations, unifications and connections that can be established between the elements of experience. Thus, not only the appearance of speech, but the onset of the major stages in its development, are critical to the development of the child's imagination.

Thus, empirical research does not support the thesis that the child's imagination is a form of non-verbal, autistic or undirected thought. On the contrary, these studies consistently demonstrate that the development of the child's imagination, like the development of other higher mental functions, is linked in an essential way with the child's speech. The development of imagination is linked to the development of speech, to the development of the child's interaction with those around him, to the basic forms of the collective social activity of the child's consciousness.

Bleuler advanced yet another important thesis concerning the nature of imagination, a thesis that has also been verified by empirical research. Specifically, he argued that imagination can be a directed form of activity, that the individual can often describe the goals and motives that impel this activity.

Consider, for example, what are commonly called utopian constructions. These are deliberate representations of fantasy, representations that are clearly differentiated in consciousness from realistic planes of thought. Clearly, these representations are developed not subconsciously but consciously. The subject manifests a clear psychological set associated with the task of constructing a fantasy image relating either to the future or the past. We could also consider the domain of artistic creativity in this domain. This domain of activity is accessible to the child at a young age. If we consider the products of this creativity in drawing or storytelling, it quickly becomes apparent that this imagination has a directed nature. It is not a subconscious activity. Finally, if we consider the child's constructive imagination, the creative activity of consciousness associated with technical-constructive or building activity, we see consistently that real inventive imagination is among the basic functions underlying this activity. In this type of activity, fantasy is highly directed. From beginning to end, it is directed toward a goal that the individual is pursuing.

Cumulatively, these facts provide a clear demonstration that the way that the child's imagination has been defined as unique – like the very concept of its primal nature – is false.

I would like briefly to consider another issue related to the domain of imagination: specifically, the emotional aspect of imagination.

Child psychologists have made some important empirical observations related to the problem of imagination, observations that are reflected in what has been called *the law of real feeling* in fantasy. The essence of this law is simple. Briefly, the movement of our feelings is closely connected with the activity of imagination. A certain construction may turn out to lack reality from a rational perspective. Nonetheless, this construction is real in the emotional sense.

This can be illustrated using a common and rather crude example. Suppose that on entering a room I mistake a hanging cloak for a thief. I know that my fright was false. Nonetheless, the feeling of fear was a real experience. There is no real sensation of fear in comparison to which this sensation appears as fantasy. This is an important component in the explanation of the unique development of the emotions in childhood and in the explanation of the multitude of the forms of fantasy in adult life. The activity of imagination has exceedingly rich emotional aspects. Indeed, it was on this foundation that psychologists argued for the primal nature of imagination, assuming that the primary mover of imagination was affect.

★ ★ ★

However, if we consider the form of imagination that is associated with invention and other forms of action on reality, we find that imagination is not subordinated to the subjective caprice of emotional logic. An inventor who has used his imagination to construct a sketch or plan of what must be done differs radically from the individual whose thinking is directed by the subjective logic of the emotions. We find very different systems, very different forms of complex activity, in the two cases.

Approaching this issue from the perspective of classification, it becomes apparent that we cannot view imagination as a function existing alongside other functions. It is not a homogenous, recurrent form of brain activity. Imagination is a complex form of mental activity that is based on the unification of several functions in unique relationships. This kind of complex activity, one that exceeds the boundaries of the processes that we habitually call functions, can be called a *psychological system*. It is a complex functional system. The essential characteristics of this kind of system are the inter-functional connections and relationships that dominate it. The analysis of the varied forms of imagination and thinking demonstrates that it is only by approaching these forms of activity as systems that we can begin to describe the very important changes that occur in them, that we can begin to describe the dependencies and connections that are manifested in them.

I will now attempt to draw some conclusions from what we have said up to this point. First, does the kind of consistent antagonism or opposition that has been established between directed realistic thought and daydreaming, fantasy or autistic thought actually exist? As we have seen, the verbal character of thought is inherent to both imagination and realistic thinking. We have also seen that the directedness or consciousness of thought, the presence of motives and goals, is found in both autistic and realistic forms of thinking. Moreover, the individual frequently lacks full conscious awareness of his true motives, goals and tasks in realistic thinking. Finally, both imagination and realistic thinking are often characterised by high levels of affect or emotion. There is no opposition between the two in this connection. Not all forms of imagination are subordinated to the logic of emotions and feelings. In sum, the apparent, metaphysical and primal opposition that has been established between realistic and autistic thinking is both fictive and false. The differences between realistic and autistic thinking are not absolute but relative.

If we now attempt to characterise the relationship between thinking and imagination in positive rather than negative terms, we must emphasise two important points. First, we must emphasise the extraordinary kinship that exists between thinking and imagination. The basic achievements of both are manifested in the same genetic features. The key transition point in the development of both thinking and imagination corresponds with the appearance of speech; the school age is the critical point in the development of the child's realistic thinking as well as the development of his autistic thinking. There is an intimate interconnection in the development of these two forms of thinking. A careful analysis might permit a bolder formulation of this statement. In brief, the two processes develop as a unity. There is no essential independence of the two developmental processes. Moreover, by observing the forms of imagination that are linked with creativity, that is, the forms of imagination that are directed toward reality, we find that the boundary between realistic thinking and imagination is erased. Imagination is a necessary, integral aspect of realistic thinking.

There is a contradiction in the problem as it actually exists. No accurate cognition of reality is possible without a certain element of imagination, a certain flight from the immediate, concrete, solitary impressions in which this reality is presented in the elementary acts of consciousness. The processes of invention or artistic creativity demand a substantial participation by both realistic thinking and imagination. The two act as a unity.

Nonetheless, it would be a serious error to identify realistic thinking and imagination or overlook the opposition that does exist between them. The essential feature of imagination is that consciousness departs from reality. Imagination is a comparatively autonomous activity of consciousness in which there is a departure from any immediate cognition of reality. Alongside the images that are constructed in the immediate cognition of reality, man constructs images that he recognises as part of the domain of imagination. At advanced levels in the development of thinking, we find the construction of images that are not found in complete form in reality. By recognising this, we can begin to understand the complex relationship between the activity of realistic thinking and the activity of advanced forms of imagination. Each step in the child's achievement of a more profound penetration of reality is linked with his liberation from earlier, more primitive forms of cognition. A more profound penetration of reality demands that consciousness attain a freer relationship to the elements of that reality, that consciousness depart from the external and apparent aspect of reality that is given directly in perception. The result is that the processes through which the cognition of reality is achieved become more complex and richer.

Finally, I would add that the internal connection that exists between imagination and realistic thinking brings us to a new problem associated with volition or freedom in human activity and consciousness. The potential for free action that we find associated with the emergence of human consciousness is closely connected with imagination, with the unique psychological set of consciousness vis-à-vis reality that is manifested in imagination. Thus, interconnected in this single knot, we find three of the greatest problems of contemporary psychology, and of contemporary child psychology in particular: the problem of thinking, the problem of imagination, and the problem of will.

Imagination and creativity in childhood (Vygotsky, 2004), from which the third group of extracts in this chapter is taken, is a short book, or monograph, with chapters. It was published during Vygotsky's lifetime by GIZ, a state publisher, and much more recently, in English, as a journal article. Here, we present extracts from two of its chapters.

For Vygotsky, the facility and use of imagination is central to being human and to human achievement: 'the entire world of human culture, as distinct from the world of nature, all this is the product of human imagination and of creation based on this imagination'. Furthermore, 'it is easy to see that the creative processes are already fully manifest in earliest childhood'. In play, children don't simply rework experiences they have already had; they creatively rework them. This is 'the combinatorial operation of the imagination'.

Imagination and reality (or real experience), though distinct, are closely linked. Imagination builds on reality: '...the creative activity of the imagination depends directly on the richness and variety of a person's previous experience because this experience provides the material from which the products of fantasy are constructed'. And this has an important implication for education: '...if we want to build a relatively strong foundation for a child's creativity, what we must do is broaden the experiences we provide him with'. Sometimes, the exercise of the imagination results in the invention of physical things: 'any technical device, machine or instrument'.

The exercise of the imagination is shaped and constrained by a person's social and physical environment, which is itself a product of the historical forces which have brought that environment to its current stage and state of development.

From *Imagination and creativity in childhood*, chapter 1, 'Creativity and imagination'

Any human act that gives rise to something new is referred to as a creative act, regardless of whether what is created is a physical object or some mental or emotional construct that lives within the person who created it and is known only to him. If we consider a person's behaviour and all of his activity, we are readily able to distinguish two basic types. One type of activity we could call reproductive, and is very closely linked to memory; essentially it consists of a person's reproducing or repeating previously developed and mastered behavioural patterns or resurrecting traces of earlier impressions. When I recall the house where I spent my childhood or the distant lands I have visited in the past, I retrieve traces of the impressions that I formed in early childhood or in my travels. In exactly the same way, when I draw from life, write or do something following a specific model, I am merely reproducing what exists in front of me or what I have mastered and developed earlier. What is common to all these instances is the fact that my actions do not create anything new, but rather are based on a more or less accurate repetition of something that already exists.

It is easy to understand what enormous significance such retention of previous experience has in a person's life insofar as it facilitates his adaptation to the world around him, giving rise to and fostering development of habits that are repeated under a particular set of conditions.

The organic basis for such reproductive activity or memory is the plasticity of our neural substance. Plasticity is a term denoting the property of a substance that allows it to change and retain the traces of that change. Thus, in this sense, wax is more plastic than, let us say, iron or water, because it undergoes changes more readily than iron, and retains the traces of these changes better than water. The plasticity of our nervous system depends on both of these properties taken together. Our brain and our nerves, possessing enormous plasticity, readily alter their finest structure under the influence of one or another type of stimulation, and if the stimulation is strong enough or is repeated a sufficient number of times, retain memory traces of these changes. Something analogous to what happens to a piece of paper when we fold it in the middle takes place in the brain; a crease remains where the fold was made, and this trace, resulting from the change that was made, makes it easier to repeat the same change in the future. One need only blow on this paper for it to bend at the crease.

The same thing happens with the trace made by a wheel on soft earth: a track forms, which bears the imprint of the changes made by the wheel and facilitates movement of the wheel along this track in the future. Similarly, strong or frequently repeated stimulation lays down new tracks in our brain.

Thus, our brain proves to be an organ that retains our previous experience and facilitates the reproduction of this experience. However, if the brain's activity were limited merely to retaining previous experience, a human being would be a creature who could adapt primarily to familiar, stable conditions of the environment. All new or unexpected changes in the environment not encountered in his previous experience would fail to induce the appropriate adaptive reactions in humans.

In addition to its function of storing previous experience, the brain has another, no less important function. Aside from reproductive activity, we can readily observe another type of activity in human behaviour, what can be called combinatorial or creative activity. When, in my imagination, I draw myself a mental picture of, let us say, the future life of humanity under socialism or a picture of life in the distant past and the struggle of prehistoric man, in both cases I am doing more than reproducing the impressions I once happened to experience. I am not merely recovering the traces of stimulation that reached my brain in the past. I never actually saw this remote past, or this future; however, I still have my own idea, image, or picture of what they were or will be like.

All human activity of this type, activity that results not in the reproduction of previously experienced impressions or actions but in the creation of new images or actions, is an example of this second type of creative or combinatorial behaviour. The brain is not only the organ that stores and retrieves our previous experience, it is also the organ that combines and creatively reworks elements of this past experience and uses them to generate new propositions and new behaviour. If human activity were limited to reproduction of the old, then the human being would be a creature oriented only to the past and would only be able to adapt to the future to the extent that it reproduced the past. It is precisely human creative activity that makes the human being a creature oriented toward the future, creating the future and thus altering his own present.

This creative activity, based on the ability of our brain to combine elements, is called imagination or fantasy in psychology. Typically, people use the terms imagination or fantasy to refer to something quite different than what they mean in science. In everyday life, fantasy or imagination refer to what is not actually true, what does not correspond to reality, and what, thus, could not have any serious practical significance. But in actuality, imagination, as the basis of all creative activity, is an important component of absolutely all aspects of cultural life, enabling artistic, scientific and technical creation alike. In this sense, absolutely everything around us that was created by the hand of man, the entire world of human culture, as distinct from the world of nature, all this is the product of human imagination and of creation based on this imagination.

[Theodule] Ribot[5] (1906) says:

> Every invention, whether large or small, before being implemented, embodied in reality, was held together by the imagination alone. It was a structure erected in the mind through the agency of new combinations and relationships ...
>
> The overwhelming majority of inventions were created by unknown inventors; only a few names of great inventors are extant. The imagination forever remains true to its nature, whether it manifests itself individually or collectively. No one knows how many acts of imagination it took to transform the plough, which started out as a simple piece of wood with a fire-sharpened end, from this simple manual tool into what it became after a long series of alterations that are described in the works devoted to this subject. In the same way, the dim flame from a branch of resinous wood, which was the first crude primitive torch, led us, through a long series of inventions, to gas and electric lighting. All the objects used in everyday life, including the simplest and most ordinary ones, are, so to speak, crystallised imagination.

★ ★ ★

The overwhelming majority of inventions were produced by unknown individuals, as Ribot rightly says. A scientific understanding of this phenomenon thus compels us to consider creativity as the rule rather than the exception. Of course, the highest expressions of creativity remain accessible only to a select few human geniuses; however, in the everyday life that surrounds us, creativity is an essential condition for existence and all that goes beyond the rut of routine and involves innovation, albeit only a tiny amount, owes its existence to the human creative process.

From *Imagination and creativity in childhood*, chapter 2, 'Imagination and reality'

Let us take as an example the image of the fairy tale world as Pushkin depicts it:

> Beside the bow-shaped shore a green oak grows, an oak engirt with golden chain, and day and night, leashed by this chain, a learned cat in circles goes. When he goes right he sings a folksong, when he goes left a tale he tells.

What wonders there: the wood sprite wanders, a mermaid sits upon a bough; strange creatures stalk forgotten trails; a hut stands there on chicken legs that has no windows and no door.

We could go through this whole excerpt word for word and demonstrate that it is only the combination of elements that is fantastic in this tale, while the elements themselves were taken from reality. An oak, a gold chain, a cat, songs – all these things exist in reality; it is only the image of the learned cat who circles on a golden chain and tells tales, only the combination of all these elements that is fantastic. As for the pure fairy-tale images in the next lines, the wood sprite and hut on chicken legs – these too are only complex combinations of certain elements hinted at by reality. In the image of the mermaid, for example, the idea of a woman meets the idea of a bird sitting on a branch; in the enchanted hut the idea of chicken legs is combined with the idea of a hut, and so forth.

Thus, imagination always builds using materials supplied by reality. It is true, as can be seen from the excerpt cited, that imagination may create more and more new levels of combination, combining first the initial elements of reality (cat, chain, oak), then secondarily combining fantastic elements (mermaid, wood sprite), and so forth and so on. But the ultimate elements, from which the most fantastic images, those that are most remote from reality, are constructed, these terminal elements will always be impressions made by the real world.

Now we can induce the first and most important law governing the operation of the imagination. This law may be formulated as follows: the creative activity of the imagination depends directly on the richness and variety of a person's previous experience because this experience provides the material from which the products of fantasy are constructed. The richer a person's experience, the richer is the material his imagination has access to. This is why a child has a less rich imagination than an adult, because his experience has not been as rich.

If we trace the history of great works, great discoveries, then we can almost always establish that they were the result of an enormous amount of previously accumulated experience. Every act of imagination starts with this accumulation of experience. All else being equal, the richer the experience, the richer the act of imagination.

★ ★ ★

The implication of this for education is that, if we want to build a relatively strong foundation for a child's creativity, what we must do is broaden the experiences we provide him with. All else being equal, the more a child sees, hears, and experiences, the more he knows and assimilates, the more elements of reality he will have in his experience, and the more productive will be the operation of his imagination.

Even this primitive form of linkage between fantasy and reality clearly shows how unjustified it is to consider them to be opposites. The combinatorial function of our brain is not something completely different from its memory storage function, but is merely a further elaboration of the latter. Fantasy is not the opposite of memory, but depends on it and utilises its contents in ever-new combinations. The combinatorial action of the brain is ultimately based on the same process by which traces of previous stimuli are stored in the brain, and the only new thing about this function is that, in operating on the traces of these stimuli, the brain combines them in ways that are not encountered in actual experience.

The second linkage between fantasy and reality is quite different. It involves a more complex association, not between the elements of an imaginary structure and reality, but between the final product of imagination and some complex real phenomenon. When on the basis of study and stories of historians or travel, I construct a picture for myself of the French Revolution or the African desert, then in both cases the picture is the result of creative activity of the imagination. It does not reproduce what I perceived in my previous experience, but creates new combinations from that experience.

In this sense, it is completely governed by the first law that we have just described. These products of the imagination also consist of transformed and reworked elements of reality and a large store of experience is required to create these images out of these elements. If I did not have a concept of lack of water, sand, enormous spaces, animals that live in deserts, and so forth, I, of course, could not generate the concept of this desert. If I did not possess a large number of historic concepts, I also would not be able to create a picture of the French Revolution in my imagination.

★ ★ ★

The third type of association between the functioning of imagination and reality is an emotional one. This association manifests itself in two ways. On the one hand, every feeling, every emotion seeks specific images corresponding to it. Emotions thus possess a kind of capacity to select impressions, thoughts and images that resonate with the mood that possesses us at a particular moment in time. Everyone knows that we see everything with completely different eyes depending on whether we are experiencing at the same time grief or joy. Psychology has long noted the fact that every feeling has not only an external, physical expression, but an internal expression associated with the choice of thoughts, images and impressions. This phenomenon has been named the dual expression of feeling. Fear, for example, is expressed not only through pallor, trembling, dry throat, and changes in respiration and heart rate, but also in the fact that all the impressions a person receives during the time he is fearful and all the thoughts in his head are typically permeated by the feeling that possesses him. When the proverb says that a scared raven takes fright even at a bush, it means that the influence of the emotion we are experiencing colours our perception of external objects. Just as people long ago learned to express their internal states through external expressions, so do the images of imagination serve as an internal expression of our feelings. Human sorrow and mourning is indicated by the colour black, happiness by white, serenity by light blue, and rebellion by red. The images of imagination also provide an internal language for our emotion. The emotion selects separate elements from reality and combines them in an association that is determined from within by our mood, and not from without by the logic of the images themselves.

★ ★ ★

The passions and fates of imaginary characters, their joys and sorrows, move, disturb and excite us, despite the fact that we know these are not real events, but rather the products of fantasy. This occurs only because the emotions that take hold of us from the artistic images on the pages of books or from the stage are completely real and we experience them truly, seriously and deeply. Frequently, a simple combination of external impressions, such as a musical composition, induces a whole complex world of experiences and feelings in a person listening to the music. This expansion and deepening of feelings, their creative restructuring, constitutes the psychological basis for the art of music.

We must still mention the fourth and last type of association between imagination and reality. This last type is, on the one hand, intimately associated with the one just described, and, on the other, very different from it. The essence of this association is that a construct of fantasy may represent something substantially new, never encountered before in human experience and without correspondence to any object that actually exists in reality; however, once it has been externally embodied, that is, has been given material form, this crystallised imagination that has become an object begins to actually exist in the real world, to affect other things.

In this way imagination becomes reality. Examples of such crystallised or embodied imagination include any technical device, machine or instrument. These were created by the combinatory imagination of human beings and do not correspond to any model existing in reality, but they have the most persuasive, active and practical association with reality in that once they have been given material form, they become just as real as other things and affect the surrounding real environment.

Such products of the imagination have a very long history, which perhaps it would be worthwhile to outline briefly. One could say that their development takes a circular path. The elements out of which they are constructed were taken by the human inventor from reality. Within the mind of this inventor, in his thoughts, these elements underwent complex reworking and were transformed into products of the imagination.

Finally, once they were given material form, they returned to reality, but returned as a new active force with the potential to alter that reality. This is the complete cycle followed by the creative operation of the imagination.

It would be incorrect to suppose that only in the area of technology, in the area of practical effects on nature, is imagination capable of completing this full cycle. Such a circle can also be found in the area of emotional imagination where it is not difficult to trace.

It is a fact that precisely when we confront a full circle completed by the imagination do we find that both factors – the intellectual and the emotional – are equally necessary for an act of creation. Feeling as well as thought drives human creativity.

Notes

1. In this paragraph, *smysl* or *znachenie* or their plurals are not specified as translations of 'meaning' or 'meanings'.
2. Kurt Koffka (1886–1941) was a German psychologist. Together with Max Wertheimer and Wolfgang Köhler, he founded Gestalt psychology.
3. David Katz (1884–1953) was a German-born Swedish educator and psychologist, specialising in Gestalt psychology and phenomenology.
4. Eugen Bleuler (1857–1939) was a Swiss psychiatrist and psychologist best known for his studies of mental illness. He introduced the terms 'autism' and 'schizophrenia', among others, into the vocabulary of psychology.
5. Theodule Ribot (1839–1916) was a French psychologist, recognised as the founder of scientific psychology in France.

References

Barrs, M. (2022). *Vygotsky the teacher*. Abingdon, Oxon and New York, NY: Routledge.

Ribot, T. (1906). *Essay on the creative imagination*. Trans. (from French, *Essai sur l'imagination créatrice* [1900]) A. Baron. Russian translation 1901. Available online at www.gutenberg.org/cache/epub/26430/pg26430-images.html

Vygotsky, L.S. (1987). *The collected works of L.S. Vygotsky. Volume 1, Problems of general psychology*. Trans. and intro. N. Minick; Rieber, R.W. and Carton, A.S. (eds). New York, NY: Plenum Press.

Vygotsky, L.S. (1987a). 'Lecture 5. Imagination and its development in childhood' [1932], in Vygotsky, L.S. (1987). *The collected works of L.S. Vygotsky. Volume 1, Problems of general psychology*, pp. 339–349.

Vygotsky, L.S. (2004). Imagination and creativity in childhood [1930]. *Journal of Russian and East European Psychology*, 42(1), pp. 7–97. Also available online in the Marxist Archive: www.marxists.org/archive/vygotsky/works/1927/imagination.pdf

Vygotsky, L.S. (2016). 'Play and its role in the mental development of the child' [1933]. Trans. N. Veresov and M. Barrs. *International Research in Early Childhood Education*, 7(2), pp. 3–25. Also available online at https://files.eric.ed.gov/fulltext/EJ1138861.pdf

Chapter 9

The zone of proximal/proximate development

The zone of proximal/proximate development [ZPD] is Vygotsky's best-known concept (type it into Google and you get about seventeen million mentions) but it is also 'perhaps one of the most used and least understood constructs to appear in contemporary educational literature' [Palinscar, 1998, p. 370].

(Barrs, 2022)

Vygotsky discusses the concept several times in different texts (Chaiklin [2003] identifies eight such places). This chapter contains extracts from three of those discussions, culminating in Stanley Mitchell's recent translation of 'The problem of teaching and mental development at school age' (Vygotsky, 2017), which is now the most authentic version in English of this text. Prior to this, the translation most easily available in English was the highly edited and misleading version included in *Mind in society* (Vygotsky, 1978). The ZPD is also discussed in Chapters 8 and 10.

We must briefly deal with the question of the most appropriate English translation of the term. 'Zone of proximal development' is the formulation most commonly used, and it originated in *Mind in society*. But, as Luciano Mecacci (2017) explains, 'proximal' is an obscure term from anatomy: 'the Russian original (*"blizhayshego"*) simply means "nearest", and the equivalent of "proximate" was the translation used in other languages (e.g. "*zona di sviluppo prossimo*" in Italian)' (Barrs, 2022, pp. 143–144). Despite the editors' preference for 'proximate' over 'proximal', however, we are obliged to leave 'proximal' as it is in two of the extracts which follow.

The reason why the ZPD has become Vygotsky's most famous concept, despite the fact that it occupies a very limited amount of space in his oeuvre, is that it offers a means of assessing, indeed of measuring, potential, through a comparison of children's performance in supported and unsupported contexts. This of course had major implications for assessment, and also for teaching, although the emphasis Vygotsky put on teaching and pedagogy in this paper did not fully emerge until the publication of the Mitchell translation. But not all the versions of the ZPD focused on its potential for refining teaching-learning relationships and encouraging responsive teaching. Some, such as Vygotsky (2011), presented it mainly as a more accurate form of measurement for assessing individuals and grouping and streaming children. Here the administrative uses of the ZPD for pedologists charged with assessing large groups of children are uppermost. The ZPD is a powerful and generative concept, but it seems likely that Vygotsky was still developing it in his last years. Modern interpretations of the ZPD have expanded wildly beyond anything to be found in Vygotsky's formulations.

In 'The problem of age and the diagnostics of development' (Vygotsky, 2021a), Vygotsky discusses the potential value of the ZPD as a diagnostic or assessment tool, and its significance for '*obucheniye*', the Russian word which combines teaching with learning, and which Kellogg and Veresov, the translators of the lecture from which this extract is taken, render as 'learning-and-teaching'. Vygotsky proposes the term 'imitation', not in any slavish sense, but as referring 'to all sorts of activities of a particular type being performed by a child not independently, but in collaboration with adults or with another child.'

From 'The problem of age and the diagnostics of development'

When we speak here of imitating, we have in mind not mechanically, automatically, and senselessly, but rational imitative performance of a given intellectual operation based on understanding. In this regard, we have narrowed the meaning of this term, using it to refer to an area of operations that are more or less directly linked to the rational activity of the child. On the other hand, we have deepened the meaning of the term by using 'imitation' to [refer to] all sorts of activities of a particular type being performed by a child not independently, but in collaboration with adults or with another child. Everything that a child cannot do independently but which can be *learnt* or which can *be performed under the guidance or in collaboration with the help of leading questions or with the help of assistance in difficult points*, we will treat as the sphere of *imitation*.

With this definition of the concept, we may at once establish the symptomatic significance of this intellectual imitation widely used in the diagnostics of mental development. It is completely clear that what a child can do by himself, without any aid from outside, may be indicative of already matured capabilities and functions. These are identified with the aid of tests usually employed to determine the real level of mental development, as these tests are based exclusively on solving problems independently.

But, as we have already said, it is always important to define not only the matured processes but also the maturing ones. In relation to the child's mental development, we can solve this task with the help of determining what the child is capable of in the area of intellectual imitation, if we understand this term as meaning the definition given above. Research shows that there exists a strict genetic relationship between what the child is capable of in this area and his mental development. What the child is able to do today in collaboration and under guidance, he will tomorrow become capable of performing independently. This means that by investigating the potential of the child working in collaboration, we define thereby the area of maturing intellectual functions that in the near stage of his development should bear their fruits and thereby move to the level of real mental development.

In this way, by investigating what the child is capable of performing independently, we investigate the development of the bygone day. Exploring what the child is able to perform in cooperation, we define the development of the day to come. This whole area of immature but maturing processes makes up the zone of proximal development of the child.

We will explain with a simple example how we determine the zone of proximal development. We assume that as a result of our inquiry we have established with respect to two given children that they are at the same year in their mental age. Let us say that both are 8-year-olds. This means that both of them handle tasks of the degree of difficulty which corresponds to the standard for 8-year-olds by themselves. In this way, we have identified the real level of their intellectual development. However, we do not cease our inquiry with this, but rather continue it. With the help of specifically developed techniques for each given method, we examine how capable both children are in handling tasks which somewhat exceed the standard for 8-year-olds. We show the child how to handle the task, and we see whether he can, imitating this demonstration, manage it; or we begin the solution of the task and allow the child to complete it. Or we offer the child some cases of solutions of problems that go beyond his mental age, in collaboration with other, more developed children, or, finally, we explain to the child the principle of handling the task; we put leading questions to him, we divide the task into parts, etc. In short, we offer to the child various forms of cooperation for handling those tasks that exceed his mental age, and we determine how far the opportunity for intellectual cooperation extends the intellectual sphere for the given child and how far it goes beyond his mental age.

It then turns out that one child can solve in collaboration tasks at, say, the 12-year-old standard. His zone of proximal development exceeds his mental age by 4 years. The other child turns out to advance with cooperation only to the 9-year-old standard age. His zone of proximal development covers only one year of development.

Now ask yourself: are these two children, who find themselves at the same age level established by their real level of development, the same with regard to the entire picture of their development to the present day as a whole? Obviously, the similarity is only limited to the area of already matured functions, capable of independent application. But in relation to maturing processes, one child went four times as far as the other.

The editors included lengthy extracts from 'Play and its role in the mental development of the child' (Vygotsky, 2016) in Chapter 8. We repeat here part of one of those extracts, linking play to the ZPD.

From 'Play and its role in the mental development of the child'

Is it possible to suppose that a child's behaviour is always guided by meaning, that a pre-schooler's behaviour is so arid that he never behaves with candy as he wants to, simply because he thinks he should behave otherwise? This kind of subordination to rules is quite impossible in life, but in play it does become possible; thus, play creates the zone of proximal development of the child. In play a child is always above his average age, above his daily behaviour; in play it is as though he were a head taller than himself. As in the focus of a magnifying glass, play contains all developmental tendencies in a condensed form; in play it is as though the child is trying to jump above the level of his normal behaviour.

The relationship can be compared with the instruction-development relationship, but play provides changes in needs and in consciousness of a much wider nature. Play is the source of development and creates the zone of proximal development. Action in the imaginative field, in an imaginary situation, the creation of voluntary intentions and the formation of real-life plans and volitional motives – all appear in play and make it the highest level of pre-school development.

The child moves forward essentially through play activity. It is in this way that play can be termed a leading activity that determines the child's development.

The third extract is from 'The problem of teaching and mental development at school age', in the recent translation (Vygotsky, 2017) mentioned at the beginning of the chapter. It was originally the first chapter in a posthumously published book of Vygotsky's writings, *Children's mental development in the process of learning/teaching* (Vygotsky, 1935). As so often in his work, Vygotsky begins the article by describing and disposing of psychological theories he regards as inadequate to the task in hand, which is to grasp how children's pre-school understandings interact with and are changed by the introduction of school learning, and from there to propose the most effective kinds of teaching.

Vygotsky first dismisses the theory that 'the processes of child development are independent of the processes of education' (Vygotsky, 2017, p. 359). The implication of this position is that teaching achieves nothing: 'Any possibility of discussing what role teaching might have in the development and maturing of these functions and in their activation is thereby excluded in advance' (ibid., p. 360). Then he dismisses a theory which seems at first sight to be the opposite of the first: that child development and teaching are the same thing. This second idea is based on reflexology: 'development is nothing other than the education of conditioned reflexes, and ... the teaching process is completely and inseparably at one with the process of child development' (ibid.). He has more sympathy for a third theory, which 'seeks to overcome the extremes of the previous two by simply aligning them' (ibid., p. 362). However, this third theory is associated with teaching as formal discipline, and 'It is common knowledge that this theory of formal discipline has led to the most reactionary practical results in the sphere of pedagogy' (ibid.).

Once he has cleared the ground, Vygotsky proceeds.

Whereas in the *Mind in society* version of this paper (Vygotsky, 1978), references to pedagogy are ignored and omitted, in this translation 'pedagogy' features prominently (15 mentions). Similarly, while the word 'teaching' occurs rarely in the *Mind in society* translation, usually being replaced by 'learning', or omitted, in the Mitchell translation it appears throughout (64 mentions).

From 'The problem of teaching and mental development at school age'

Having examined these three theories with their different versions of the relationship between learning and development, we are now free to suggest a more correct solution to the problem. The first thing to consider is the fact that a child's education begins long before it goes to school. School never starts in an empty space. Whatever a child learns in school has its prehistory. For instance, a child begins to learn arithmetic at school. However, long before school it will have had some experience of quantity, it will have come across one or another form of division, magnitude, addition and subtraction; thus the child will already be in possession of a pre-school arithmetic which only short-sighted psychologists do not notice, and ignore.

A careful examination will show that pre-school arithmetic is extremely complex, which means that the child pursues its arithmetical development long before it studies arithmetic at school. Of course, this pre-school prehistory does not entail a strict succession between the two stages of the child's arithmetic development.

The line of school learning does not directly continue that of pre-school development in any sphere. It may turn aside in certain respects, even contradict the line of pre-school development. But whether pre-school learning is directly continued or rejected at school, we cannot ignore the fact that school education never starts from an empty space, but is always confronted with a definite stage of development experienced by the child before school.

★ ★ ★

Doesn't the child learn to speak from its parents? Through question and answer doesn't the child acquire a whole range of knowledge and information from adults? By imitating adults and receiving direction from them on how to behave doesn't it develop a whole range of skills?

Obviously, this learning process that takes place before school age differs fundamentally from the process of school education, whose job it is to impart the basics of scientific knowledge. But even when the child asks its first questions and learns the names of surrounding objects, it goes through a definite cycle of education. Thus, learning and development are not encountered for the first time at school, but are in fact connected with one another from the first day of a child's life.

Hence, the question which we have to ask ourselves is doubly problematic. It divides as it were into two separate questions. We have first of all to understand the relationship between learning and development in general, and then the specific peculiarities of this relationship at school age.

Let us begin with the second question, which will help us to clarify the first question. To define this we shall look at the results of several studies that we believe have a fundamental significance for our problem as a whole and can offer the educational field a new concept of extreme importance without which our question cannot be properly answered. We are referring to the so-called zone of proximate development.

That teaching has in one way or another to synchronise with the child's level of development is an empirically established and frequently attested fact, which cannot be gainsaid. That reading can only be taught at a particular age, that only at a particular age can a child study algebra – this does not require any proof. Thus, the correlation of developmental level with potentialities of learning constitutes an unshakeable and fundamental fact which we can boldly take as our starting point.

However, it is only recently that the developmental level on its own has been judged insufficient for defining the real relationships of development to learning. We need to define at least two levels of a child's development, which we must know before we can find the true relationship between the child's development and its capacity to learn in each concrete instance. The first we shall call the level of actual development. We have in mind the level of development of the child's psychological functions formed by definite developmental cycles already having taken place.

Basically, we almost always encounter this actual level of development when we try to define the mental age of a child by means of tests. However, simple experience shows that this level of actual development does not as yet adequately define the condition of child development at the present day. Imagine that we have examined two children and set their mental age at seven. This would mean that each child is capable of solving problems accessible to seven-year olds. However, when we try to move these children on with further tests, we find a serious difference between them. One child, with the help of leading questions, examples, demonstrations, will easily answer the tests that are two years in advance of its developmental level. The second child will able to answer tests that are only six months in advance of its level.

Here we come straight to the central concept that is necessary for defining the zone of proximal development. This central concept is in turn linked with a reconsideration of the problem of imitation in contemporary psychology.

In the past, the established view took the fixed position that the indicator of the level of a child's development was only its independent activity in which imitation played no part. This view found its expression in all contemporary systems of test investigations. Only those tests were considered that the child answers independently, without outside help, without examples, without leading questions.

However, this view, as research has shown, does not hold water. Even experiments with animals have proved that actions which the animal is able to imitate lie in the zone of the animal's own potentialities. This means that the animal can imitate only those actions which in one or another form it finds accessible, and, as Köhler's (1925) studies have established, the ability of an animal to imitate does not go beyond the limits of the actions it is capable of. This means that if the animal is capable of imitating an intellectual action, then in certain circumstances it will by its independent activity show an ability to perform a completely analogous action. Thus, imitation is closely bound up with understanding; it is only possible in the sphere of those actions accessible to the animal's understanding.

A child's ability to imitate is different, and in a series of actions it can go beyond its own capacities, although these are not limitless. With the help of imitation in a collective sphere, under the guidance of adults, a child is able to do much more and to do it with understanding and independently. The difference between the level at which it solves a problem under guidance, with the help of adults, and the level at which it acts on its own defines the zone of proximate development.

Take the example just quoted. We have two children of an equal mental age, seven, but one of them with a minimum of help solves a problem of a nine-year old, while the other reaches only seven-and-a-half. Is the mental development of these two children the same? From the point of view of their independent activity it is the same, but from the point of view of proximate possibility it differs sharply. What the child is able to do with the help of an adult points to its zone of proximate development. This means that with the help of this method we can take into consideration not only the process of development up to the present moment, not only the cycles completed, not only the processes of maturation, but also those processes which are taking place now and are beginning to grow and develop.

What the child can do today with the help of adults, it will be able to carry out tomorrow on its own. In this way the zone of proximate development will help us to define tomorrow's achievements and the dynamics of the child's development, taking into account not only what it has already mastered, but also its process of growth. The two children in our example show the same mental age from the point of view of the developmental cycles they have completed, but the dynamic of their development is quite different. So the child's mental development can at least be defined by clarifying its two levels – the level of actual development and the zones of its proximate development.

This fact, apparently of little importance in itself, nevertheless has a decisive and fundamental significance, revolutionising the whole science of the relationship between the learning process and the development of the child. First of all, it changes the traditional point of view on the drawing of pedagogical conclusions from a diagnosis of development. In the past the matter was seen as follows. By means of testing we define the level of the child's mental development which pedagogy has to take into account and beyond which it must not go. Thus, in the very posing of this question the idea is that teaching should orient itself, in the development of the child, towards yesterday, towards stages that have already been gone through and completed.

The mistakenness of such a view was revealed in practice sooner than in theory. This can be shown most clearly in the teaching of mentally backward children. As is known, studies have established that a mentally backward child has little aptitude for abstract thought. For this reason pedagogy in auxiliary schools seems to have drawn the right conclusion[1] that the teaching of such a child should be based on visual aids. However, experience brought deep disappointment to this special kind of pedagogy. It turned out that such a system, based exclusively on visual aids and excluding anything to do with abstract thinking, not only does not help the child to overcome its inborn deficiency, but strengthens this inadequacy still further, accustoming the child exclusively to visual thinking and extinguishing those elements of abstract thinking which every child has. Precisely because the mentally backward child, left to itself, will never attain any developed forms of abstract thinking, the task of the school is to do all it can to encourage it in this direction, to develop what by itself will remain inadequate. And in the contemporary pedagogy of the auxiliary school we observe this beneficial turning away from the kind of understanding of visual education,[2] which gives their methods their true meaning. The use of visual aids is necessary and unavoidable only as a step towards the development of abstract thinking, as a means, not an end in itself.

Something very close to this occurs in the development of the normal child, too. Teaching oriented on already completed cycles of development is futile from the point of view of a child's general development. Rather than advancing a process of development, it remains tied to its tail.

As against this old point of view, the concept of the zone of proximate development gives prominence to the opposite formula which states that the only good method of teaching is that which runs ahead of development.

★ ★ ★

We have no hesitation, after all that has been said, in stating the essential characteristic of teaching to be the creation of the zone of proximate development. Teaching engages the child with life, awakens and puts in motion a whole range of inner developmental processes which, initially depending on relations with others in his intimate circle, then undergo an inner development and become part of the child's own self.

In this sense teaching is not development, but teaching organised on the right basis will facilitate the child's mental development, bring to life a whole range of developmental processes which outside of teaching would not be at all possible. Teaching therefore is an inwardly necessary and universal moment in the process of developing in a child not the innate but the historical characteristics of a human being. Just as a child of deaf-and-dumb parents, who does not hear the spoken word in his presence, must remain dumb although he has all the natural instincts for speech, and will not develop those higher psychic functions connected with speech, so every process of teaching is the source of development, calling into being a series of processes, which in the absence of teaching would not arise at all.

★ ★ ★

We can now try to sum up what we have said and give a general formulation of the relationship we have found between processes of learning and those of development. Jumping ahead, let us say that all experimental research regarding the psychological nature of the processes of teaching arithmetic, writing, natural science and other subjects in a primary school shows that all these processes revolve as if on an axis round the basic new formations occurring at school age, interweaving with the central nerves of the pupil's development. The very lines of school education awaken inner processes of development. To trace the origin and fate of these inner developmental lines that school education promotes constitutes a primary task for the psychological analysis of the pedagogic process.

Most important about this hypothesis is its position that developmental processes and learning processes do not coincide, that the former follow the latter, creating zones of proximate development.

From this point of view the traditional attitude to the relationship between teaching and development has to change. From the traditional point of view, as soon as the child has learnt the meaning of a particular word, for example 'revolution', or mastered a particular operation, for example addition or writing, its development is essentially complete. From the new point of view it only begins at this moment. To show how the mastery of four arithmetical sums can give rise to a whole series of very complex inner processes in the development of a child's thinking constitutes the basic task of pedology in analysing the pedagogic process.

Our hypothesis establishes the unity, but not the identity, of learning processes and the inner processes of development. It presupposes the transition from one to the other. To show how outward meaning and outward ability in the child become inward is a primary object for pedagogic research.

Pedagogic analysis is not a psycho-technology in regard to school. The child's school work is not a profession, analogous to those of adults. To open up the real processes of development behind the teaching means opening the doors to a scientific analysis of the pedagogic process.

The question is what kind of reality is reflected in psychological analysis. It is that of the real inner connections in the processes of development, awakened to life by teaching at school. In this sense pedological analysis will always look within, like Röntgen's X-ray. It should enable the teacher to watch the processes of development as they occur in the head of each child during the course of instruction. To lay bare this inner, subterranean, genetic network of school subjects constitutes the primary task of psychological analysis.

The second important moment of the hypothesis is the notion that although teaching connects directly with a child's development, nevertheless it does not occur evenly and in parallel to the latter. The child's development never follows school education like a shadow. This is why tests of achievement never reflect the real course of a child's development. Indeed, the most complex, dynamic dependencies assert themselves between the process of development and that of teaching, and these cannot be fitted into a single, speculative, *a priori* formula given in advance.

Each subject has its own concrete relationship to a child's development and this relationship changes as the child moves from one step to another. This takes us immediately to a review of the problem of formal discipline, i.e. to the role and significance of each individual subject from the point of view of the child's overall mental development. This cannot be decided using a single formula, and opens the space for the widest and most varied concrete studies.

We can presuppose that the coefficient of formal discipline, inhering in every subject, will not remain the same in the various stages of teaching and development. The task of pedological research in this sphere is the determination of the inner structure of school subjects from the point of view of the child's development, and the change that takes place in this structure along with methods of school education.

We believe that together with this hypothesis we have introduced into pedology the potential for a boundless field of concrete research, which can alone solve our problem in all its plenitude.

Notes

1. 'The right conclusion' seems confusing here. Perhaps Vygotsky was being ironic. Luciano Mecacci has translated the article into Italian (Vygotsky, 2022). Helpfully, where the English has 'the right conclusion', he has *'la conclusione, apparentemente corretta'* ('the apparently correct conclusion').
2. A 'beneficial turning away', that is, from the former overreliance on visual aids.

References

Barrs, M. (2022) *Vygotsky the teacher*. Abingdon, Oxon and New York, NY: Routledge.

Chaiklin, S. (2003). 'The zone of proximal development in Vygotsky's analysis of learning and instruction', in Kozulin, A., Gindis, B., Ageyev, V.S. and Miller, S.M. (eds) (2003). *Vygotsky's educational theory in cultural context*, pp. 39–64.

Köhler, W. (1925). *The mentality of apes*. Trans. E. Winter. London: Kegan Paul, Trench, Trubner; New York: Harcourt Brace and Co.

Mecacci, L. (2017). *Lev Vygotskii: sviluppo, educazione e patologia della mente*. Florence: Giunti.

Palinscar, A.S. (1998). 'Keeping the metaphor of scaffolding fresh: a response to C. Addison Stone's "The metaphor of scaffolding: its utility for the field of learning disabilities"'. *Journal of Learning Disabilities*, 31(4), pp. 370–373.

Vygotsky, L. S. (1935). '*Problema obučenija i umstvennogo razvitija v škol'nom vozraste*' ['The problem of teaching and mental development at school age']. In *Umstvennoe razvitie detej v processe obučenija* [*Children's mental development in the process of learning/teaching*]. Moscow: Gosudarstvennoie Uchebno-pedagogicheskoie Izdatel'stvo, pp. 3–19.

Vygotsky, L.S. (1978). *Mind in society*. Cole, M., John-Steiner, V., Scribner S. and Souberman, E. (eds). Cambridge, MA: Harvard University Press.

Vygotsky, L.S. (2011). 'The dynamics of the schoolchild's mental development in relation to teaching and learning' [1928]. Trans. A. Kozulin. *Journal of Cognitive Education and Psychology*, 10(2), pp. 198–211.

Vygotsky, L.S. (2016). 'Play and its role in the mental development of the child' [1933]. Trans. N. Veresov and M. Barrs. *International Research in Early Childhood Education*, 7(2), pp. 3–25.

Vygotsky, L.S. (2017). 'The problem of teaching and mental development at school age' [1935]. ('*Problema obucheniya i umstvennogo razvitiya v shkol'nom vozraste*'). Trans. S. Mitchell. *Changing English*, 24(4), pp. 359–371. Also available online in the Marxist Archive: www.marxists.org/archive/vygotsky/works/1931/school-age.htm

Vygotsky, L.S. (2021). *L.S. Vygotsky's pedological works. Volume 2, The problem of age*. Trans. and notes D. Kellogg and N. Veresov. Singapore: Springer.

Vygotsky, L.S. (2021a). 'The problem of age and the diagnostics of development' [1932–1934], in Vygotsky, L.S. (2021). *L.S. Vygotsky's pedological works. Volume 2, The problem of age*, pp. 50–63.

Vygotsky, L.S. (2022). '*Il problema dell'insegnamento/apprendimento e dello sviluppo mentale nell'età scolare*', in *La mente umana: Cinque saggi* (2022). Mecacci, L. (ed. and trans.) Milan: Giangiacomo Feltrinelli Editore, pp. 107–135.

Chapter 10

Word meaning develops
Extracts from *Thinking and speech*, Chapters 1, 2, 4 and 6

This is the first of two chapters presenting extracts from Vygotsky's profound last book, *Thinking and speech* (Vygotsky, 1987a). The argument of the book is a complex one, though Vygotsky's focus is made very clear from the outset: his principal theme is the development of *word meaning*. Vygotsky pursues this topic through three main developmental 'sites': young children's language development; concept development; and the internalisation of language as inner speech. Vygotsky writes (ibid., p. 51): 'What unifies all these investigations is *the idea of development*, an idea that we attempt to apply in our analysis of word meaning as the unity of speech and thinking.'

It seems clear that the only full translation from the original 1934 Russian edition of *Thinking and speech*, which was published a few months after Vygotsky's death, is Luciano Mecacci's Italian translation, *Pensiero e linguaggio* (Vygotsky, 1992). Mecacci's translation sometimes seems to the editors more successful in clarifying Vygotsky's meaning than the English translation we use here. In a few of the most striking cases, Mecacci's Italian alternative, with our English translation from the Italian, appear as notes to this and the next chapter.

The first extract describes a key aspect of Vygotsky's methodology, which he used in *The psychology of art* (Vygotsky, 1971). In studying a complex whole, a common approach is to analyse it by breaking it down into its component parts: a form of analysis that 'begins with the decomposition of the complex mental whole into its elements' (Vygotsky, 1987a, p. 45). Vygotsky argues that such a method risks destroying the very thing you're investigating. He wants a holistic approach that will preserve the character of the whole.

From Chapter 1, 'The problem and the method of investigation'

In our view, an entirely different form of analysis is fundamental to further development of theories of thinking and speech. This form of analysis relies on the partitioning of the complex whole into *units*. In contrast to the term 'element', the term 'unit' designates a product of analysis that possesses *all the basic characteristics of the whole.* The unit is a vital and irreducible part of the whole. The key to the explanation of the characteristics of water lies not in the investigation of its chemical formula but in the investigation of its molecule and its molecular movements. In precisely the same sense, the living cell is the real unit of biological analysis because it preserves the basic characteristics of life that are inherent in the living organism.

A psychology concerned with the study of the complex whole must comprehend this. It must replace the method of decomposing the whole into its elements with that of partitioning the whole into its units. Psychology must identify those units in which the characteristics of the whole are present, even though they may be manifested in altered form. Using this mode of analysis, it must attempt to resolve the concrete problems that face us.

What then is a unit that possesses the characteristics inherent to the integral phenomenon of verbal thinking and that cannot be further decomposed? In our view, such a unit can be found in the inner aspect of the word, in its meaning ...

The word does not relate to a single object, but to *an entire group or class of objects*. Therefore, every word is a concealed *generalisation*. From a psychological perspective, word meaning is first and foremost a generalisation. It is not difficult to see that generalisation is a *verbal act of thought*; its reflection of reality differs radically from that of immediate sensation or perception.

It has been said that the dialectical leap is not only a transition from matter that is incapable of sensation to matter that is capable of sensation, but a transition from sensation to thought. This implies that reality is reflected in consciousness in a qualitatively different way in thinking than it is in immediate sensation. This qualitative difference is primarily a function of a *generalised reflection of reality*. Therefore, generalisation in word meaning is an act of thinking in the true sense of the word. At the same time, however, meaning is an inseparable part of the word; it belongs not only to the domain of thought but [also] to the domain of speech. A word without meaning is not a word, but an empty sound. A word without meaning no longer belongs to the domain of speech. One cannot say of word meaning what we said earlier of the elements of the word taken separately. Is word meaning speech or is it thought? It is both at one and the same time; it is a *unit of verbal thinking*. It is obvious, then, that our method must be that of semantic analysis. Our method must rely on the analysis of the meaningful aspect of speech; it must be a *method for studying verbal meaning*.

We can reasonably anticipate that this method will produce answers to our questions concerning the relationship between thinking and speech because this relationship is already contained in the unit of analysis. In studying the function, structure and development of this unit, we will come to understand a great deal that is of direct relevance to the problem of the relationship of thinking to speech and to the nature of verbal thinking.

The second extract concerns the tendency of psychological investigation to focus solely on the cognitive aspect of mind and of thinking. Vygotsky was living at a time when experimental psychology was based on the study of animals, and when, in Russia, Pavlov, with his focus on the conditional reflex, ruled the field. In the West, behavioural psychology led to cognitive psychology, with its close focus on cognition. We are familiar with the relentless focus on the cognitive that has been characteristic of educational psychology, especially its tendency to isolate, privilege and test one aspect of thinking. Vygotsky always wanted to consider and include in psychology other aspects of mind that were just as important – emotion, affect and 'volition' (or will) – and here he stresses those aspects.

From Chapter 1, 'The problem and the method of investigation'

The first issue that emerges when we consider the relationship of thinking and speech to the other aspects of the life of consciousness concerns the connection between *intellect and affect*. Among the most basic defects of traditional approaches to the study of psychology has been the isolation of the intellectual from the volitional and affective aspects of consciousness. The inevitable consequence of the isolation of these functions has been the transformation of thinking into an autonomous stream. Thinking itself became the thinker of thoughts. Thinking was divorced from the full vitality of life, from the motives, interests and inclinations of the thinking individual. Thinking was transformed either into a useless epiphenomenon, a process that can change nothing in the individual's life and behaviour, or into an independent and autonomous primeval force that influences the life of consciousness and the life of the personality through its intervention.

By isolating thinking from affect at the outset, we effectively cut ourselves off from any potential for a causal explanation of thinking. A causal analysis of thinking presupposes that we identify its motive force, that we identify the needs, interests, incentives and tendencies that direct the movement of thought in one direction or another. In much the same way, when thinking is isolated from affect, investigating its influences on the affective or purposive aspects of mental life is effectively precluded. A causal analysis of mental life cannot begin by ascribing to thought a magical power to determine human behaviour, a power to determine behaviour through one of the individual's own inner systems. Equally incompatible with a causal analysis is the transformation of thought into a superfluous appendage of behaviour, into its feeble and useless shadow.

The direction we must move in our attempt to resolve this vital problem is indicated by the method that relies on the analysis of the complex whole into its units. There exists a dynamic meaningful system that constitutes *a unity of affective and intellectual processes*. Every idea contains some remnant of the individual's affective relationship to that aspect of reality which it represents. In this way, analysis into units makes it possible to see the relationship between the individual's needs or inclinations and his thinking.[1]

The first developmental 'site' through which Vygotsky pursues the topic of word meaning is young children's language development.

Most contemporary theories of young children's language development were theories of language acquisition, which supposed that young children acquired words and meanings by association. Vygotsky's theory, by contrast, is developmental. He advances his theory via a long debate with Jean Piaget. Vygotsky admires Piaget as a researcher but utterly disagrees with him as a theorist.

Piaget's model of young children's earliest language presents it as 'autistic'. From this private form of language Piaget shows children moving to 'egocentric speech'. Subsequently, for him, egocentric speech 'atrophies', 'dies off', and is replaced by its final form: social speech modelled on adult speech.

Vygotsky, on the other hand, believes that early language is learned in social interaction with adults. This social speech, in Vygotsky's theory, is taken over into their private play, and then internalised as inner speech.

This next extract, though lengthy, is only a sample of Vygotsky's exhaustive intellectual quarrel with Piaget.

From Chapter 2, 'The problem of speech and thinking in Piaget's theory', sections 3, 4 and 5

Our first step will be to clarify Piaget's own ideas, to define as precisely as possible what it is that he sees as the empirical foundation for his theory. This foundation appears in his research on the functions of the child's speech.

Piaget classifies all the child's conversation as either egocentric or social speech. When he speaks of egocentric speech, Piaget is concerned with a speech form that is distinguished primarily by its function. Piaget writes that 'This talk is ego-centric, partly because the child speaks only about himself, but chiefly because he does not attempt to place himself at the point of view of his hearer' [Piaget, 1959, p. 9].[2] The child is not interested in whether anyone is listening to him; he does not expect an answer; he does not wish to influence his partner or to inform him of something. This is monologue, reminiscent of monologue in drama. Its essence can be expressed in a single formula: 'The child talks to himself as though he were thinking aloud. He does not address anyone' [ibid.]. When he is occupied with something, the child accompanies his action with a variety of utterances. It is this verbal accompaniment of activity that Piaget designates with the term 'egocentric speech'. The child's socialised speech has an entirely different function. In this speech, the child actually exchanges thoughts with others; he requests, orders, threatens, informs, criticises, or asks questions.

In his careful clinical isolation and description of the child's egocentric speech, in his extensive survey of the phenomenon, and in his efforts to trace its fate, Piaget has unquestionably performed a valuable service. In the egocentric nature of the child's speech, Piaget sees the first, basic, and most direct proof of egocentrism in the child's thought. His survey of the phenomenon demonstrated that the coefficient of egocentric speech was extremely high with young children. Before the age of 6 or 7, more than half of the child's utterances were egocentric.

★ ★ ★

Leaving issues of fact aside for the moment, the basic outline of Piaget's theory of egocentric speech is sufficiently clear. It is his contention that the majority of the young child's speech is egocentric. It is not a means of social interaction. It does not have a communicative function. It provides a rhythm for the child's activity and experience, accompanying it in the sense that an accompaniment is provided for a basic melody in music. Egocentric speech contributes nothing essential to the child's activity or experience, any more than the course or structure of a basic melody is influenced by its accompaniment. There is agreement but no internal connection.

For Piaget, the child's egocentric speech is an accessory of the activity, a reflection of the egocentric nature of the child's thinking. The highest law for the child is play. His thinking is primarily an illusory imagination, a form of imagination expressed in egocentric speech.

Thus, the first postulate of Piaget's views on egocentric speech is that it has no necessary, objective, or useful function in the child's behaviour. This concept will play an important role in our analysis of Piaget's work. For Piaget, egocentric speech is speech for itself, for the sake of its own satisfaction. It is speech that cannot and does not change anything significant in the child's activity. Egocentric speech is completely subordinated to egocentric motives and nearly incomprehensible to others. It is the child's verbal dream, a product of his mind that stands closer to the logic of dream and fantasy than to the logic of realistic thinking.

★ ★ ★

Of interest to us here is ... the question of the function and fate of egocentric speech. Our interpretation of the fact that egocentric speech disappears in the school-age child is dependent on our analysis of its function. It is extremely difficult to address the roots of this question experimentally. The data that we gather in the experiment can serve only indirectly as a foundation for building our hypothesis that egocentric speech is a transitional stage in the development of speech from external to inner.

Piaget, of course, does not provide us with a foundation for this concept. He does not indicate that egocentric speech should be considered a transitional stage of this kind. On the contrary, it is Piaget's view that the fate of egocentric speech is to atrophy. In Piaget's work, the question of the development of the child's inner speech remains the least clarified of all issues concerning the child's speech. In fact, one gets the impression that inner speech – understood as speech that is psychologically inner and that functions in a manner analogous to external egocentric speech – precedes external or socialised speech.

Though from a genetic perspective this position may be ludicrous, Piaget must reach precisely this kind of conclusion if he consistently develops his thesis that socialised speech arises after egocentric speech, that socialised speech asserts itself only after egocentric speech has atrophied.

However, in spite of Piaget's theoretical views, there is a good deal of empirical data in his research (as there is in our own) which supports our assumption concerning the function and fate of egocentric speech. Of course, at this point, this assumption is only an hypothesis. However, this hypothesis is more consistent with what we know of the development of the child's speech than is Piaget's.

* * *

Our hypothesis obligates us to represent the overall process of development in the following way. The initial function of speech is social, that of social interaction or social linkage. Speech affects those in the immediate environment and may be initiated by either the adult or the child. The first form of speech in the child, then, is purely social. The notion that speech is socialised is incorrect in that this implies that speech was originally non-social, that it becomes social only through development and change.

The social speech of the child is a phenomenon with multiple functions, a phenomenon that develops in accordance with the law of functional differentiation. It is only after an initial stage where the child's speech is a purely social phenomenon, only in subsequent growth and development, that we begin to see a sharp differentiation of social speech into egocentric and communicative speech. We prefer the term 'communicative' rather than 'socialised' speech partly because of the considerations discussed above. In addition, our *hypothesis indicates* that egocentric and communicative speech are equally social; they simply have different functions. In accordance with this hypothesis, egocentric speech develops in a social process that involves the transmission of social forms of behaviour to the child. Egocentric speech develops through a movement of social forms of collaboration into the sphere of individual mental functions.

* * *

It is our view, then, that the most important point in the transition from external to inner speech is the egocentric speech of the child as described by Piaget. Though not himself aware of it, a careful analysis of Piaget's empirical data indicates that he has provided a graphic demonstration of how external speech is transformed into inner speech.

Piaget showed that egocentric speech is inner in its mental function but external in its physiological nature. In this sense, speech becomes mentally 'inner' earlier than physically 'inner'. This allows us to clarify the dynamics involved in the formation of inner speech. Briefly, the process occurs through a differentiation of speech functions.

It involves the isolation of egocentric speech from social speech through a gradual process of abbreviation and the subsequent transformation of egocentric speech into inner speech.

Egocentric speech is a form critical to the transition from external to inner speech. This is why it is of such tremendous theoretical interest. Our entire scheme can be represented in the following way:

social speech – egocentric speech – inner speech

This scheme can be usefully contrasted with that assumed by the traditional theory of inner speech development and with that inherent in Piaget's proposals. Traditional theory assumed the following sequence:

external speech – whispered speech – inner speech

Piaget's scheme assumes a different sequence, one related to the development of logical verbal thinking:

inner autistic thinking
|
egocentric speech and egocentric thinking
|
socialised speech and logical thinking

We include the traditional schema here to demonstrate that despite the great differences between its empirical content and the content of Piaget's schema, the two are methodologically similar. Watson[3] assumes that the transition from external speech to inner speech requires an intervening stage such as whispered speech. In the same way, Piaget identifies the egocentric stage of speech and thinking as the transitional stage in the development from autistic to logical forms of thinking.

One and the same point in the development of the child's thinking, that is, the phenomenon of egocentric speech, is placed in entirely different developmental sequences by Piaget and ourselves. For Piaget, egocentric speech acts as a transitional stage in the development from autism to logic, in the development from the intimately individual to the social. For us, egocentric speech acts as a transitional form in the movement from external to inner speech, in the movement from social to individual speech. We would include autistic verbal thought as an aspect of the latter.

Thus, our perspective on the developmental process is very different from Piaget's. This is a consequence of the difference in our understanding of the phenomenon of egocentric speech because it is on this basis that we proceed to reconstruct the whole.

Vygotsky credits the German psychologist and philosopher William Stern with the 'first and best description' of the crossover point between language and thought in the young child's consciousness.

From Chapter 4, 'The genetic roots of thinking and speech', section 2

… the most important event in the development of the child's thinking and speech occurs at approximately two years of age. It is at this point that the lines representing the development of thinking and speech, lines that up to this point have moved in isolation from one another, cross and begin to coincide. This provides the foundation for an entirely new form of behaviour, one that is an essential characteristic of man.

Stern[4] provided the first and best description of this extraordinarily important event in the child's mental life. He demonstrated that a vague consciousness of the significance of language and the will to master it is awakened in the child. The child makes what is the most significant discovery of his life, the discovery that 'every thing has a name' [1924, p. 162]. This critical moment, the moment when speech becomes intellectual and thinking verbal, is marked by two clear and objective symptoms. These signs provide a foundation for reliable judgments concerning whether this turning point in speech development has occurred. In cases of abnormal or arrested development, they make it possible to determine the extent to which development has been delayed, since these two symptoms are closely linked. First, the child who has attained this level of development begins to *actively expand his vocabulary* by asking the name of each new thing he encounters. Second, these efforts result in an extremely rapid increase in the child's vocabulary.

★ ★ ★

Our conclusions can be briefly summarised in the following way:

1. As we found in our analysis of the phylogenetic [evolutionary] development of thinking and speech, we find that these two processes have different roots in ontogenesis [individual development].

2. Just as we can identify a 'pre-speech' stage in the development of the child's thinking, we can identify a 'pre-intellectual stage' in the development of his speech.
3. Up to a certain point, speech and thinking develop along different lines and independently of one another.
4. At a certain point, the two lines cross: thinking becomes verbal and speech intellectual.

Vygotsky's second 'site' examining the development of word meaning focuses on concept development. Here, he leaps forward to the adolescent years to explore how students come to understand meanings of the 'scientific' concepts (formal concepts, that is, not confined to science) that make up school knowledge.

From Chapter 6, 'The development of scientific concepts in childhood', section 1

How do scientific concepts develop in the course of school instruction? What is the relationship between instruction, learning, and the processes involved in the internal development of scientific concepts in the child's consciousness? Are these simply two aspects of what is essentially one and the same process? Does the process involved in the internal development of concepts follow instruction like a shadow follows the object which casts it, not coinciding with it but reproducing and repeating its movement, or do both processes exist in a more complex and subtle relationship which requires special investigation?

In contemporary child psychology, we find two answers to these questions. First, we find the position that *scientific concepts do not have their own internal history*, that they do not undergo a process of development in the true sense of the word. Rather, they are simply learned or received in completed form through the processes of understanding, learning, and comprehension. They are adopted by the child in completed form from the domain of adult thinking. From this perspective, the problem of the development of scientific concepts is essentially exhausted[5] by that of teaching scientific concepts to the child and by that of learning concepts. This is the most widely accepted – indeed the generally accepted – perspective on this issue in contemporary child psychology. Until recently, it has provided the foundation for the construction of most theories and methods of school instruction.

Even the most rudimentary scientific critique makes the theoretical and practical inadequacy of this view apparent. We know from research on concept formation that the concept is not simply a collection of associative connections learned with the aid of memory. We know that the concept is not an automatic mental habit, but a *complex and true act of thinking* that cannot be mastered through simple memorisation. The child's thought must be raised to a higher level for the concept to arise in consciousness.

At any stage of its development, the concept is an *act of generalisation*. The most important finding for all research in this field is that the concept – represented psychologically as word meaning – develops. The essence of the development of the concept lies in the transition from one structure of generalisation to another. Any word meaning, at any age, is a generalisation. However, word meaning develops. When the child first learns a new word, the development of its meaning is not completed but has only begun. From the outset, the word is a generalisation of the most elementary type. In accordance with the degree of his development, the child moves from elementary generalisations to higher forms of generalisation. This process is completed with the formation of true concepts.

The development of concepts or word meanings presupposes the development of a whole series of functions. It presupposes the development of voluntary attention, logical memory, abstraction, comparison and differentiation. These complex mental processes cannot simply be learned. From a theoretical perspective, then, there is little doubt concerning the inadequacy of the view that the concept is taken by the child in completed form and learned like a mental habit.

The inadequacy of this view is equally apparent in connection with practice. No less than experimental research, pedagogical experience demonstrates that direct instruction in concepts is impossible. It is pedagogically fruitless. The teacher who attempts to use this approach achieves nothing but a mindless learning of words, an empty verbalism that simulates or imitates the presence of concepts in the child. Under these conditions, the child learns not the concept but the word, and this word is taken over by the child through memory rather than thought. Such knowledge turns out to be inadequate in any meaningful application. This mode of instruction is the basic defect of the purely scholastic verbal modes of teaching which have been universally condemned. It substitutes the learning of dead and empty verbal schemes for the mastery of living knowledge.

Vygotsky engages in an intellectual contest with Piaget on concept development which parallels their contest on young children's language development.

From Chapter 6, 'The development of scientific concepts in childhood', section 1

If we review the scientific literature, it quickly becomes apparent that nearly all studies of concept formation in childhood have focused on the development of what we call everyday concepts. As we mentioned earlier, our work is one of the first systematic attempts to study the development of scientific concepts. All the established laws and regularities of the development of the child's concepts have been derived from studies of everyday concepts. In spite of the differences in the internal conditions under which these two types of concepts develop, these findings have been extended to the domain of the child's scientific thinking. No attempt has been made to verify the validity of such an extension. That the extension of these findings to the domain of scientific concepts has occurred without any attempt to assess its validity is primarily a function of the fact that the question of the propriety of this extension has never been raised.

Recently, several particularly insightful researchers (including Piaget) have found that they could not ignore this question. Moreover, when the problem presented itself, these researchers were obliged to differentiate sharply between representations that develop primarily through the operation of the child's own thought and those that arise under the decisive and determining influence of knowledge the child acquires from those around him.

Piaget refers to the first of these two types of representations as spontaneous representations.

Piaget demonstrated that these two types of representations have a good deal in common. They both: (1) manifest a resistance to external suggestion; (2) have deep roots in the child's thought; (3) manifest a certain commonality among children of the same age; (4) are maintained in the child's consciousness over a period of several years (giving way to new concepts gradually rather than disappearing suddenly); and (5) manifest themselves in the child's first true answers. These characteristics differentiate these two types of representations from suggested representations and from answers that are provided to the child through leading questions.

In our view, these positions are correct. They recognise that the child's scientific concepts (which clearly belong to the second group of representations discussed by Piaget) undergo a true process of development rather than arising spontaneously. This is made clear by the five features of these representations listed above. Piaget goes further and deeper than other researchers into the problem which interests us. He even recognises that this group of concepts can become an independent object of investigation.

However, Piaget makes several mistakes that detract from the positive aspect of his argument. *Three interrelated aspects of Piaget's thought are mistaken* and of special interest to us.

The first mistake, for Vygotsky, is that Piaget asserts that only spontaneous concepts, and not scientific concepts, 'can serve as the source of direct knowledge of the unique qualities of the child's thought' (Vygotsky, 1987a, p. 174). The second is that 'there exists an impassable, solid, eternal barrier which excludes any mutual influence' (ibid.) between the two kinds of concept. The third, as we see in the following paragraph, is that Piaget seems to exclude any role for school instruction in concept development.

Inevitably, these two mistakes tangle Piaget's theory in contradiction and lead to a third mistake. On the one hand, Piaget asserts that the child's non-spontaneous concepts do not reflect the characteristics of his thought. He asserts that this privilege belongs exclusively to spontaneous concepts. This implies that knowledge of these characteristics of the child's thought can have no practical significance, since the acquisition of non-spontaneous concepts is not dependent on them. On the other hand, a basic thesis of his theory is the recognition that the essence of the child's mental development lies in the progressive socialisation of the child's thought. As we have seen, one of the basic and most concentrated contexts for the formation of non-spontaneous concepts is school instruction. If we accept Piaget's views on this matter, the process involved in the socialisation of thought that we find in instruction (among the most important processes in the child's development) turns out to be entirely independent of the child's own internal processes of intellectual development. On the one hand, the internal development of the child's thought is deprived of any significance in explaining the socialisation of the child in instruction. On the other, the socialisation of the child's thought (which moves to the forefront in the process of instruction) is represented as unconnected with the internal development of the child's representations and concepts.

This contradiction constitutes the weakest link in Piaget's theory ...

Vygotsky presses the contradictions inherent in Piaget's position to an absurd conclusion, before presenting his own understanding of the relationship between spontaneous and scientific concepts, and the role of school instruction in the development of that relationship.

From Chapter 6, 'The development of scientific concepts in childhood', section 2

How do we explain the school-age child's manifestation of a capacity for conscious awareness or mastery of important intellectual functions such as memory and attention while he is incapable of the mastery or conscious awareness of his own thinking? How do we explain the fact that during the school age all the intellectual functions except intellect are intellectualised and become volitional?

To resolve this paradox, we must consider the basic laws of mental development in children of this age. Elsewhere, we have considered the changes in the connections and relationships among functions that occur in the course of the child's mental development. In that context, we were able to demonstrate empirically that the child's mental development consists not so much in the development or maturation of separate functions as in changes in the connections and relationships among these functions. Indeed, the development of each mental function depends on these changes in inter-functional relationships. Consciousness develops as a whole. With each new stage in its development, its internal structure – the system of connections among its parts – changes.

Development is not a sum of the changes occurring in each of the separate functions. Rather, the fate of each functional part of consciousness depends on changes in the whole.

Of course, the idea that consciousness is a unified whole with the separate functions existing in insoluble connection with one another is nothing new for psychology. Indeed, it is as old as psychology itself. Nearly all psychologists note that the mental functions act in unbroken connection with one another. Remembering presupposes the activity of attention, perception, and the attribution of meaning. Perception requires attention, recognition (or memory), and understanding. In both traditional and contemporary psychology, however, this concept of the functional unity of consciousness – of the insoluble connections among the various aspects of its activity – has consistently remained on the periphery.

★ ★ ★

Change in these inter-functional connections – *change in the functional structure of consciousness – is the main and central content of the entire process of mental development.* That which served as a postulate for traditional psychology must become psychology's central problem. Traditional psychology proceeded from the postulate that the mental functions are connected and did not pursue the question further. Neither the nature of these inter-functional connections nor their development became an object of investigation. For the new psychology, this change in inter-functional connections and relationships becomes the central problem. If we fail to resolve this problem, we will not be able to understand the changes we observe in the isolated functions. This conception of developmental change in the structure of consciousness must be considered if we are to resolve the question that interests us in the present context, the question of how the school-age child becomes consciously aware of attention and memory, and gains voluntary control over them while his intellect remains outside conscious awareness.

★ ★ ★

Thus, *the foundation of conscious awareness is the generalisation or abstraction of the mental processes, which leads to their mastery.* Instruction has a decisive role in this process. Scientific concepts have a unique relationship to the object. This relationship is mediated through other concepts that themselves have an internal hierarchical system of interrelationships. It is apparently in this domain of the scientific concept that conscious awareness of concepts or the generalisation and mastery of concepts emerges for the first time. And once a new structure of generalisation has arisen in one sphere of thought, it can – like any structure – be transferred without training to all remaining domains of concepts and thought. Thus, *conscious awareness enters through the gate opened up by the scientific concept.*

★ ★ ★

On this basis alone, we can state the core of our hypothesis (we will discuss this hypothesis in more detail later in summarising our experiments): *only within a system can the concept acquire conscious awareness and a voluntary nature. Conscious awareness and the presence of a system are synonyms when we are speaking of [scientific] concepts, just as spontaneity, lack of conscious awareness, and the absence of a system are three different words for designating the nature of the child's [spontaneous]*[6] *concept.*

A striking example of a competence dependent on the development of scientific concepts is writing. Vygotsky here discusses writing at length, pointing out in particular the different demands made on a writer as opposed to those made on a speaker, and mapping the relationships between inner speech, written speech and external oral speech.

From Chapter 6, 'The development of scientific concepts in childhood', section 4

In writing, [the child] constructs the phrase in the same voluntary and intentional way as he creates the word from separate letters. That is, the child's syntax is as voluntary as his phonetics. The semantic aspect of written speech also requires voluntary work on word meanings. It requires that they be arranged in a particular syntactic and phonetic sequence. This reflects the fact that written speech stands in a different relationship to inner speech than does oral speech. While the development of external speech precedes the development of inner speech, written speech emerges only after the development of the latter. Written speech presupposes the existence of inner speech. According to Jackson and Head,[7] written speech is the key to inner speech. The transition from inner to written speech requires what we have called voluntary semantics, which is associated with the voluntary phonetics of written speech. The grammar of thought characteristic of inner and written speech do not coincide; the meaningful syntax of inner speech is completely different from that of either oral or written speech. Entirely different laws govern the construction of the whole and of meaningful units. In a certain sense, the syntax of inner speech is the polar opposite of that of written speech. The syntax of oral speech stands somewhere between these two poles.

Inner speech is maximally contracted, abbreviated, and telegraphic. Written speech is maximally expanded and formal, even more so than oral speech. Written speech does not contain ellipses while inner speech is filled with them. Syntactically, inner speech is almost entirely predicative. In oral (audible) speech, syntax becomes predicative where the subject and related parts of the sentence are known to the interlocutors. This is consistent with the nature and structure of inner speech. With inner speech, the subject – indeed the whole conversational situation – is known to the individual who is thinking. Here, speech consists almost entirely of predicates. We do not have to tell ourselves what this speech is about. That is always implied, forming the background of consciousness. This explains the predicative nature of inner speech. Even if inner speech were made audible to the outsider, only the speaker would understand it. No one else would know the mental field in which it flows. Inner speech is, therefore, completely idiomatic.

In contrast, written speech requires the situation to be established in full detail so it can be understood by the interlocutor. Written speech is the most expanded form of speech. Even things that can be omitted in oral speech must be made explicit in written speech. Written speech must be maximally comprehensible to the other. Everything must be laid out fully. This transition from a maximally contracted inner speech (i.e. from speech for oneself) to a maximally expanded written speech (i.e. to speech for the other) requires a child who is capable of extremely complex operations in the voluntary construction of the fabric of meaning.

The second basic characteristic of written speech (i.e. its greater *consciousness*) is closely linked with its *volitional nature*. Wundt[8] noted that the intentional and conscious nature of written speech is among the most important features that distinguishes it from oral speech. In his view, the difference between the development of language and of writing is that the latter is directed by consciousness and intention almost from the outset. This is why change in sign systems can be voluntary (as in the development of cuneiform writing systems, for example) while the processes involved in language change are always unconscious.

In our research, we were able to establish that this is as true of the ontogenesis [individual development] of written speech as it is of its phylogenesis [genetic development]. From the very beginning, consciousness and intention direct the child's written speech. The child learns the signs of written speech and the use of these signs consciously and volitionally. In contrast, oral speech is learned and used unconsciously. Written speech forces the child to act more intellectually. It requires conscious awareness of the very process of speaking. The motives of written speech are more abstract, intellectualistic, and separated from need.

In summarising this brief discussion of our study of the psychology of written speech, we can say that the mental functions which form written speech are fundamentally different from those which form oral speech. Written speech is the algebra of speech. It is a more difficult and a more complex form of intentional and conscious speech activity. Two conclusions follow: (1) this explains the radical difference between the child's oral and written speech (this difference is a function of differences in the level of development required by activities that are spontaneous, involuntary, and without conscious awareness, and those that are abstract, voluntary, and characterised by conscious awareness); and (2) *when instruction in written speech begins, the basic mental functions that underlie it are not fully developed; indeed, their development has not yet begun.* Instruction depends on processes that have not yet matured, processes that have just entered the first phases of their development.

Vygotsky uses a metaphor, that of a growing plant or tree, to depict the interactive relationship between spontaneous and scientific concepts. He sees each type of concept as having its own strengths and weaknesses, and shows how each supports the other. The strength of *spontaneous concepts* is their rootedness in concrete experience. The *scientific concepts* are, like the plant or tree, the culmination of the structure, but they need to reach down to the roots for nourishment. Spontaneous concepts and scientific concepts are all part of a whole, and interdependent.

In Vygotsky's discussion of scientific concepts, he insists on the central importance of pedagogy in their development and in the development of mind. He says that the link between the lines of development of spontaneous and scientific concepts 'is *the link of the zone of proximal and actual development*'.

From Chapter 6, 'The development of scientific concepts in childhood', section 5

The scientific concept grows downward through the everyday concept and the everyday concept moves upward through the scientific. In this assertion, we are only stating our experimental findings in more general terms. Let us review these findings. The everyday concept must reach a certain level of spontaneous development for the superior scientific concept to emerge. As we have seen, this potential is present for the concept 'because' by the second grade, while for the concept 'although' it only emerges in the fourth grade. Everyday concepts, however, move quickly along the upper section of the path which was blazed by scientific concepts. In this process, they are restructured in accordance with the structures prepared by the scientific concept. This is reflected in the sharp upward movement in the curve representing everyday concepts to the level of that representing scientific concepts.

We can now state our findings in more general terms. *The strength of the scientific concept lies in the higher characteristics of concepts, in conscious awareness and volition.* In contrast, this is the weakness of the child's everyday concept. The strength of the everyday concept lies in spontaneous, situationally meaningful, concrete applications; that is, in the sphere of experience and the empirical. The development of scientific concepts begins in the domain of conscious awareness and volition. It grows downward into the domain of the concrete, into the domain of personal experience. In contrast, the development of spontaneous concepts begins in the domain of the concrete and empirical. It moves toward the higher characteristics of concepts, toward conscious awareness and volition. The link between these two lines of development reflects their true nature. This is *the link of the zone of proximal and actual development.*

It is indisputable that conscious awareness and the volitional use of concepts (i.e. the characteristics of the school child's spontaneous concepts that remain underdeveloped) lie entirely within the school child's zone of proximal development. They emerge or become actual in his collaboration with adults. This is why the development of scientific concepts presupposes a certain level in the development of spontaneous concepts, in connection with which conscious awareness and volition emerge in the zone of proximal development. Scientific concepts restructure and raise spontaneous concepts to a higher level, forming their zone of proximal development. What the child is able to do in collaboration today, he will be able to do independently tomorrow.

Thus, the development of scientific concepts does not coincide with that of spontaneous concepts. Precisely because of this, there exist extremely complex relationships between them. If scientific concepts simply repeated the developmental history of spontaneous concepts, these relationships would not be possible. The links between the two processes and the tremendous influence they have on one another are possible because their development takes such different paths.

If the development of scientific concepts repeated that of spontaneous concepts, the acquisition of a system of scientific concepts would contribute only an increase or broadening of the circle of concepts, only an enrichment of the child's vocabulary. However, our theory and research indicate that scientific concepts provide a segment of development which the child has not yet passed through; they indicate that the scientific concept moves ahead into a zone where the corresponding potentials have not yet matured in the child. This allows us to begin to understand that instruction in scientific concepts plays a decisive role in the child's mental development.

Notes

1. Mecacci's Italian has more detail in this sentence, and makes it clear that the movement from a person's needs and impulses (*'il movimento diretto dai bisogni e dagli impulsi dell'uomo'*) towards the act of thinking is in one direction, while the movement from the dynamic of a finished thought to a person's behaviour and concrete activity (*'alla dinamica del comportamento e all'attività concreta della persona'*) is in the opposite direction (*'il movimento inverso'*). So there is a genuinely dynamic and contested relationship between affect and thought.
2. Vygotsky's reference here and a few lines further down are to the 1932 Russian translation of Piaget's *Le langage et la pensée chez l'enfant.* The editors have referred to the English translation of the book (Piaget, 1959), which is in the reference list.
3. John Watson (1878–1958) was an American psychologist. He established behaviourism as a school of thought in psychology.
4. See Chapter 3, note 2.
5. Mecacci's translation – '*deve essere ricondotto*', 'must be brought back to, reduced to' – is a much clearer rendering of Vygotsky's criticism of contemporary child psychology's understanding of how children take on the school's scientific concepts. According to

contemporary child psychology, scientific concepts are 'simply learned or received in completed form'.
6. The editors have introduced the terms 'scientific' and 'spontaneous' in this sentence to make Vygotsky's intended meaning clearer.
7. John H. Jackson (1835–1911) and Henry Head (1861–1940) were English neurologists.
8. Wilhelm Wundt (1832–1920) was a German psychologist, philosopher and physiologist, widely regarded as the person who established psychology as an independent discipline.

References

Piaget, J. (1959). *The language and thought of the child* [1923]. London: Routledge and Kegan Paul.

Stern, W. (1924). *Psychology of early childhood up to the sixth year of age* [1914]. London: George Allen and Unwin.

Vygotsky, L.S. (1971). *The psychology of art*. Intro. A.N. Leontiev; commentary V.V. Ivanov. Cambridge, MA: MIT Press.

Vygotsky, L.S. (1987). *The collected works of L.S. Vygotsky. Volume 1, Problems of general psychology*. Trans. and intro. N. Minick; Rieber, R.W. and Carton, A.S. (eds). New York, NY: Plenum Press.

Vygotsky, L.S. (1987a). *Thinking and speech* [1934], in Vygotsky, L.S. (1987). *The collected works of L.S. Vygotsky. Volume 1, Problems of general psychology*, pp. 37–285.

Vygotsky, L.S. (1992). *Pensiero e linguaggio* [1934]. Trans. L. Mecacci, Bari-Roma: Gius. Laterza e Figli Spa.

Chapter 11

The final 'why'

Extracts from *Thinking and speech*,
Chapter 7, 'Thought and word'

We come now to the last chapter of *Thinking and speech* (Vygotsky 1987a), which focuses on the third area in the development of word meaning. Previously in the book, development has been seen as the broadening and refining of external language, verbal speech, first by young children as social talk, and then, increasingly, in formal learning contexts. Vygotsky's subsequent account of concept development describes how, with teaching, students develop formal 'scientific' concepts which are capable of carrying more abstract meanings, and which give access to formal knowledge.

Now Vygotsky turns to the internalisation of language, first from verbal speech to inner speech, and then its subsequent transformations into 'verbal thought', 'thought itself' and ultimately what lies beyond thought. The chapter carries one of the richest, most complex arguments in all Vygotsky's work. In its first section, he reiterates a major claim.

From Chapter 7, 'Thought and word', section 1

Our experimental studies have ... shown that by taking word meaning as a unit of verbal thinking we create the potential for investigating its development and explaining its most important characteristics at the various developmental stages. The primary result of this work, however, is not this thesis itself but a subsequent conclusion that constitutes the conceptual centre of our investigation, that is, the finding that word meaning *develops*. The discovery that word meaning changes and develops is our new and fundamental contribution to the theory of thinking and speech. It is our major discovery, a discovery that has allowed us to overcome the postulate of constancy and unchangeableness of word meaning which has provided the foundation for previous theories of thinking and speech.

In the second section of the chapter Vygotsky describes the nature of the development of word meaning in detail, insisting that 'the relationship of thought to word is not a thing but a process, a movement from thought to word and from word to thought.'

From Chapter 7, 'Thought and word', section 2

The discovery of the changeable nature of word meanings and their development is the key to liberating the theory of thinking and speech from the dead end where it currently finds itself. Word meaning is inconstant. It changes during the child's development and with different modes of the functioning of thought. It is not a static but a dynamic formation. To establish the changeable nature of meaning, we must begin by defining it correctly. The nature of meaning is revealed in generalisation. The basic and central feature of any word is generalisation. All words generalise.

It is important to emphasise, however, that the fact that the internal nature of word meaning changes implies that the relationship of thought to word changes as well. To understand the changeable and dynamic relationship of thought to word, we need to take a cross-section of the genetic scheme of changes in meaning that we developed in our basic research. We need to clarify *the functional role of verbal meaning in the act of thinking*.

We have not yet had the opportunity to consider the process of verbal thinking as a whole. However, we have brought together all the information necessary to outline the basic features of this process. At this point, we will attempt to outline the complex structure of the actual process of thinking, the complex movement from the first vague emergence of a thought to its completion in a verbal formulation. For this purpose, we must move from a genetic to a functional plane of analysis. That is, we must now analyse not the development of meanings and their structure, but the process through which *meanings function in the living process of verbal thinking*. If we succeed in this, we will have shown that with each stage in development there exists not only a specific structure of verbal meaning, but a special relationship between thinking and speech that defines this structure. Functional problems are resolved most easily when we are studying the higher, developed forms of some activity, where the whole complexity of the functional structure appears in a well-articulated, mature form. Therefore, we will consider issues of development only briefly, turning then to the study of the relationships of thought to word in the development of consciousness.

When we attempt to realise this goal, a grand and extraordinarily complex picture emerges before us, a picture that surpasses in subtlety the architectonics of researchers' richest expressions. In the words of Tolstoy, 'the relationship of word to thought and the formation of new concepts is the most complex, mysterious, and delicate process of the spirit' (1903, p. 143).

Before moving on to a schematic description of this process, we will state our leading concept. This central idea – a concept we will develop and clarify in the following discussion – can be expressed in the following general formula: the relationship of thought to word is not a thing but a process, a movement from thought to word and from word to thought. Psychological analysis indicates that this relationship is a developing process which changes as it passes through a series of stages. Of course, this is not an age-related development but a functional development. The movement of thinking from thought to word is a developmental process. Thought is not expressed but completed in the word. We can, therefore, speak of the establishment[1] (i.e. the unity of being and non-being) of thought in the word. Any thought strives to unify, to establish a relationship between one thing and another. Any thought has movement. It unfolds. It fulfils some function or resolves some task. This flow of thought is realised as an internal movement through several planes, as a transition from thought to word and from word to thought. Thus, the first task in an analysis of the relationship of thought and word as a movement from thought to word is to analyse the phases that compose this movement, to differentiate the planes through which thought passes as it becomes embodied in the word. To paraphrase Shakespeare, much opens up before us here of which 'even wise men have not dreamed'.

Our analysis leads first to the differentiation of two planes of speech. Though they form a unity, the inner, meaningful, semantic aspect of speech is associated with different laws of movement than is its external, auditory aspect. The unity of speech is complex, not homogeneous. This differentiation in the movement of the semantic and sound aspects of speech is reflected in several factors related to the ontogenesis of speech development. In the present context, we will note only two major factors.

First, we know that the development of the external aspect of speech in the child begins with the initial single-word utterance and moves to the coupling of two or three words, then to the simple phrase and the coupling of phrases, and still later to the complex sentence and connected speech composed of a series of complex sentences. Thus, in mastering the external aspect of speech, the child moves from the part to the whole. In its meaning, however, we know that the child's first word is not a one-word sentence but a whole phrase. Thus, in the development of the semantic aspect of speech, the child begins with the whole – with the sentence – and only later moves to the mastery of particular units of meaning, to the mastery of the meanings of separate words. The child begins with the whole and only subsequently partitions its fused thought which is expressed in the one-word sentence into a series of separate though interconnected verbal meanings. Thus, the development of the semantic and external aspects of speech moves in opposite directions. The semantic aspect of speech develops from the whole to the part or from the sentence to the word. The external aspect of speech moves from the part to the whole or from the word to the sentence.

In section 2, Vygotsky has also described the interactive relationship (but non-correspondence) between two 'planes of speech': the 'semantic aspect of speech' and 'its external, auditory aspect'. But as language travels inward, 'sense' increasingly comes to predominate over 'meaning'.

From Chapter 7, 'Thought and word', section 3

We must take an additional step to penetrate the internal aspect of speech more deeply. The semantic plane is only the first of the internal planes of speech. Beyond it lies the plane of inner speech. Without a correct understanding of the psychological nature of inner speech, we cannot clarify the actual complex relationships between thought and word.

★ ★ ★

... we must begin with the thesis that *inner speech is a psychological formation that has its own unique nature*, the thesis that inner speech is a unique form of speech activity that has unique characteristics and stands in complex relationships to other speech forms. To study the relationships of inner speech to thought and to the word, we must identify what distinguishes inner speech from thought and word. We must clarify its unique function.

In our view, it is important in this connection that in one case I am speaking to myself and in the other to another. Inner speech is speech for oneself. External speech is speech for others. This is a fundamental functional difference in the two types of speech that will have inevitable structural consequences. In our view, then, it is incorrect to view the difference between inner and external speech as one of degree rather than of kind (as Jackson and Head,[2] 'among others, have done). The presence or absence of vocalisation is not a cause that explains the nature of inner speech. It is the consequence of its nature. Inner speech is not merely what precedes or reproduces external speech. Indeed, in a sense, it is the opposite of external speech. External speech is a process of transforming thought into word; it is the materialisation and objectivisation of thought. Inner speech moves in the reverse direction, from without to within. It is a process that involves the evaporation of speech in thought. This is the source of the structure of inner speech, the source of all that structurally differentiates it from external speech.

Inner speech is among the most difficult domains of psychological research. As a consequence, most theories of inner speech are arbitrary and speculative constructions based on little empirical data. The experiment has been used primarily as a demonstration or illustration. Research has centred on attempts to identify subtle shifts in articulation and respiration, factors that are at best three stages removed from the phenomenon of inner speech. This problem has remained almost inaccessible to the experiment because genetic methods have not been utilised. Development is the key to understanding this extremely complex internal function of human consciousness. By identifying an adequate method for investigating inner speech, we can move the entire problem from its current stalemate. The first issue we must address, then, is that of method.

Piaget was apparently the first to recognise the special function of egocentric speech in the child and to understand its theoretical significance. Egocentric speech is a common phenomenon in the child, one familiar to all who deal with children. Piaget did not overlook its significance. He attempted to study it and interpret it theoretically. However, he remained entirely blind to the most important characteristics of egocentric speech, that is, to its genetic origins and its connections with inner speech. As a consequence, his interpretation of its nature was false in functional, structural and genetic terms.

Using Piaget as a point of departure, our research has focused on the relationship between egocentric and inner speech. As a consequence, we have identified a means for studying inner speech experimentally.

Earlier, we outlined the basic considerations that caused us to conclude that *egocentric speech passes through several stages that precede the development of inner speech.* These considerations can be classed in three groups. First, in functional terms, we found that egocentric speech fulfils an intellectual function similar to that of inner speech. Second, we found that the structure of egocentric speech is similar to that of inner speech. Third, in our genetic analysis, we combined Piaget's observation that egocentric speech atrophies in the school-age child with several facts that forced us to associate this event with the initial development of inner speech. This led to the conclusion that as egocentric speech atrophies it is transformed into inner speech.

In the next group of extracts, Vygotsky discusses some characteristics of inner speech. One is 'predicativity': the need for less explicit language in intimate contexts. Like the abbreviated speech between intimates, inner speech requires less language to express meaning and privileges a word's sense over its meaning.

From Chapter 7, 'Thought and word', section 5

It is no surprise that written speech is the polar opposite of oral speech. The situation that is clear to the interlocutors in oral speech, and the potential for expressive intonation, mimic and gesture, is absent in written speech. The potential for abbreviation is excluded from the outset. Understanding must be produced through words and their proper combination. Written speech facilitates speech as a complex activity. This underlies the use of the rough draft. The path from the rough to the final draft is a complex activity. However, even without the rough draft, the process of reflecting on one's work in written speech is extremely powerful. Frequently, we say what we will write to ourselves before we write. What we have here is a rough draft in thought. As we have tried to show in the preceding chapter, this rough draft that is constructed in thought as part of written speech is inner speech. Inner speech acts as an internal rough draft in oral as well as in written speech. We must, therefore, compare the tendency for abbreviation in inner speech with that of oral and written speech.

We have seen that the tendency for abbreviation and pure predicativity of expression arises in two circumstances in oral speech – where the situation being referred to is clear to the interlocutors and where the speaker expresses the psychological context of his expression through intonation. We have also seen that both circumstances are excluded in written speech. Again, this is why written speech does not manifest the tendency for predicativity characteristic of oral speech. This is why it is the most expanded speech form.

What do we find if we analyse inner speech from this perspective? Our detailed discussion of predicativity in oral speech permits the clear expression of one of the most subtle and complex theses to which our research on inner speech has led us: the thesis that inner speech is predicative. This thesis is fundamental to the resolution of all related issues. In oral speech, the tendency for predicativity arises frequently and regularly in particular types of situations. In written speech, it never arises. In inner speech, it is always present. It is the basic and indeed the only form assumed by inner speech. Inner speech consists entirely of psychological predicates. We do not find a predominance of predicate over subject. We find absolute predicativity. As a rule, written speech consists of expanded subjects and predicates. In inner speech, however, the subject is always dropped. Only the predicate is preserved.

★ ★ ★

... in inner speech, we find a predominance of the word's sense over its meaning. Paulhan[3] significantly advanced the psychological analysis of speech by introducing the distinction between a word's sense and meaning. A word's sense is the aggregate of all the psychological facts that arise in our consciousness as a result of the word. Sense is a dynamic, fluid and complex formation which has several zones that vary in their stability. Meaning is only one of these zones of sense that the word acquires in the context of speech. It is the most stable, unified and precise of these zones. In different contexts, a word's sense changes. In contrast, meaning is a comparatively fixed and stable point, one that remains constant with all the changes of the word's sense that are associated with its use in various contexts. Change in the word's sense is a basic factor in the semantic analysis of speech. The actual meaning of the word is inconstant.[4] In one operation, the word emerges with one meaning; in another, another is acquired. The dynamic nature of meaning leads us to Paulhan's problem, to the problem of the relationship between meaning and sense. Isolated in the lexicon, the word has only one meaning. However, this meaning is nothing more than a potential that can only be realised in living speech, and in living speech meaning is only a cornerstone in the edifice of sense.

★ ★ ★

Gogol's work *Dead Souls* provides a remarkable example of [the] law of sense influence. Initially, these words designate dead serfs who have not been removed from official lists, dead serfs that can therefore be bought and sold like the living. These words are used in this sense throughout the poems,[5] poems that focus on the trafficking in these dead souls. As they pass through the poems, however, these two words acquire an entirely new and an immeasurably richer sense. As a sponge absorbs the ocean mist, these words absorb the profound sense of the various chapters. Only toward the end do they become completely saturated with sense. By this time, however, these words designate something entirely different than they did initially. 'Dead souls' refers not only to the dead, yet still counted, serfs, but to all the poems' central characters, characters who live but who are spiritually dead.

There is an analogous phenomenon in inner speech, though it is again taken to the extreme. Here, the word assumes the sense of preceding and subsequent words, extending the boundaries of its meaning almost without limit. In inner speech, the word is much more heavily laden with sense than it is in external speech. Like the title of Gogol's poems, it is a concentrated clot of sense. To translate this meaning into the language of external speech, it must be expanded into a whole panorama of words. This is why the full revelation of the sense of the title of Gogol's poems requires the entire text of *Dead Souls* for its development. However, just as the entire sense of the poems can be included in these two words, tremendous sense content can be fitted into a single word in inner speech.

These characteristics of the meaningful aspect of inner speech result in the incomprehensible nature of egocentric and inner speech that has been noted by all who have observed them. It is impossible to understand the child's egocentric expression if you do not know what is referred to by the predicates that constitute it, if you do not see what the child is doing and seeing. Watson[6] suggested that inner speech would remain completely incomprehensible even if one were to succeed in recording it. Though noted by all observers, the incomprehensible nature of inner speech – like its abbreviated nature – has not been subjected to analysis. What analysis indicates is that, like the abbreviation of inner speech, its incomprehensible nature is a product of many factors. It is the summary expression of a wide variety of phenomena.

A sufficient explanation and clarification of the psychological nature of the incomprehensibility of inner speech has been provided by our discussion of its characteristics, that is, its unique syntax, its phonetic reduction, and its special semantic structure. Nonetheless, we will consider two additional factors that lead to the incomprehensible nature of inner speech. The first is the integral consequence of all the characteristics of inner speech listed above. It stems from the unique function of inner speech. Inner speech is not meant for communication. It is speech for oneself. It occurs under entirely different internal conditions than external speech and it fulfils an entirely different function. Thus, we should not be surprised by the fact that inner speech is incomprehensible but by the fact that we expect it to be comprehensible.

The second is associated with the unique nature of the sense structure of inner speech. We will again clarify our thought through an illustration from external speech. In *Childhood, Boyhood, Youth*, Tolstoy notes that among people who live the same life a special dialect or jargon often emerges that is comprehensible only to those who have participated in its development. The brothers Irten'ev had their own dialect, as do street children. Under certain conditions, the usual sense and meaning of a word changes and it acquires a specific meaning from the conditions that have led to this change. It should be no surprise that this kind of inner dialect also arises in inner speech. In its internal use, each word gradually acquires different colourations, different sense nuances, that are transformed into a new word meaning as they become established. Our experiments show that word meanings are always *idiomatic* in inner speech, that they are always untranslatable into the language of external speech. The meaning of the word in inner speech is an individual meaning, a meaning understandable only in the plane of inner speech. It is as idiomatic as an elision or password.

Inner speech stands between the external word in one direction and, in the other, 'the next stable plane of verbal thinking': 'thought itself'.

From Chapter 7, 'Thought and word', section 5

We can now return to the definition of inner speech and the contrast of inner and external speech which served as the point of departure for our analysis. We said then that inner speech is a unique function that can be considered the polar opposite of external speech. We rejected the view that inner speech is what precedes external speech, that it is the latter's internal aspect. External speech is a process that involves the transformation of thought into word, that involves the materialisation and objectivisation of thought. Inner speech involves the reverse process, a process that moves from without to within. Inner speech involves the evaporation of speech into thought. However, speech does not disappear in its internal form. Consciousness does not evaporate and dissolve into pure spirit. Inner speech is speech. It is thought that is connected with the word. However, where external speech involves the embodiment of thought in the word, in inner speech the word dies away and gives birth to thought. To a significant extent, inner speech is thinking in pure meanings, though as the poet says, 'we quickly tire of it'.[7] Inner speech is a dynamic, unstable, fluid phenomenon that appears momentarily between the more clearly formed and stable poles of verbal thinking, that is, between word and thought. Consequently, its true role and significance can be clarified only if we take an additional analytic step inward, only if we establish some general representations about the next stable plane of verbal thinking.

This plane is thought itself. The first task of our analysis is to isolate this plane, to partition it from the unity where we always encounter it. We have said that any thought strives to unite something with something else. Thought is characterised by a movement, an unfolding. It establishes a relationship between one thing and another. In a word, thought fulfils some function. It resolves some task. Thought's flow and movement do not correspond directly with the unfolding of speech. The units of thought and speech do not coincide. The two processes manifest a unity but not an identity. They are connected with one another by complex transitions and transformations. They cannot, however, be superimposed on one another.

★ ★ ★

... thought does not immediately coincide with verbal expression. Thought does not consist of individual words like speech. I may want to express the thought that I saw a barefoot boy in a blue shirt running down the street today. I do not, however, see separately the boy, the shirt, the fact that the shirt was blue, the fact that the boy ran, and the fact that the boy was without shoes. I see all this together in a unified act of thought. In speech, however, the thought is partitioned into separate words. Thought is always something whole, something with significantly greater extent and volume than the individual word. Over the course of several minutes, an orator frequently develops the same thought. This thought is contained in his mind as a whole. It does not arise step by step through separate units in the way that his speech develops. *What is contained simultaneously in thought unfolds sequentially in speech.* Thought can be compared to a hovering cloud which gushes a shower of words.

Therefore, the transition from thought to speech is an extremely complex process which involves the partitioning of the thought and its recreation in words. This is why thought does not correspond with the word, why it doesn't even correspond with the word meanings in which it is expressed. The path from thought to word lies through meaning. There is always a background thought, a hidden subtext in our speech. The direct transition from thought to word is impossible. The construction of a complex path is always required. This is what underlies the complaint of the word's incompletion,[8] the lamentation that the thought is inexpressible:

How can the heart express itself,
How can the other understand ...

or:

If only it were possible to express the spirit without words!

To overcome this, attempts arise to fuse words, to create new paths from thought to word through new word meanings.

There is a plane even beyond 'thought itself': 'the motivating sphere of consciousness', the 'affective and volitional tendency' – wishing, feeling and needing. Near the end of the book, Vygotsky offers a summative description of the extraordinary, complex two-way journeys which thought and word take 'from the most external to the most internal plane'. And, in the book's last words, he asserts his conviction that thinking and speech, the words of the book's title, are fundamental to 'understanding the nature of human consciousness'.

From Chapter 7, 'Thought and word', section 5

We must now take the final step in the analysis of the internal planes of verbal thinking. Thought is not the last of these planes. It is not born of other thoughts. Thought has its origins in the motivating sphere of consciousness, a sphere that includes our inclinations and needs, our interests and impulses, and our affect and emotion. The affective and volitional tendency stands behind thought. Only here do we find the answer to the final 'why' in the analysis of thinking. We have compared thought to a hovering cloud that gushes a shower of words. To extend this analogy, we must compare the motivation of thought to the wind that puts the cloud in motion. A true and complex understanding of another's thought becomes possible only when we discover its real, affective-volitional basis. The motives that lead to the emergence of thought and direct its flow can be illustrated through the example ... of discovering the subtext through the specific interpretation of a given role. Stanislavskii teaches that behind each of a character's lines there stands a desire that is directed toward the realisation of a definite volitional task. What is recreated here through the method of specific interpretation is the initial moment in any act of verbal thinking in living speech.

Because a volitional task stands behind every expression, Stanislavskii notes the desire that underlies the character's thought and speech in each line of a play. As an example, we will present the text and subtext in an interpretation that is similar to that of Stanislavskii's.

Text of the play[9]	Parallel desires
Sophia:	
Oh Chatskii, I am glad to see you.	Wants to hide her confusion.
Chatskii:	
You're glad, that's good.	Wants to appeal to her conscience
Though, can one who becomes glad	through mockery. Aren't you ashamed!
in this way be sincere?	Wants to elicit openness.
It seems to me that in the end,	
people and horses are shivering,	
and I have pleased only myself.	

Liza: But, sir, had you been behind the door, not five minutes ago, you'd have heard us speak of you. Miss, tell him yourself!	Wants to calm Chatskii and to help Sophia in a difficult situation.
Sophia: It is always so – not only now. You cannot reproach me so.	Wants to calm Chatskii. I am guilty of nothing!
Chatskii: Let's assume it is so. Blessed is the one who believes, and warm his life.	Let us cease this conversation.

Understanding the words of others also requires understanding their thoughts. And even this is incomplete without understanding their motives or why they expressed their thoughts. In precisely this sense we complete the psychological analysis of any expression only when we reveal the most secret internal plane of verbal thinking – its motivation.

With this, our analysis is finished. We will now briefly consider the results to which it has led. In our analysis, verbal thinking has emerged as a complex dynamic whole where the relationship between thought and word is manifested as a movement through several internal planes, as a transition from one plane to another. We carried our analysis from the most external to the most internal plane. In the living drama of verbal thinking, movement takes the reverse path. It moves from the motive that gives birth to thought, to the formation of thought itself, to its mediation in the internal word, to the meanings of external words, and finally, to words themselves. However, it would be a mistake to imagine that this single path from thought to word is always realised. On the contrary, the current state of our knowledge indicates that extremely varied direct and reverse movements and transitions from one plane to another are possible. We also know in general terms that it is possible for movement to be broken off at any point in this complex path in the movement from the motive through the thought to inner speech, in the movement from inner speech to thought, or in the movement from inner to external speech. However, our task was not to study the varied movements that are actually realised along the trajectory from thought to word. Our goal was merely to show that the relationship between thought and word is a dynamic process. It is a path from thought to word, a completion and embodiment of the thought in the word.

★ ★ ★

In concluding, we should say a few words about the prospects that lie beyond the present study. Our investigation has brought us to the threshold of a problem that is broader, more profound, and still more extraordinary than the problem of thinking. It has brought us to the threshold of the problem of consciousness. In our investigation, we have tried to consistently keep in view that aspect of the word which has been unfamiliar ground for experimental psychology.[10] We have tried to study the word's relationship to the object, its relationship to reality. We have tried to study the dialectical transition from sensation to thinking and show that reality is reflected in thinking differently than it is reflected in sensation. We have tried to show that the word's distinguishing feature is a generalised reflection of reality. In the process, however, we have touched on an aspect of the word's nature whose significance exceeds the limits of thinking as such, an aspect of the word that can be studied only within the framework of a more general problem, the problem of the relationship between the word and consciousness.

The consciousness of sensation and thinking are characterised by different modes of reflecting reality. They are different types of consciousness. Therefore, *thinking and speech are the key to understanding the nature of human consciousness*. If language is as ancient as consciousness itself, if language is consciousness that exists in practice for other people and therefore for myself,[11] then it is not only the development of thought but the development of consciousness as a whole that is connected with the development of the word. Studies consistently demonstrate that the word plays a central role not in the isolated functions but [in] the whole of consciousness. In consciousness, the word is what – in Feuerbach's [1843] words[12] – is absolutely impossible for one person but possible for two. The word is the most direct manifestation of the historical nature of human consciousness.

Consciousness is reflected in the word like the sun is reflected in a droplet of water. The word is a microcosm of consciousness,[13] related to consciousness like a living cell is related to an organism, like an atom is related to the cosmos. The meaningful word is a microcosm of human consciousness.

Throughout this last chapter of Thinking and speech, Vygotsky 'seems to turn with pleasure, perhaps some relief, to the world of literature.' (Barrs, 2022, p. 187) He refers to and/or quotes from works of literature by Mandelstam, Dostoevsky, Heine, Tolstoy, Krylov, Gogol, Shakespeare, Cervantes, Pushkin and Griboyedov. Vygotsky's

> study of word meaning and of the deep semantics of inner speech [has] here mainly [been] carried on in relation to literary discourse, which is admitted as completely legitimate evidence of the workings of mind. Vygotsky seems not to acknowledge that he is making any kind of statement through this approach, and yet it must have been a very challenging demonstration of his belief that psychology should not

Thinking and speech, Chapter 7   165

confine itself to the study of behaviour in experimental contexts, but should study mind in all its manifestations, including works of art.

(ibid., pp. 187–188)

In the closing pages of this last chapter Vygotsky celebrates the fact that his 'unit of analysis', the development of word meaning, has enabled him to investigate so many aspects of the development of the human mind and indeed the construction of consciousness: '… consciousness is constructed through language and consciousnesss has a radical transforming power' (Barrs, 2016, p. 246). He quotes from an earlier paper, 'The problem of consciousness' (Vygotsky, 1997a): 'Of course life defines consciousness. Consciousness is only one of its moments. But once it has emerged, consciousness itself starts to define life' (in Kozulin, 1990, p. 245).

In this chapter, as in all his work, Vygotsky aims to change psychology:

'By enlarging the boundaries of psychology to take in more than external behaviour and activity, he laid the basis of a new and humanistic psychology, which we are only just beginning to inhabit' (Barrs, 2016, p. 246).

Notes

1. Mecacci's translation (Vygotsky, 1992; see the introduction to Chapter 10) has the much more illuminating '*un divenire*' ('a becoming') to describe the development of the relationship between thought and word, rather than 'the establishment', which does not imply a gradual process.
2. See Chapter 10, note 7.
3. Frédéric Paulhan (1856–1931) was a French philosopher and psychologist, author of *The double function of language* (1929) and of the article '*Qu'est-ce le sens des mots?*' in the *Journal de psychologie*, 25, 1928, to which Vygotsky refers here.
4. The reader may be forgiven for feeling confused here. 'Meaning' has gone, in the space of a few sentences, from being 'stable, unified and precise', to being 'comparatively fixed and stable' (in both these cases in opposition to 'sense'), to being 'inconstant'. 'Actual meaning' in this sentence may refer to a level of general signification inclusive of both 'meaning' and 'sense'.
5. Although *Dead Souls* is now generally described as a novel, Gogol saw his work as 'an epic poem in prose'. The word '*Poema*' appears on the cover page of the original edition. Mecacci's translation also has '*poema*' (singular).
6. See Chapter 10, note 3.
7. Mecacci's translation "'*ci stanchiamo presto del cielo*'" ('we soon tire of the sky') is more poetic and appropriate. The poet is not named.
8. 'Incompletion' here seems to the editors to be simply wrong. It fails to catch Vygotsky's 'lamentation that the thought is inexpressible'. Mecacci's '*della imperfezione della parola*' ('of the imperfection of the word'), on the other hand, reflects the spirit of lamentation.
9. The example is from Griboyedov's play *Woe from wit*.
10. Mecacci's translation of this sentence is much fuller: '*La nostra ricerca ci ha portato … a quell'aspetto della parola, a quel lato della parola, che, come l'altra faccia della luna, è rimasta una terra sconosciuta per la psicologia sperimentale.*' ('Our research has brought us … to that aspect of the word, to that side of the word, which, like the other side of the moon, has remained *terra incognita* for experimental psychology.')

11. The English translation presents the words from the beginning of this sentence as Vygotsky's. In fact, they are from Marx and Engels' *The German ideology*. Mecacci's translation carries a direct and longer quotation.
12. Vygotsky is referring to Feuerbach's statement: '*The essence* of man is contained only in the community, in the *unity of man with man* – a unity, however, that rests on the reality of the distinction between "I" and "You"' (Feuerbach, 1843).
13. Mecacci's '*La parola sta alla coscienza come un piccolo mondo ad uno grande*' ('The word is to consciousness as a small world is to a large one') is a much more vivid rendering of this thought.

References

Barrs, M. (2016). 'Vygotsky's "Thought and word"'. *Changing English*, 23(3), pp. 241–256.
Barrs, M. (2022). *Vygotsky the teacher*. Abingdon, Oxon and New York, NY: Routledge.
Feuerbach, L. (1843). *Principles of the philosophy of the future*, section 59. Available online in the Marxist Archive: www.marxists.org/reference/archive/feuerbach/works/future/index.htm
Kozulin, A. (1990). *Vygotsky's psychology: a biography of ideas*. Hemel Hempstead: Harvester Wheatsheaf.
Tolstoy, L.N. (1903). *Pedagogičeskie stat'y (Pedagogical articles)*. Moscow: [publisher not found].
Vygotsky, L.S. (1987). *The collected works of L.S. Vygotsky. Volume 1, Problems of general psychology*. Trans. and intro. N. Minick; Rieber, R.W. and Carton, A.S. (eds). New York, NY: Plenum Press.
Vygotsky, L.S. (1987a). *Thinking and speech* [1934], in Vygotsky, L.S. (1987). *The collected works of L.S. Vygotsky. Volume 1, Problems of general psychology*, pp. 37–285.
Vygotsky, L.S. (1992). *Pensiero e linguaggio* [1934]. Trans. L. Mecacci, Bari-Roma: Gius. Laterza e Figli Spa.
Vygotsky, L.S. (1997). *The collected works of L.S. Vygotsky. Volume 3, Problems of the theory and history of psychology*. Trans. and intro. R. Van der Veer; Rieber, R.W. and Wollock, J. (eds). New York, NY: Plenum Press.
Vygotsky, L.S. (1997a). 'The problem of consciousness' [1933], in Vygotsky, L.S. (1997). *The collected works of L.S. Vygotsky. Volume 3, Problems of the theory and history of psychology*, pp. 129–138.

Index

Titles in *italics* or inverted commas are writings by Vygotsky unless otherwise indicated. A letter n following a page number indicates a reference in the notes.

abstraction/abstract thought 29, 53, 111, 131, 144
action, and speech 68–70
adaptation: human versus animal 2–3, 41; social, physically handicapped children 31–34
Adler, A. 23–24, 25, 36n3
adolescence xvii, 91–92, 94–97; attention in 91, 96; concept development in 92, 94, 96–97, 143–144; interests, development of 94, 95–96; memory in 91, 92, 96; thought and thinking in 91–92, 94, 96–97
aesthetic reaction 11, 19–20
affect *see* emotion and affect
age periodisation and child development xvii, 95, 100–105; crisis periods xvii, 100, 101–105; stable ages xvii, 100, 102
Akhutina, T. 106n3
animal behaviour 52, 69; adaptation to the environment 2–3, 41; conditional reflexes 1, 2, 38, 39, 40, 46; and human behaviour, distinction between 1–4; imitation 130; inherited reactions 2; sign and symbolic operations 57; unconditional reflexes 40
animal psychology 46
apes xvi, 46, 70n2; practical intelligence 57; tool use 56, 57, 59
aphasia xvii, 68, 69–70
applied psychology xv, 50–51
Aristotle 19
arithmetical development 78, 85–86, 128
art xviii, 46; aesthetic reaction to 11, 19–20; as catharsis 19–20, 21; and emotion xiv, 19–20, 21; form and content 17, 20; as perception 11; and psychoanalysis 11; psychology of xii, xiv, xxi, 10–21, 46–47; social significance of 21; as technique 11; work of, as basis for analysis 10–11;
see also drama; literature; music; poetry
assessment: of special needs children xv; and zone of proximal/proximate development (ZPD) xix, 124–125, 126
attention 24; in adolescence 91, 96; conscious awareness of 146, 147; voluntary xvi, 29, 66, 73, 75, 80, 91, 144
autistic thinking 115, 138, 141, 142
auxiliary signs and symbols 65–67; internalisation of 66–67, 68

Bacon, F. 87, 88n9
Baldwin, J.M. 81, 88n5
banning of works 105
Barrs, M. 165; *Vygotsky the teacher* xii, xiii, 108, 124, 164
'Bases for working with mentally retarded and physically handicapped children' 30–31
behaviour: social 44–45; *see also* animal behaviour; human behaviour
behaviourism 38, 67, 110
Bekhterev, V. 46, 47, 54n6
Belinskii, V. 12, 21n1
Bergson, H. 92
Bernays, J. 19, 21n6
Binet, A. 34, 36n5
Bleuler, E. 113, 123n4
blind/blind deaf-mute children 24; compensatory processes 23, 25, 26;

cultural development 26, 28; education of 26–27, 28, 30–31; language, access to 26–27, 28; and mainstream schooling 26, 27; reading 26–27, 28; speech development 28, 31; symbol and sign systems 26, 27; writing 28
Blonsky, P. 38, 54n1
Braille 26, 27, 28, 31
brain 92–93; combinatorial action of 118–119, 121; and consciousness xiv; plasticity 117–118
Bridgeman, Laura 31
Bruner, J. xii
Bühler, C. 88n7
Bühler, K. 79, 88n4
Bunin, I., 'Gentle breath' 14–17
Byford, A. xi

catharsis 19–20, 21
censorship 105
Chaiklin, S. 124
character development: deaf children 31–34; *see also* personality
Chekhov, A. 35
child development xvii, 47; actual level of 129–130, 131; adolescence *see* adolescence; age periods in xvii, 95, 100–105; arithmetical development 78, 85–86, 128; and consciousness 8, 113, 114, 146–147, 149, 154; crisis periods (critical ages) xvii, 100, 101–105; cultural development 26, 28–30, 72, 73, 76, 77, 78–87; and defect *see* defectology; developmental diagnostics *see* developmental diagnostics; embryonal development 76–77; higher mental functions xvi, xvii, 72, 73, 75–77, 78, 80; imagination xviii, 112–116; interactive nature of xvi; and interests 4–6, 24, 94, 95–96; and language/speech xvi, xvii, xx, xxi, 28, 29, 30, 56–57, 58–60, 61–63, 66, 67, 78, 80, 83, 90, 111, 112, 135, 138–143, 148–149, 157, 159; and learning 129–133; and play *see* play; practical intelligence 56–60, 63; self-control xvi, xvii, 72, 73, 86–87; and social relationships xvi, 60–61; stable ages xvii, 100, 102; and teaching 127–133; thought and thinking *see* thought and thinking; tool use, function of speech in 56–57, 58–60; written language xvii, xxi, 28, 78, 81–85; zone of proximal development *see* zone of proximal/ proximate development (ZPD)
child-rearing xvii
Childhood, Boyhood, Youth (Tolstoy) 106n4 160
children: research with *see* experimental research; with special needs *see* blind/ blind deaf-mute children; deaf/ deaf-mute children; defectology; mentally backward children; physically handicapped children
Children's mental development in the process of learning/teaching 127
choice experiments (Morozova) 63–65
chronological approach xiii–xiv
classical education 6
cognition 97; and emotion and affect xiv; *see also* thought and thinking
cognitive psychology 137
collaboration, and learning 125, 126
Collected works xi, xii, xiii, 97
'collective as a factor in the development of the abnormal child, The' 30
combinatorial operation of imagination 116, 118–119, 121
communicative speech 140
Communism 46
Communist Party xi, 105
comparative-genetic method 67, 94
compensation: by withdrawal into illness 33; and defect 23, 24, 25–26, 29–30, 32–34; fictitious 32; real 32–33
concept development xvii, xx, 29, 75, 80, 135, 143–148, 153; in adolescence 92, 94, 96–97, 143–144; and conscious awareness xx, 148, 150–151; everyday concepts 144–145, 150; and school instruction 145–146, 147; scientific concepts xx, 143–145, 147–148, 150–151, 151–152n5, 153; spontaneous concepts 145–146, 150–151; volitional use of concepts 150–151
conditional reactions, in humans 1, 2, 4, 43, 44
conditional reflexes 46, 137; in animals 1, 2, 38, 39, 46
connotative meaning xx, 108
conscious awareness 41–42, 43, 149; of attention and memory 146, 147; and concept development xx, 148, 150–151
consciousness xiv, 8–9, 116, 156, 165; children 8, 113, 114, 146–147, 149, 154; 'Consciousness as a problem in the

psychology of behavior' xv, 38–45; and emotion and affect 10; as function of brain activity xiv; functional unity of 146–147; and human behaviour 1, 3, 4, 38–45; knowledge of other persons' consciousness 40, 45; self-consciousness 40, 43, 45, 92; and speech 44, 45, 162, 164; and thought and thinking 162, 164
constructive imagination 114
contamination, theory of 21
creativity xiv, xviii, 113–114, 115, 116, 117, 118–119, 120
'crisis at three years of age, The' 103–105
crisis periods (critical ages), in development xvii, 100, 101–105
crystallised imagination xviii, 122–123
cultural development 26, 28–30, 72, 73, 76, 77, 78–87; social nature of 78–80
cultural languages xvii, xix, 78, 89

dactylology (finger spelling) 27–28, 31
Darwin, C. 40, 75, 77
daydreaming 113, 115
Dead Souls (Gogol) 159, 165n5
deaf/deaf-mute children: character development 31–34; compensatory processes 25, 32–34; cultural development 26, 28–29; education 28, 30–31; and imagination 112; language, access to 26, 27–29, 30; sign systems 27–28, 31; social adaptation 31–34; speech development 28, 30; writing 28
death of Vygotsky 105
defect: and compensation 23, 24, 25–26, 29–30, 32–34; and personality 24
defectology xiv–xv, xix, 22–37; 'detours' in xv, xvi, xix; as a term 22; *see also* blind/ blind deaf-mute children; deaf/deaf-mute children; mentally backward children; physically handicapped children
'Defectology and the study of the development and education of abnormal children' 27–30
denotative meaning 108, 109
developmental diagnostics 34–36, 125–126; and zone of proximal/proximate development (ZPD) 126
diagnostics *see* developmental diagnostics
'diagnostics of development and the pedological clinic for difficult children, The' 34–35, 36
'difficult child, The' 31–34

Dostoyevsky, F. 46
double (or two-fold) stimulation 56, 64, 67–68
doubled experience 3, 4, 39, 41
drama xiv, xviii, xix, xxi; *Hamlet* (Shakespeare) 17–19
drawing 63, 78, 82, 84, 114
dual expression of feeling 121–122

education: classical 6; of the feelings 7; physically handicapped children 26–31
Educational psychology xii, xiv, 1–9
egocentric speech xvi, xx, 58, 61–62, 83, 138–142, 157, 159
Einfühlung (empathy) 8, 45
embryonal development 76–77
emotion and affect xviii, xxi, 2, 7, 8, 105, 137; and art xiv, 19–20, 21; and cognition xiv; and consciousness 10; and imagination 114, 115, 121–122, 123; lived-through experience (*perezhivanie*) xvii; and thought and thinking 137; *see also* feeling(s)
empathy (*Einfühlung*) 8, 45
Engels, F. 49, 86, 87, 88n10, 166n11
environment *see* physical environment; social environment
ethnic psychology 46–47
everyday concepts 144–145, 150
everyday life, teaching and 6
evolutionary development xvi, 75, 76, 77, 89
experience 118; doubled 3, 4, 39, 41; of experiences 42; historical 2, 4, 39, 40, 41; and imagination 117, 120, 121; immediate 48–49; inherited 2, 40, 52; lived-through (*perezhivanie*) xvii, 98–99; social 1, 2, 4, 38, 39, 40, 41; subjective xv, 39
experimental design xv
experimental method 51–53, 56, 59, 60–68
experimental psychology xvii, 1, 53, 137
experimental research with children 56, 59, 60–68, 132; choice experiments 63–65; 'forbidden colours' game 65–66; sign or symbolic activity xvi, 56–58, 65–66; speech/language development xvi, 56, 59–60, 61–63; written language development 83–84
experimental-genetic method 67, 68
external oral speech xx–xxi, 66, 67, 84–85, 141, 142, 148, 149, 155, 156, 157, 158, 160
exteroceptive field 42

fables, 'The wolf in the kennel' (Krylov) 12–14
fantasy 113, 114, 115, 118, 120, 121
feeling(s) 40; dual expression of 121–122; education of the 7; and imagination 114; *see also* emotion and affect
Feuerbach, L. 164, 166n12
finger spelling (dactylology) 27–28, 31
'forbidden colours' game 65–66
formalism 11
freedom of will 87, 116
Freud, S. 47
Freudians 11
Froebel, F. 6
'future-directed' pedagogy xix–xx

game-like/play experiments xvi, 56, 63–66
generalisation in word meaning 136, 144, 154
'Gentle breath' (Bunin) 14–17
Gestalt psychology 46–47, 54n8, 70n2, 123n2
gesture 78, 157; pointing gesture 78–79; and written language 82–83
Gettser, G. 83–84, 88n7
Goethe, J.W. von 110
Gogol, N., *Dead Souls* 159, 165n5
Goldberg, E., *wisdom paradox, The* 70n1
Gomel Teachers' College, Vygotsky's psychology lectures at xiv, 1
Griboyedov, A. 165n9
Gutzmann, H. 69, 71n7

Hamlet (Shakespeare) 17–19
handicapped children *see* blind/blind deaf-mute children; deaf/deaf-mute children; defectology; mentally backward children; physically handicapped children
Head, H. 148, 152n7, 156
Hegel, G. 51, 54n13, 74, 77, 78, 87
Herzen Pedagogical Institute, Leningrad 98, 103, 108, 112
higher mental functions xvi–xvii, xix, 26, 72, 73, 75–77, 78, 80, 90; external stage of development 79; *history of the development of higher mental functions, The* xvi–xvii, 72–88, 89; and lower mental functions, relationship between 72, 77
historical development of behaviour xvi, 90
historical experience 2, 4, 39, 40, 41
historical meaning of the crisis in psychology, The xi, xv, 38, 45–54

history, study of 10–11, 48
history of the development of higher mental functions, The xvi–xvii, 72–88, 89
human behaviour 69; adaptation/control of the environment 3, 41, 87; and animal behaviour, distinction between 1–4; conditional reactions 1, 2, 4, 43, 44; and consciousness 1, 3, 4, 38–45; and doubled experience 3, 4, 39, 41; and historical experience 2, 4, 39, 40, 41; and social experience 1, 2, 4, 38, 39, 40, 41
Hyman, L. xv

idealistic philosophical psychology 38, 53, 67
imagination xiv, xviii, 3, 112–116, 127, 139; combinatorial operation of 116, 118–119, 121; constructive 114; crystallised xviii, 122–123; as directed form of activity 113–114; emotional aspect of 114, 115, 121–122, 123; and experience 117, 120, 121; and reality 119–123; and speech 112, 113, 115; and thinking 112, 115–116
Imagination and creativity in childhood xii, xviii, 116–123
'Imagination and its development in childhood' xviii, 113–116
imitation: and learning xix, 125–126, 130; *see also* mimicry
indirect method 49
inductive method 51–52
industrial psychology 46
inherited experience 2, 40, 52
inner speech xxi, 66, 67, 90, 111, 135, 138, 139, 140, 141, 142, 148–149, 153, 156–158, 159–160; abbreviation in 158; incomprehensible nature of 159; predicativity in 157, 158
instincts 2, 4
instrumental method xvi, 56
intelligence, practical 56–60, 63, 70
interactive nature of development xvi
interests: in adolescence 94, 95–96; children's 4–6, 24
internalisation of language 135, 153; *see also* inner speech; verbal thought
internalising behaviour 79
interoceptive field 42
interpretive methods xv
introspection 43
intuition 24

invention xviii, 114, 115, 119, 122
Ivanovsky, D. 48, 54n10

Jackson, J.H. 148, 152n7, 156
James, W. xv

Kapital, Das (Marx) 3, 53, 55n15, 74, 87n2
Katz, D. 111, 123n3
Keller, Helen 31
Kellogg, D. xi, xiii, 97, 105, 125
knowledge, assimilation of 6
Koffka, K. 47, 54n8, 70n2, 111, 123n2
Köhler, W. 47, 54n8, 56, 57, 59, 70n2, 123n2, 130
Kozulin, A. 165
Kravisova, E. xi
Kretschmer, E. 79, 87n3
Kroh, O. 103, 106n8
Krylov, I., 'wolf in the kennel, The' 12–14, 17

language: and child development xvi, 56, 135, 138–143; and concept development xvii, xx; and higher mental functions xvi; internalisation of xviii, xx, 135, 153, *see also* inner speech; verbal thought; of mathematics *see* mathematics; physically handicapped children, access to 26–29, 30; spoken xvii; and thought xx–xxi, 8–9; written *see* written language; *see also* speech; *Thinking and speech*
Learned, B.W. 57
learning 128; and collaboration 125, 126; and development 129–133; and imitation xix, 125–126, 130; pre-school 127, 128–129; with a teacher (*obuchenie*) xix
Leonardo da Vinci 46
Leontiev, A.N. xi, 65–66, 91
Leopoldoff Martin, I. xiii
Lessing, G. 19, 21n4
Levina, R.E. 59
literature xiv, xviii, xxi, 10, 12–19, 164–165; emotional component of teaching of 7; *see also* drama; poetry
lived-through experience (*perezhivanie*) xvii, 98–99
Locke, J. 43, 54n5
logical memory xvi, 29, 73, 75, 80, 91, 111, 144
logical thinking 141
lower mental functions, and higher mental functions, relationship between 72, 77

Luria, A. xi, xii, 106n3; *making of mind, The* 63; *Tool and symbol in child development* xvi, 56–71, 72

making of mind, The (Luria) 63
Marx, K. 54n13, 166n11; *Das Kapital* 3, 41, 53, 55n15, 74, 87n2
Marxists 51
Marxists Internet Archive xii
mastery of behaviour by internal processes *see* self-control
mathematics: language of xvii, 78; *see also* arithmetical development
maturation 96, 97, 100, 130
meaning: connotative xx, 108; denotative 108, 109; and object, in play 109–111; and sense 155, 158; *see also* word meaning
Mecacci, L. xiii, 124, 133n1, 135, 151n1, 151n5, 165n1, 165n7, 165n8, 165n10, 166n13
mediating activities 73, 74
memorisation 6, 68
memory 24, 112, 117, 118, 121; in adolescence 91, 92, 96; conscious awareness of 146, 147; logical xvi, 29, 73, 75, 80, 91, 111, 144
mental age 126, 129–130, 130–131
mentally backward children 131
method/methodology xv, 48–49; comparative-genetic 67, 94; of double (or two-fold) stimulation 56, 64, 67–68; experimental 51–53, 56, 59, 60–68, 132; experimental-genetic 67, 68; indirect 49; inductive 51–52; instrumental xvi, 56; of speech education 30; units of analysis xv, 51–53, 135–136, 137–138
mimicry: language of, deaf children 26, 29, 30; *see also* imitation
Mind in society xii, xix, 124, 128
Minkova, E. 105
Mitchell, S. 124, 128
Morozova, N. 63–65
Moscow Experimental-Defectological Institute xvii
Moscow Institute of Psychology 56
Moscow State University Clinic of Nervous Diseases 89
Müller, A. 19, 21n5
music 122
Mutter-Hexkomplex (mother-witch complex) 99

narrow-mindedness 7
nature: control of 86, 87; laws of 87
negativism 104–105
nervous system 1, 2; plasticity of 117–118
neuropsychology 106n3
non-verbal thought xxi

observation: and assessment of special needs children xv; empirical 48; self-observation 43
occultism 46
'On psychological systems' lecture xvii, 89–94
ontogenesis 75
ontological development xvi
oral speech *see* external oral speech

Palinscar, A.S. 124
Parkinson's disease xvii, 93
Paulhan, F. 158, 165n3
Pavlov, I. 1, 40, 52, 53, 54n2, 137
pedagogy xix, 36, 124, 128, 131, 133; for blind children 26–27; 'future-directed' xix–xx; *see also* teaching
Pedological works xiii
pedology xi, xiii, xvii, xix, 22, 34–36, 46, 89–107, 125, 132, 133; banning or censorship of works on 105; 'crisis at three years of age, The' 103–105; 'On psychological systems' xvii, 89–94; *Pedology of the adolescent* xvii, 94–97; 'problem of age periodisation in child development, The' 100–103; 'problem of the environment in pedology, The' xvii, 98–99
perception 96, 136, 147; art as 11; inner 43; sense 48, 49
perezhivanie (lived-through experience) xvii, 98–99
personalism 46, 47
personality xvii, 47, 92, 95, 100, 101; physical handicap and formation of 23, 24–25; *see also* character development
Petrazhitskii, L. 17, 21n3
philistinism 7
philosophical idealistic psychology 38, 53, 67
phoniatrics 71n7
phylogenesis *see* evolutionary development
physical environment, control of/adaptation to 2–3, 41, 86, 87
physical inheritance 2, 40
physically handicapped children 22–34; compensatory processes 23, 24, 25–26, 29–30; cultural development 26, 28–30; education 26–31; language, access to 26–29; personality formation 23, 24–25; social adaptation 31–34; *see also* blind/blind deaf-mute children; deaf/deaf-mute children; defectology
physics 48
Piaget, J. xii, xx, 58, 138–142, 144, 145–146, 151n2, 157
Planck, M. 48, 54n11
play xviii, xix, 78, 108–112, 116, 139; pretend xx; separation of meaning and object in 109–111; symbolic function of 82–84; transference to real life 111–112; and zone of proximal/proximate development (ZPD) 112, 127
'Play and its role in the mental development of the child' xviii, 108–112
play/game-like experiments xvi, 56, 63–66
Poetica (Aristotle) 19
poetry xiv, xxi
pointing gesture 78–79
polyglossia 30
Potebnya, A. 106n1
practical intelligence 56–60, 63, 70
praxis/practice xv, 50–51
pre-school learning 127, 128–129
predicativity 157, 158
pretend play xx
'problem of age and the diagnostics of development, The' 125–126
'problem of age periodisation in child development, The' 100–103
'problem of the environment in pedology, The' xvii, 98–99
'problem of teaching and mental development at school age, The' xix, 124, 127–133
proprioceptive field 41, 42–43
psyche 8, 11, 18, 27
psychoanalysis 11, 44, 46
psychological systems xvii, xviii, 38, 89–94, 115
psychology xv, xix; animal 46; applied xv, 50–51; of art xii, xiv, xxi, 10–21, 46–47; behaviourism 38, 67, 110; cognitive psychology 137; ethnic 46–47; experimental xvii, 1, 53, 137; Gestalt psychology 46–47, 54n8, 70n2, 123n2; *historical meaning of the crisis in psychology, The* xi, xv, 38, 45–54; idealistic philosophical 38, 53, 67; industrial 45; personalism 46, 47; poles

of 49–50; psychoanalytic school 11, 44, 46; reflexology xiv, 1, 38, 39, 46, 67, 72, 128; as a science 54; subjective 46; Vygotsky's roots in xiv, 1–9
psychology of art, The xii, xiv, xxi, 10–21, 135
'psychology and pedagogy of children's handicaps, The' 26–27
psychopathology 46, 47
Pushkin, A. 119–120

reading 85; blind children 26–27, 28
realistic thinking xviii, 112, 115–116
reality 136; and imagination 119–123
reflexes 41–44; conditional *see* conditional reflexes; non–manifest 44; reversible 44–45; speech 43; thought 43–44; unconditional 40
reflexology xiv, 1, 38, 39, 46, 67, 72, 128
repetition 6
reproductive activity 117, 118
research with children *see* experimental research
research methodology *see* method/methodology
Ribot, T. 119, 123n5
Rossolimo, G. 34, 36n6

Sakharov, L. xx
Schneuwly, B. xiii, xx
schools, special 26, 27
scientific concepts xx, 143–145, 147–148, 150–151, 151–152n5, 153
scribbling 78, 82
self-consciousness 40, 43, 45, 92
self-control xvi, xvii, 72, 73, 86–87
self-observation 43
sensation 136
sense perceptions 48, 49
sense, word 155, 157, 158–159; and meaning 155, 158
sensibility 24
sensory-motor functions 64–65
sex and sexuality 46, 47
sexual maturation 96
Shakespeare, W., *Hamlet* 17–19
Shcherbina, N. 27, 36n4
Sherrington, C.S. 41, 42, 52, 54n4
sign and symbol systems 149; blind children 26, 27; deaf/deaf-mute children 27–28, 31
sign or symbolic activity 80; auxiliary 65–67, 68; development of xvi, 56–58;

internalisation of auxiliary signs 66–67, 68; as inwardly directed 73, 75; as mediating activity 73, 74; play 82–84; and tool use, relationship between 73–75; *see also* speech
social adaptation, physically handicapped children 31–34
social behaviour 44–45
social environment xvii, 98–99, 108
social experience 1, 2, 4, 38, 39, 40, 41
social inheritance 2
social relationships, and child development xvi, 60–61
social significance of art 21
social speech xx, 61–62, 138–139, 140, 141, 142
special education, of blind children 26–27
special needs children *see* blind/blind deaf-mute children; deaf/deaf-mute children; defectology; mentally backward children; physically handicapped children
special schools 26; antisocial nature of 27
speech: and action 68–70; blind and deaf children 28, 29, 30; communicative 140; and consciousness 44, 45, 162, 164; development of xvi, xvii, xviii, xx, 28, 29, 30, 56–57, 58–60, 61–63, 78, 80, 83, 90, 111, 112, 135, 138–143, 148–149, 157, 159; difficulties with *see* aphasia; egocentric xvi, xx, 58, 61–62, 83, 138–142, 157, 159; external oral xx–xxi, 66, 67, 84–85, 141, 142, 148, 149, 155, 156, 157, 158, 160; and imagination 112, 113, 115; inner *see* inner speech; planning function 62–63; pre-intellectual stage 143; reflexes 43; semantic aspect of xx, 148, 155; social xx, 61–62, 138–139, 140, 141, 142; and social behaviour 44, 45; as system of auxiliary symbols 67; and thought and thinking xx–xxi, 89–90, 115, 135, *see also Thinking and speech*; tool use and development of 56–57, 58–60; whispered 141; written *see* written language
Spinoza, B. 47, 53, 54n9
spontaneous concepts 145–146, 150–151
stable ages xvii, 100, 102
Stalin, J. xi, 105
Stanislavsky, K.S. xxi, 162
Stern, W. 23, 36n2, 47, 48, 54n7, 54n12, 57, 82, 100, 101, 103, 106n6, 142

storytelling 114
subject disciplines 133
subjective experience xv, 39
subjective psychology 46
symbol systems *see* sign and symbol systems
symbolic activity *see* sign or symbolic activity

teaching xix, 124–125; and child development 127–133; and children's interests 4–6; and creation of zone of proximal/ proximate development (ZPD) 132; emotionally felt 7; and everyday life 6; mentally backward children 131; written language 84; *see also* pedagogy
Thinking and speech/Thought and language xi, xii, xiii, xiv, xx–xxi, 106n1, 135–152, 153–166
Thorndike, E. L. 4, 9n
thought and thinking xiv, 40; abstract 29, 53, 111, 131, 144; in adolescence 91–92, 94, 96–97; autistic 115, 138, 141, 142; concept development *see* concept development; and consciousness 162, 164; and emotion and affect 137; and imagination 112, 115–116; inner planes of xiv, xxi, 155, 156, 162, 163; and language xx–xxi, 8–9; logical 141; non-verbal xxi; pre-speech stage 143; realistic xviii, 112, 115–116; reflexes 43–44; and speech 8–9, 89–90, 115, 135; 'thought itself' 153, 160–161, 163; verbal xxi, 136, 141, 142, 143, 153, 154–155, 160–161, 162, 163; *see also Thinking and speech*
Tolstoy, L.N. 96, 103, 154; *Childhood, Boyhood, Youth* 106n4 160
Tool and symbol in child development (Vygotsky and Luria) xvi, 56–71, 72
tool use xvi, 3; apes 56; as mediating activity 73, 74; as outwardly directed 73, 75; and sign or symbolic activity, relationship between 73–75; and speech development 56–57, 58–60
totem 46
tragedy 17–19
two-fold (or double) stimulation 56, 64, 67–68

Ukhtomsky, A. 52, 55n14
unconscious 40, 48

units of analysis xv, 51–53, 135–136, 137–138
utopian constructions xviii, 113

Van der Veer, R. xii
Vasileysky, S.M. 103, 106n7
verbal thought xxi, 136, 141, 142, 143, 153, 154–155, 160–161, 162, 163
Veresov, N. xi, xiii, 105, 108, 125
visual aids, and teaching of mentally backward children 131
Vokelt, J. 106n7
volition *see* will
voluntary attention xvi, 29, 66, 73, 75, 80, 91, 144
Vygotsky reader, The (Van der Veer and Valsiner [eds]) xii
Vygotsky the teacher (Barrs) xii, xiii, 108, 124, 164

Watson, J. 141, 151n3, 159
Wertheimer, M. 47, 54n8, 70n2, 123n2
whispered speech 141
will (volition) xiv, xvi, 8, 29, 40, 69, 73, 86–87, 103, 112, 127, 137, 146, 149, 150–151, 162; freedom of 87, 116
Wisdom paradox, The (Goldberg) 70n1
'wolf in the kennel, The' (Krylov) 12–14, 17
wonder 7
word meaning, development of xx, 135–152, 153–157; concept development 135, 143–148, 150–151, 153; external language development 135, 138–143; internalisation of language 135, 153, *see also* inner speech; verbal thought
word sense 155, 157, 158–159
world view 92
written language xvii, xxi, 28, 78, 81–85, 148–150, 157, 158; and gesture 82–83; teaching 84; volitional nature of 149
Wundt, W. 106n7, 149, 152n8

Yasnitsky, A. xii
Yerkes, R.M. 57

Zeller, E. 19, 21n7
zone of proximal/proximate development (ZPD) xviii, xix–xx, 124–134, 151; and assessment xix, 124–125, 126; and play 112, 127; and teaching 132; translation of the term 124

For Product Safety Concerns and Information please contact our EU
representative GPSR@taylorandfrancis.com
Taylor & Francis Verlag GmbH, Kaufingerstraße 24, 80331 München, Germany